The Tyndale New Testament Commentaries

General Editor: PROFESSOR R. V. G. TASKER

THE REVELATION OF ST. JOHN

THE

REVELATION

OF ST. JOHN

AN INTRODUCTION AND COMMENTARY

by

THE REV. CANON LEON MORRIS,
M.Sc., M.Th., Ph.D

Principal, Ridley College, Melbourne

Inter-Varsity Press,
Leicester, England

William B. Eerdmans Publishing Company
Grand Rapids, Michigan

Inter-Varsity Press
38 De Montfort Street, Leicester LE1 7GP, England
Wm. B. Eerdmans Publishing Company
255 Jefferson S.E., Grand Rapids, MI 49503

© The Tyndale Press

Reprinted 1983

Published and sold only in the USA and Canada by
Wm. B. Eerdmans Publishing Co.

IVP PAPERBACK EDITION 0 85111 869 0
EERDMANS EDITION 0-8028-1419-0

Printed in the United States of America

Inter-Varsity Press is the publishing division of the Universities and Colleges Christian Fellowship (formerly the Inter-Varsity Fellowship), a student movement linking Christian Unions in universities and colleges throughout the British Isles, and a member movement of the International Fellowship of Evangelical Students. For information about local and national activities in Britain write to UCCF, 38 De Montfort Street, Leicester LE1 7GP.

GENERAL PREFACE

ALL who are interested in the teaching and study of the New Testament today cannot fail to be concerned with the lack of commentaries which avoid the extremes of being unduly technical or unhelpfully brief. It is the hope of the editor and publishers that this present series will do something towards the supply of this deficiency. Their aim is to place in the hands of students and serious readers of the New Testament, at a moderate cost, commentaries by a number of scholars who, while they are free to make their own individual contributions, are united in a common desire to promote a truly biblical theology.

The commentaries are primarily exegetical and only secondarily homiletic, though it is hoped that both student and preacher will find them informative and suggestive. Critical questions are fully considered in introductory sections, and also, at the author's discretion, in additional notes.

The commentaries are based on the Authorized (King James) Version, partly because this is the version which most Bible readers possess, and partly because it is easier for commentators, working on this foundation, to show why, on textual and linguistic grounds, the later versions are so often to be preferred. No one translation is regarded as infallible, and no single Greek manuscript or group of manuscripts is regarded as always right! Greek words are transliterated to help those unfamiliar with the language, and to save those who do know Greek the trouble of discovering what word is being discussed.

There are many signs today of a renewed interest in what the Bible has to say and of a more general desire to understand its meaning as fully and clearly as possible. It is the hope of all those concerned with this series that God will graciously use what they have written to further this end.

R. V. G. TASKER.

5

CONTENTS

CHIEF ABBREVIATIONS

Abbott   *Johannine Grammar* by Edwin A. Abbott, 1906.

AG   *A Greek-English Lexicon of the New Testament and Other Early Christian Literature* edited by William F. Arndt and F. Wilbur Gingrich, 1957.

Alford   *The Greek Testament*, Vol. IV by Henry Alford, 1875.

ANF   *The Ante-Nicene Fathers* (American reprint of the Edinburgh edition), n.d.

AS   *A Manual Greek Lexicon of the New Testament* by G. Abbott-Smith, 1954.

Atkinson   *The War with Satan* by Basil F. C. Atkinson, n.d.

AV   English Authorized Version (King James), 1611.

Barclay   *The Revelation of John* by William Barclay (*Daily Study Bible*), 2 vols., 1960.

BDF   *A Greek Grammar of the New Testament and Other Early Christian Literature* by F. Blass and A. Debrunner, translated and revised by Robert W. Funk, 1961.

Beckwith   *The Apocalypse of John* by Isbon T. Beckwith, 1967.

Caird   *A Commentary on the Revelation of St. John the Divine* by G. B. Caird (*Black's New Testament Commentaries*), 1966.

Charles   *A Critical and Exegetical Commentary on the Revelation of St. John* by R. H. Charles (*International Critical Commentary*), 2 vols., 1920.

9

EB	*Encyclopaedia Biblica* edited by T. K. Cheyne and J. Sutherland Black, 1914.
ET	*The Expository Times.*
Farrer	*The Revelation of St. John the Divine* by Austin Farrer, 1964.
Glasson	*The Revelation of John* by T. F. Glasson (*Cambridge Bible Commentary*), 1965.
GNT	*The Greek New Testament*, being the text translated in The New English Bible, edited with Introduction, Textual Notes and Appendix by R. V. G. Tasker, 1964.
HDB	*A Dictionary of the Bible* edited by James Hastings, 5 vols., 1898–1904.
Hendriksen	*More than Conquerors* by W. Hendriksen, 1962.
Hort	*The Apocalypse of St. John I–III* by F. J. A. Hort, 1908.
IB	*The Interpreter's Bible.*
IBNTG	*An Idiom Book of New Testament Greek* by C. F. D. Moule, 1953.
ISBE	*The International Standard Bible Encyclopaedia* edited by James Orr, 5 vols., 1937.
Kepler	*The Book of Revelation* by Thomas S. Kepler, 1957.
Kiddle	*The Revelation of St. John* by Martin Kiddle (*Moffatt New Testament Commentary*), 1940.
Love	*I, II, III John, Jude, Revelation* by J. P. Love (*Layman's Bible Commentaries*), 1960.
LS	*A Greek-English Lexicon* by Henry George Liddell and Robert Scott, revised by Sir Henry Stuart Jones and Roderick McKenzie, 1940.

LXX   The Septuagint Version.

M   *A Grammar of New Testament Greek:* Vol. I, *Prolegomena* by James Hope Moulton, 1906
Vol. II, *Accidence and Word-Formation* edited by Wilbert Francis Howard, 1919
Vol. III, *Syntax* by Nigel Turner, 1963.

MM   *The Vocabulary of the Greek Testament* by James Hope Moulton and George Milligan, 1914–29.

Moods   *Syntax of the Moods and Tenses in New Testament Greek* by Ernest de Witt Burton, 1955.

MS(s)   Manuscript(s).

NBD   *The New Bible Dictionary* edited by J. D. Douglas *et al.*, 1962.

NEB   The New English Bible: The New Testament, 1961.

Newell   *The Book of the Revelation* by William R. Newell, 1947.

Niles   *As Seeing the Invisible* by D. T. Niles, 1962.

Preston and Hanson   *The Revelation of Saint John the Divine* by Ronald H. Preston and Anthony T. Hanson (*Torch Bible Commentaries*), 1957.

Rossetti   *The Face of the Deep* by Christina G. Rossetti, 1911.

RSV   American Revised Standard Version, 1946–52.

RV   English Revised Version, 1881.

S Bk   *Kommentar zum Neuen Testament aus Talmud und Midrasch* by Herman L. Strack and Paul Billerbeck, 4 vols., 1922–28.

Simcox   *The Revelation of S. John the Divine* by William Henry Simcox (*Cambridge Bible for Schools and Colleges*), 1894.

CHIEF ABBREVIATIONS

Smith   *A Revelation of Jesus Christ* by J. B. Smith, 1961.

Swete   *The Apocalypse of St John* by Henry Barclay Swete, 1907.

TDNT   *Theological Dictionary of the New Testament,* a translation by Geoffrey W. Bromiley of *Theologisches Wörterbuch zum Neuen Testament,* Vols. I–, 1964–.

Tenney   *Interpreting Revelation* by Merrill C. Tenney 1959.

TNTC   *Tyndale New Testament Commentary.*

Torrance   *The Apocalypse Today* by Thomas F. Torrance, 1960.

Walvoord *The Revelation of Jesus Christ* by John F. Walvoord, 1966.

The following translations are cited by the translator's surname or the title, whichever is appropriate: Amplified, Berkeley, Ferrar Fenton, Goodspeed, Knox, Moffatt, Phillips, Schonfield, Twentieth Century, and Weymouth. The Pseudepigrapha are cited from the edition of R. H. Charles; Philo and Josephus from the Loeb edition; and the Talmud from the Soncino translation.

AUTHOR'S PREFACE

THE book of Revelation is, I fear, a very neglected book. Its symbolism belongs to the first century, not to our own age. Twentieth-century men accordingly find it difficult and tend to dismiss it as irrelevant. This is unfortunate because its theology of power is of the utmost importance to an age as preoccupied with the problems of power as is ours. In this Commentary I have tried to explain the significance of the symbolism and to show the bearing of the message of Revelation on the problems of the day. Some of the problems of this book are enormously difficult and I certainly have not the capacity to solve them. But it is my hope that I have been able to point towards the solution of enough of the more obvious difficulties for some modern readers to be able to discern the main thrust of the book.

One difficulty is that there are various schools of interpretation. Many exegetes are quite sure that only their own particular approach will yield the correct interpretation. As best I can I have carefully weighed the contentions of those who have written before me, or at least of such of them as I have had time to read. The literature on this book is enormous, and I make no claim to have mastered it all, though I can say that I have profited very much from what I have read. While I have not felt able to align myself with any one of the usual schools of interpretation, I would like it to go on record that I have not differed from accepted points of view without a careful weighing of the issues involved. In the process I have become indebted to many, to so many, indeed, that I hesitate to single out names. I must content myself with a general expression of indebtedness and with the specific acknowledgments I have made in the body of the Commentary and in the footnotes.

While this Commentary has been on the way for many years, and therefore I have had time to think a good deal about some of its problems, it has had to be written in the intervals (all too few and short) in a busy life as college principal. I ask the reader's pardon accordingly for its many infelicities. I would like to express my appreciation of the patience of the publishers and General Editor. Though they commissioned this book years ago and had every right to expect it long since they have treated my failure to produce it earlier with kindness and understanding. I am grateful.

LEON MORRIS.

INTRODUCTION

THE Revelation (or the Apocalypse as it is often called, from its opening word in the Greek) is by common consent one of the most difficult of all the books of the Bible. It is full of strange symbolism. There are curious beasts with unusual numbers of heads and horns. There are extraordinary phenomena like the turning of one third of the sea into blood (viii. 8), which are impossible to envisage. Modern readers find it strange. They are moreover not usually attracted by the fantastic schemes of prophecy which some exegetes profess to find in it, and whose ingenuity is matched only by their improbability.

The result is that for many modern men Revelation remains a closed book. Except for one or two passages, like the vision of the redeemed in chapter vii, or that of the heavenly Jerusalem in the final two chapters, it remains largely unread. We know it is there. We recognize that it is part of the Canon of Scripture and therefore we accord it formal recognition. But we remain uneasy and we do not make use of it. We turn our backs on its mysteries and luxuriate in John's Gospel or the Epistle to the Romans.

This is a great pity. This book has much to teach us in the twentieth century.[1] J. B. Phillips tells us that he found the task of translating this book 'in the true sense of that threadbare word, thrilling. For in this book the translator is carried into another dimension—he has but the slightest foot-hold in the Time-and-space world with which he is familiar. He is carried, not into some never-never land of fancy, but into the Ever-ever land of God's eternal Values and Judgments.'[2]

---

[1] Cf. A. M. Hunter, 'Revelation, beyond all other books, has made people feel that heaven is real; and in the strength of that blessed conviction go forth anew to do battle with the world and all its evils' (*Introducing the New Testament*, 1945, p. 113). [2] *The Book of Revelation*, 1960, p. 9.

It is of the utmost importance for modern man that he does not lose touch with the eternal realities so stressed in Revelation. Perhaps there is no age for which its essential teaching is more relevant. These are days when the decisions of the great powers have far-reaching effects on ordinary men and women. We may have no great interest in ideologies, yet find that our lives are affected by decisions reached in Moscow or in Washington, decisions in which we have had no voice, nor conceivably could have. Are we then no more than pawns caught up in a great ideological conflict? Nobody wants a nuclear holocaust, but are our lives destined to be snuffed out in a world-wide inferno brought about almost against the will of those controlling the destinies of the nations? Is there something demonic about those evil forces which even our most powerful statesmen seem unable to control? Revelation speaks to an age which is tortured by problems like these, for it was written to a minority with problems of its own about the realities of power. Indeed it has been called, not unjustly, 'a theology of power'.

This is not how it has always been seen. Through the centuries the book has been interpreted in a variety of ways. We may sum up the principal ways of viewing it as follows:

a. The 'preterist' view
This starts with the situation of the church in the first century and ends there. It sees the book as arising out of the situation of the first Christians, and that is the outstanding merit of the preterist position. The Roman Empire dominates the scene. The Seer was wholly preoccupied with the church of his day. He wrote out of its situation and indeed has nothing more in mind than its situation. In other words this view has the merit of making the book exceedingly meaningful for the people to whom it was written. And it has the demerit of making it meaningless (except for the information it gives about that early generation) for all subsequent readers.[1] It

---

[1] Cf. Merrill C. Tenney, 'The preterist has an interpretation which has a firm pedestal, but which has no finished sculpture to place on it' (p. 144).

should perhaps be added that some variant of this view is adopted by most modern scholars.[1]

b. The 'historicist' view

Those who see the book this way claim that it is an inspired forecast of the whole of human history. They see its symbols as setting out in broad outline the history of western Europe and as stretching right on until the second coming of Christ. This view does indeed make Revelation meaningful for this generation, at any rate in part. And it is a strengthening of faith to see the whole of history as under the control of God. But the early Christians could not have got much out of a book whose concern was basically for later periods. For them most of the book on this view must have been an insoluble puzzle. Yet we should surely hold that those to whom it was written had or could have had a satisfying understanding of it. It is also curious that a book forecasting human history should largely ignore the world outside western Europe. Historicist views also labour under the serious disadvantage of failing to agree. If the main points of subsequent history are in fact foreshadowed it should be possible to identify them with tolerable certainty, otherwise what is the point of it? But there are many historicist views, and no real agreement.[2]

c. The 'futurist' view

Some hold that, apart from the first few chapters, the book is exclusively concerned with happenings at the end of the age. They see the seven seals and all the rest as being concerned

---

[1] E.g. W. G. Kümmel, 'The Apocalypse is a book of its time, written out of its time and for its time, not for the distant generations of the future or even of the end-time. It is an occasional writing (Gelegenheitsschrift), as much so as are the epistles of the NT, and which, therefore, as a matter of principle should be understood in relation to the history of its time' (*Introduction to the New Testament*, 1966, p. 324).

[2] Samuel A. Cartledge points out that each adherent of this school of interpretation works things out so that the end falls in his own time. He further says, 'No one who studies the widely divergent conclusions reached by this school through the centuries is likely to become a member of this school and believe in the particular scheme which makes his own days necessarily the last days' (*A Conservative Introduction to the New Testament*, 1957, p. 206).

with the end of the world, and as prefiguring those events which will usher in the second coming of the Lord Jesus Christ. This robs the book of all significance for the early Christians, and, indeed, for all subsequent generations right up to the last. For all intermediate generations it is merely a forecast of what will happen in the last days. Until those days come it means little, except that God has an ultimate purpose.

d. The 'idealist' view

Some maintain that there are few or no references in Revelation to happenings, whether at the time of the writer or subsequently. On this view the whole book is concerned with ideas and principles.[1] It sets out in poetic form certain theological conceptions. It is not particularly concerned with the situation of the early church, nor with that of the church in later days, nor with that of the end-time. It simply sets out principles on which God acts throughout human history. This secures its relevance for all periods of the church's history. But its refusal to see a firm historical anchorage seems to most students dubious to say the least.

It seems that elements from more than one of these views are required for a satisfactory understanding of Revelation. We must always begin with the situation of the church to which it was written.[2] Indeed, we must keep that situation in mind throughout our study if we are to make sense of this difficult book, for it is the clue to many things.

The gospel had been preached throughout the Roman

---

[1] Cf. W. Milligan, 'While the Apocalypse thus embraces the whole period of the Christian Dispensation, it sets before us within this period the action of great principles and not special incidents'; 'we are not to look in the Apocalypse for special events, but for an exhibition of the principles which govern the history both of the world and the Church' (*The Revelation of St. John*, 1886, pp. 153, 154 f.).

[2] G. T. Manley notes a variety of systems of understanding this book, but concludes by urging the reader to maintain 'an open mind to deal with each portion of the book as seen in relation to its context and to other parts of Scripture' (*The Revelation of St. John*, n.d., p. 11). This is still good advice. Each passage must be interpreted in its own context, and not forced into an over-all scheme.

province of Asia (as elsewhere). Some had believed and become Christians. They had been taught that Jesus of Nazareth was the Christ, the Son of God. Being divine, He was fully in control of all situations. He had indeed been rejected by the Jews and crucified. But that was simply the way in which He brought salvation to men. He could be greeted by those in heaven with the words: 'Thou wast slain, and hast redeemed us to God by thy blood out of every kindred, and tongue, and people, and nation' (Rev. v. 9). Having died for men He rose triumphant now to die no more (Rev. i. 18). He went back to heaven, but in due course He would return. He would destroy the kingdoms of this world and set up God's perfect kingdom. It was an inspiring faith and the little group of Christians embraced it with fervour. They looked and longed for the promised consummation when God's will would be perfectly done throughout the whole earth.

And nothing happened.

The church continued to be a very tiny group, doubtless adding a few members from time to time, but not becoming, and not looking like becoming, a mighty force to take over the Empire. The Empire continued on its wicked way. Oppression and wrong abounded. Evil men prospered. Idolators persisted in their idol-worship, and the cult of the emperor flourished. Because they would not conform, the tiny band of Christians found themselves the object of suspicion and sometimes outright persecution. A few of them were killed. Some were put in gaol.

What had become of the message which had induced them to become Christians in the first place? Where was the promise of His coming? All things continued as they were from the foundation of the world. If God was active in the world it demanded a very strong faith to perceive it. And most of the Christians, as they have always been, were men with no more than an average faith. Had they been mistaken in coming to Christ in the first place? Was it all a delusion? Was Christianity a fine religion indeed for the sanctuary but totally unable to cope with the demands of the forum and the capitol? Must they conclude that it was a pretty delusion, which must inevitably be shattered on the hard rocks of social and political realities? Was real power in the hands of the emperor and his associates?

To a church perplexed by such problems Revelation was written. We must not think of it as a kind of intellectual puzzle (spot the meaning of this symbol!) sent to a relaxed church with time on its hands and an inclination for solving mysteries. It was sent to a little, persecuted, frustrated church, one which did not know what to make of the situation in which it found itself. John writes to meet the need of that church.[1]

Take for an example of his method the opening of the book sealed with seven seals. This must surely be the book of human destiny, that book which tells what is in store for mankind. The first thing to notice is that 'no man in heaven, nor in earth, neither under the earth, was able to open the book' (v. 3). The secrets of the future are not accessible to men, but remain fast sealed from men's gaze. But the Seer is assured that 'the Lion of the tribe of Juda, the Root of David, hath prevailed to open the book, and to loose the seven seals thereof' (v. 5). When John looks for this Lion he sees 'a Lamb as it had been slain' (v. 6), a clear reference to Jesus Christ in His character as the crucified One. He comes and takes the book, at which there begins a mighty chorus of praise, first from the elders and living creatures close to the heavenly throne and then taken up by myriads of angels and finally by 'every creature which is in heaven, and on the earth, and under the earth, and such as are in the sea, and all that are in them' (v. 13).

In this way John makes his point that the future belongs not to the Roman emperor, nor to any human potentate or ecclesiastic. It belongs to no man or group of men, but only to Christ, that Christ who was crucified for the salvation of

---

[1] Cf. W. C. van Unnik, 'This is not a book written to titillate or to gratify the curiosity of men anxious to tear aside the veil from the future. It is no book of riddles, although often in the past it has been treated as one. It does indeed draw veils aside and open up a vista of God's actions and his ways; for it proclaims the kingdom of God, which is here and now and yet is still to come in its fulness, bringing with it the overthrow of all that is against him' (*The New Testament*, 1964, p. 161).

mankind. He it is who can open the book of human destiny. All men, and all men's destiny, rest with Him. This will be recognized by those in highest heaven, and by all the angels, and eventually by all that live. This peep behind the scenes brings to John's readers a glimpse of the realities of power. Real power rests with Christ, the Lion. The appearances may be against it for the present. But ultimate reality is not dependent on present appearances.

Throughout the book John makes this point with emphasis. Continually he takes his readers behind the scenes. Wl•en one has due regard to all the facts it becomes plain that earthly potentates do nothing but fulfil the plan mapped out for them by God. They never manage to thwart Him. In vision after vision the truth is emphasized that God is supreme and that He brings His purposes to pass in the affairs of men. The illustrations which make the point are drawn from the contemporary Roman Empire, so that the book is securely rooted in a given historical situation. But the principles set out in it are of permanent validity. We see them in operation round us still.[1] John's conclusion as to the location of ultimate power is just as relevant for us as for the little, persecuted church of the first century.[2]

Some find themselves troubled by the symbolism, and particularly by the difficulty in visualizing some of the Seer's more complicated pieces of imagery (where does one locate ten horns and seven heads on one beast?). So, too, some pieces of imagery do not fit in very well with other pieces. It is important to realize that John is an artist in words. We are to look for the meaning conveyed by each symbol in that

---

[1] Cf. F. B. Clogg, 'The author did not look beyond his own age, but inasmuch as his visions are an expression of the truth that all human history is in God's hands, they have in a sense been fulfilled many times over' (*An Introduction to the New Testament*, 1940, p. 293).

[2] A. M. Hunter sees set forth in the book the great principle 'that all history is divinely controlled; that this world is the scene of a great conflict between good and evil; that the clue to God's character and action in history is to be found in Christ "the lamb slain from the foundation of the world"; that in the end of the day God must finally cope with evil and make an end of it; and that Heaven is the most real place of all' (*Interpreting the New Testament 1900–1950*, 1951, p. 103).

symbol itself. It is a matter of indifference whether the symbols can be visualized or reconciled. That is not their purpose. Their purpose is to convey ideas.[1]

G. B. Caird makes the point that the symbols do not all serve the same purpose. He likens them to the little flags on a map in a military headquarters where the movement of a flag may indicate something which has happened or alternatively something which is planned to happen. 'The strange and complex symbols of John's vision are, like the flags in this parable, the pictorial counterpart of earthly realities; and these symbols too may be either determinative or descriptive.'[2] The visions, in other words, sometimes lift the veil and show things as they are. But on other occasions they reveal to us what God has planned. They may even be significant events, as initiating the working out of God's plan.

II. THE REVELATION OF ST. JOHN AND APOCALYPTIC

The Revelation is commonly regarded as an example of apocalyptic. This is the name given by modern scholars to a class of literature which flourished during the last two centuries BC and the first century AD. It is not easy to define with precision, as the apocalypses varied widely and they shade off into other types of literature. But normally an apocalypse purports to be a revelation made by some celestial personage (like an angel) to a great figure of the past (such as Abraham or Moses or Ezra). The message is usually expressed in vivid symbolism, sometimes of a bizarre kind. It appears in difficult times and conveys to its readers the author's profound conviction that the troubles in which they find themselves are not the last word. God in His own good time will intervene

---

[1] Cf. M. E. Boismard, 'When the Seer describes a vision, he translates into symbols the ideas suggested by God; he goes on then, by accumulating colors, symbolic numbers etc., without giving a thought to the resulting plastic effect. His purpose is, above all, to translate the ideas received from God, not to describe a coherent vision, an *imaginable* vision. To follow him to the end on the way he has chosen, one must play his game and convert into ideas the symbols he describes without troubling oneself about their incoherence' (*Introduction to the New Testament*, ed. A. Robert and A. Feuillet, 1965, p. 697).   [2] P. 61.

catastrophically and destroy evil. Not infrequently this deliverance is associated with God's Messiah who would inaugurate the kingdom of God. The apocalyptists were usually pessimistic about the present world. They despaired of man's efforts ever overcoming evil, and they looked to God to bring the victory. Perhaps it is this stress on the divine which accounts for the small attention they give to ethical teaching. They see evil as overcome, not by better living, but by God's mighty intervention. Apocalypses abound in history rewritten as prophecy in the mouth of the great figure of the past with which they are concerned. Such 'prophecies' are, of course, precise enough up till the writer's own day, but vague thereafter (which affords scholars evidence of the dates of such writings).

There are good reasons for classing the Revelation with apocalyptic. Thus it abounds in symbolism of a typically apocalyptic character, symbolism which is quite difficult to interpret. Again, it is like the apocalypses in its expectation of the setting up of God's kingdom, and its looking for a new heaven and a new earth. So too we notice its mention of angels, or revelations made through heavenly beings. But this book also has some marked differences from typical apocalyptic which we should not overlook. The principal points are as follows:

1. The writer calls his book a prophecy and that repeatedly (i. 3, xxii. 7, 10, 18, 19). Apocalyptic is usually distinguished from prophecy, but this writer claims to be in the prophetic tradition.[1] In line with this his visions convey the 'word of God (i. 2).[2]

[1] Cf. M. Dibelius, 'A certain unique quality belongs to it, for there is here a union of apocalyptic knowledge and of the kind of prophecy which presses to an immediate effect . . . nowhere else is the union so organically carried out as in this book' (*A Fresh Approach to the New Testament and Early Christian Literature*, 1936, p. 124).

[2] A. Wikenhauser maintains that this book 'is not a product of the study or of intensive meditation on the signs of the times'. He thinks that it 'was born from the ecstatic experiences of a prophet'. He says further, 'The author is a genuine prophet. . . . The prophetic consciousness of the author is attested by the whole book' (*New Testament Introduction*, 1958, p. 545).

2. The typical prophetic insistence on moral considerations is to be found throughout the book. Typical is the series of warnings to the churches and the demand for repentance in the Seven Letters (ii. 5, 16, 21, 22, iii. 3, 19).[1]

3. Apocalypses are pseudonymous. They are written in the name of some illustrious predecessor. This writer gives his own name (i. 4).

4. The pessimism of the apocalyptists does not seem to be found here. This age is not seen as hopelessly dominated by evil, though the writer does look for an outbreak of Satanic activity at the last time. But he sees history as the place wherein God has wrought out redemption. And though evil is depicted realistically the book is fundamentally optimistic.

5. The apocalyptists characteristically retrace history in the guise of prophecy. From the standpoint of someone in the remote past they forecast what will happen up to their own day. There is no trace of this in the Revelation. Rather, in the manner of the true prophet, John takes his stand in his own days and looks resolutely to the future.

6. G. E. Ladd maintains this book 'embodies the prophetic tension between history and eschatology. The beast is Rome and at the same time an eschatological Antichrist which cannot be fully equated with historical Rome. While the churches of Asia were facing persecution, there is no known persecution in the first century A.D. which fits that portrayed in the Apocalypse. The shadow of historical Rome is so outlined against the darker shadow of the eschatological Antichrist that it is difficult if not impossible to distinguish between the two. History is eschatologically interpreted; evil at the hands of Rome is realized eschatology.'[2]

7. The apocalypses normally contain curious visions whose meaning is not clear until they are explained usually by an angelic personage. Often the whole apocalypse depends on

---

[1] Cf. Wikenhauser, 'Perhaps the strongest proof of the genuinely prophetic character of the book is the fact that the author writes under his own name to definite Christian Churches of his own time and castigates them unsparingly. There is nothing similar in the apocryphal apocalyptic writings of Judaism' (*loc. cit.*). [2] *Baker's Dictionary of Theology*, 1960, p. 53.

the contribution made by the heavenly guide. It is not unusual to have God Himself pictured as contributing to the
apocalyptic message. In Revelation this kind of explanation
appears occasionally (an angel explains the mystery of the
scarlet woman and the beast on which she rides, xvii. 7ff.).
But the general practice is simply to narrate the vision and to
allow the reader to work out the meaning.

8. In general it is the case that apocalyptists look forward
to the coming of God's Messiah. He would introduce a new
thing into human history. But for John the new thing has
already appeared. He writes of a Messiah who will come
indeed, but who has also already come and won a decisive,
resounding victory. In his unforgettable picture of the Lamb
slain from the foundation of the world he sets forth the truth
that the Messiah has already come and has paradoxically
won His triumph through crucifixion. He bears the marks of
His suffering, but is King of kings and Lord of lords.

III. AUTHORSHIP

Martin Kiddle has a notable statement on the difficulty and
unprofitableness of discussion of the authorship of the Johannine writings of the New Testament. He says:

> No subject of Biblical studies has provoked such elaborate
> and prolonged discussion among scholars as that of the
> authorship of the five books of the New Testament which
> are traditionally ascribed to 'John' (the Fourth Gospel,
> the three Epistles of John, and REVELATION). And no
> discussion has been so bewildering, disappointing, and
> unprofitable. The student who attempts to follow the
> innumerable lines of enquiry is soon caught in a maze
> of conflicting arguments brought forward to support the
> rival theories, and invariably finds himself unable to
> reach any definite conclusion concerning the authorship
> of at least some, if not all, of the books concerned. In
> fact, it is quite impossible to determine the authorship of
> any of these books from the available evidence.[1]

[1] P. xxxiii.

This may be unduly pessimistic, but the subject is certainly one of great difficulty. The following seem to be important points:

1. The writer of Revelation tells us that his name is John (Rev. i. 4). He calls himself a 'servant' (i. 1), 'your brother, and companion in tribulation' (i. 9), and apparently one of 'the prophets' (xxii. 9).

2. It is suggested that the use of the name John without qualification points to the apostle as author. No-one else, it is argued, would call himself simply John without qualification. Only one John was great enough among the Christians to need no description. The general air of authority which pervades Revelation would accord with apostolic authorship.[1]

3. Such references as there are to authorship in the early literature are unanimous in ascribing this work to John the apostle. This ascription is as early as Justin Martyr,[2] testimony which impresses Kiddle.[3] It is supported by Irenaeus,[4] while the Muratorian Fragment twice speaks of the author as John, evidently meaning the apostle.[5] Clement of Alexandria appears to support this view,[6] as does Tertullian.[7] Until Dionysius of Alexandria there is no dissenting voice in the church.[8]

[1] E. Stauffer thinks that the relationship between the apocalyptist on the one hand and the church of Ephesus and the churches attached to it in Asia Minor on the other is very much like that of the Evangelist to his disciples and his churches. He cites Rev. i. 4, ii. 1, 5 and Jn. xxi. 22, 24 as evidence (*New Testament Theology*, 1955, p. 264, n. 75).

[2] Justin says, with reference to Rev. xx, 'There was a certain man with us, whose name was John, one of the apostles of Christ, who prophesied, by a revelation. . . .' (*Dial. Try.* lxxxi, *ANF*, I, p. 240). Charles, who thinks Justin was in error, yet recognizes that this is early testimony and dates it 'as early as 135 A.D. or thereabouts' (I, p. xxxvii, n. 2).

[3] P. xxxv.

[4] In *Adv. Haer.* iv. 20. 11, iv. 30. 4, v. 26. 1 (*ANF*, I, pp. 491, 504, 554) he says the apocalypse was written by 'John, the disciple of the Lord', by which most agree that he means the apostle.

[5] See J. Stevenson, *A New Eusebius*, 1963, p. 146.

[6] He speaks of 'the Apostle John' as having been on the isle of Patmos until 'the tyrant's death' (*Who is the Rich Man . . .?*, xlii, *ANF*, II, p. 603), an apparent reference to Rev. i. 9.

[7] *Adv. Marc.* iii. 14, *ANF*, III, p. 333.

[8] Epiphanius says that the anti-Montanist Alogoi ascribed it to Cerinthus (*Haer.* li. 3, *Panarion*, 51). According to Kümmel the Roman anti-Montanist, Gaius (*c.* 210), shared this opinion (*op. cit.*, p. 330).

There was, it is true, some hesitation in certain parts of eastern Christendom in accepting the book. Eusebius is a well-known example.[1] Revelation is missing from some eastern lists of canonical books, and it was for long excluded from the Syriac canon. Indeed it first appears to have been included in the Syriac version in the revision of Philoxenus (*c.* AD 500). But the doubts appear to have been aroused as much by the subject-matter of the book as by anything.[2] There does not appear to be evidence of any early or well grounded tradition which regards anyone other than the apostle as the author.[3] Indeed, B. W. Bacon can go so far as to say, 'There is no book of the entire New Testament whose external attestation can compare with that of Revelation, in nearness, clearness, definiteness, and positiveness of statement.'[4]

4. A big objection to the apostolic authorship is that of style. R. H. Charles says that the Greek of Revelation is 'unlike any Greek that was ever penned by mortal man'.[5] The argument from difference of style is as old as Dionysius of

---

[1] See *H.E.* iii. 25. He divides the sacred writings into the recognized books (those accepted by all), the disputed books, and the spurious. He puts Revelation into the first class if the apostle wrote it, otherwise into the third. This seems to show that for Eusebius, as for others, it was dislike of its teachings that weighed. If it was simply a matter of dispute over the authorship he would surely have put it in the class of disputed works.

[2] L. Pullan points out that the Montanist sect 'taught an extravagant doctrine about the millennium when Christ would return to reign on earth. This doctrine was partly founded on Rev. xx, and was supported by pretended prophecies. It caused orthodox Christians to be more suspicious about the statements of Christian prophets, and probably made them less anxious to translate and circulate the Revelation' (*The Books of the New Testament*, 1926, p. 271).

[3] Donald Guthrie notes a number of ancient authors who testify to apostolic authorship. He proceeds: 'So strong is this evidence that it is difficult to believe that they all made a mistake in confusing the John of the Apocalypse with John the apostle. . . . It must be conceded that taken as a whole (the evidence) points very strongly to the probability that the John of the Apocalypse was, in fact, John the apostle' (*New Testament Introduction, Hebrews to Revelation*, 1962, p. 255).

[4] *The Making of the New Testament*, n.d., pp. 190f. He later says, 'One would think the case for apostolic authenticity could hardly be stronger' (*op. cit.*, p. 191). We should add that despite this Bacon goes on to the view that the work was not written by the apostle. In view of this his recognition of the force of the external evidence is noteworthy.

[5] I, p. xliv.

Alexandria. Indeed, the arguments against the apostolic authorship of Revelation are still essentially those of Dionysius. Later scholars have scarcely done more than repeat and elaborate the position he took up. In the matter of style his words are these:

> The Apocalypse is utterly different from, and foreign to, these writings (i.e. the Fourth Gospel and 1 John); it has no connexion, no affinity, in any way with them; it scarcely, so to speak, has even a syllable in common with them. Nay more, neither does the Epistle (not to speak of the Gospel) contain any mention or thought of the Apocalypse, nor the Apocalypse of the Epistle ... by means of the style one can estimate the difference between the Gospel and Epistle and the Apocalypse. For the former are not only written in faultless Greek, but also show the greatest literary skill in their diction, their reasonings, and the constructions in which they are expressed. There is a complete absence of any barbarous word, or solecism, or any vulgarism whatever. For their author had, as it seems, both kinds of word, by the free gift of the Lord, the word of knowledge and the word of speech. But I will not deny that the other writer had seen revelations and received knowledge and prophecy; nevertheless I observe his style and that his use of the Greek language is not accurate, but that he employs barbarous idioms, in some places committing downright solecisms. These there is no necessity to single out now. For I have not said these things in mockery (let no one think it), but merely to establish the dissimilarity of these writings.[1]

So greatly has this point impressed recent students that T. W. Crafer can say, 'Modern criticism has set aside altogether

[1] Eusebius, *H.E.* vii. 25, Loeb edn., II, pp. 207 f. James Orr sums up the objection in these words: 'Two works so diverse in character—the Gospel calm, spiritual, mystical, abounding in characteristic expressions as "life," "light," "love," etc., written in idiomatic Gr; the Apocalypse abrupt, mysterious, material in its imagery, inexact and barbarous in its idioms, sometimes employing solecisms—could not, it was argued, proceed from the same author' (*ISBE*, IV, p. 2583).

the authorship of the son of Zebedee, and has largely inclined to the view (e.g. Bousset), suggested by Eusebius, that there was a second John who may have been the author.'[1] This difference in style is very real. R. H. Charles has made a thorough examination and has drawn up an impressive list of stylistic differences between the style of John's Gospel and that of Revelation.[2] He notices, for example, the frequent use of the genitive absolute in John and its absence from Revelation, which is also the case with the attracted relative and other constructions. There are vocabulary differences sometimes in that the two writings use different words for the same idea (two different words for 'lamb', for 'possession', for 'until', etc.), sometimes in that words are used in different senses. The Greek of John is idiomatic, but that of Revelation is so unusual that Charles writes a special grammar for it. But it should not be overlooked that Charles also sees a connection between the two writings because of another set of linguistic resemblances.[3] The question is not simple.

Dionysius also sees a difference in approach. The Evangelist 'nowhere adds his name, nor yet proclaims himself, throughout either the Gospel or the Epistle' whereas the author of Revelation 'put himself forward'.[4]

However, there are other considerations that ought to be noted.

a. The solecisms may sometimes be deliberate. Thus R. A. Edwards says, 'It is a strange book, obviously belonging to the world of poetry rather than to that of straight prose, and, as we have been forced to learn in our own times, poets do not always observe the rules of syntax.'[5] It is worth noting that if John does on occasion break grammatical rules, on other occasions he keeps those same rules. In other words it seems

---

[1] *A New Commentary on Holy Scripture*, ed. G. Gore *et al.*, III, 1937, p. 681.
[2] *Op. cit.*, pp. xxix ff. R. H. Preston and A. T. Hanson point out that of 'the 900 or so words in both books they have fewer than half in common' (p. 24).
[3] *Op. cit.*, pp. xxxii f.
[4] Eusebius, *H.E.* vii. 25, Loeb edn., II, p. 199.
[5] *The Gospel according to St. John*, 1954, pp. 26 f.

as though his peculiar Greek is written for a purpose, and not solely through ignorance of the right forms.[1]

Caird is of opinion that the balance of probability is against common authorship, but he does not see the language differences as decisive. Revelation is written in Hebraic Greek. 'But because a man writes in Hebraic Greek, it does not inevitably follow that this is the only Greek he is capable of writing. He may have adopted this style quite deliberately for reasons of his own, as Luke appears to have imitated the style of the Septuagint in his nativity stories, and as the Jew Aquila, in a much more pedantic fashion, chose to reproduce the details of Hebrew idiom in his Greek translation of the Old Testament. John's Greek may be all his own, but it is not the product of incompetence, for he handles it with brilliant lucidity and compelling power.'[2] On the score of lucidity a comment of Farrer's is worth noting: 'We often have to wonder how he came to write what he wrote, but very seldom to wonder what he meant.'[3]

b. Undoubtedly there is much apocalyptic reading behind this work. Allusions to apocalyptic literature and typical apocalyptic expressions are everywhere. Quotations and echoes of this type of literature make for strange reading.

c. Revelation was written in exile. The writer had no access to the tools of scholarship and apparently no opportunity for a leisurely scholarly approach.

d. It was also written in excitement. The writer tells us that he was 'in the spirit'. We must not expect calm, detached, polished prose.[4]

e. It is agreed by all that the author is Aramaic-speaking. But he has obviously read a good deal of Greek and has written in it.

[1] C. F. D. Moule says that this book 'stands alone as the only New Testament writing containing considerable sections of quite barbarously ungrammatical writing, which, nevertheless, achieve a profoundly moving effect' (*The Birth of the New Testament*, 1962, p. 162). It may well have been written of set purpose in such a way as to produce this effect.

[2] P. 5.

[3] P. 50.

[4] 'The "rapt seer" will not speak and write like the self-collected, calmly brooding evangelist' (J. Orr, *op. cit.*, p. 2548).

f. The influence of an amanuensis cannot be ruled out. It is possible that one and the same author may have had the help of an amanuensis in writing the Gospel and have written Revelation without such assistance.

g. It has been pointed out that the writer writes not as an apostle but as a prophet. The less he was known the more likely the next age was to ascribe his book (which claims inspiration and a high place for itself, Rev. i. 10, xxii. 18 f.) to the greatest John it knew.

h. It is possible that some of the curious language is due to the fact that the writer is setting out visions and oracles of divine origin. There is some evidence that an ungrammatical style was held in certain circles at least to be appropriate to such inspired communication.[1]

5. If there are differences in style from the Fourth Gospel there are also resemblances. These two writings in the New Testament alone refer to the *logos* (Jn. i. 1, Rev. xix. 13); these use the imagery of 'the lamb', 'the water of life', 'he that overcometh', 'keeping the commandments', the adjective 'true' (*alēthinos*, nine times in John, four times in 1 John, ten times in Revelation, and five times in all the rest of the New Testament). These two also have a striking form of Zc. xii. 10 (Jn. xix. 37, Rev. i. 7). There is also the invitation to him that is thirsty (Jn. vii. 37, Rev. xxii. 17); a commandment received by Christ from the Father (Jn. x. 18, Rev. ii. 27); white clothing for angels (Jn. xx. 12) and the worthy (Rev. iii. 4). Crafer points out that both writings have the same sharp contrasts between absolute good and absolute evil, they both emphasize the bearing of witness and the keeping of the commandments of God.[2]

6. Some of the ideas of Revelation are said to be incom-

---

[1] A. S. Peake cites Heinrici for the information that 'the Greek oracles also are partial to barbarisms of style. The irregular, strange, and surprising are more effective' (*The Revelation of John*, n.d., pp. 59 f.). He also cites A. Harnack, 'only the mysterious appears divine' (*op. cit.*, p. 60, n.1).

[2] *Op. cit.*, p. 681. See further Godet, *Commentary on the Gospel of John*, I, n.d., pp. 182–190, Alford, pp. 224–228, G. Salmon, *A Historical Introduction to the Study of the Books of the New Testament*, 1892, pp. 211–221.

patible with those in the other Johannine writings. It is not uncommon to find scholars alleging that Revelation is sub-Christian, at least in part. For example, whereas the Gospel and the Epistles emphasize the love of God, Revelation seems to put His wrath in the prominent place. Yet here it must be borne in mind that ideas of wrath and the like would not be at all impossible for a man described as a 'son of thunder'. As R. A. Edwards says, 'We have also to remember that the idea of the "wrath of God" is a normal part of the New Testament, and to accept the idea that there is real opposition between "this world" and the world of the Kingdom.'[1] It has to be borne in mind that the Jews did write fiercely about their persecutors. They regarded them as the enemies of God, and they pulled no punches.

In similar fashion some students make a good deal of the fact that Revelation has a great concern for eschatological imagery, whereas the Gospel concentrates on this life.[2] Revelation is constantly looking for the coming of Christ, whereas in John Christ abides in believers and they in Him. But this is no more than a matter of emphasis. The Gospel sometimes does use traditional eschatological imagery (e.g. Jn. v. 25 ff.). The subject-matter of the two books is very different, and this may be sufficient to account for this point. Certainly it is going too far to say that on this score the two writings demand different authors.

7. It is often argued that John was a very common name, and that therefore we have no real reason for ascribing Revelation to the same author as the Gospel. Whatever be the truth about the use of this name among the Jews,[3] the fact is that we do not have a great number of Christian Johns

[1] *Op. cit.*, p. 26.

[2] Cf. Boismard, 'Generally speaking, it is the eschatological concept which shows deep going differences in both Gospel and Apocalypse' (*op. cit.*, p. 720).

[3] T. Zahn can say, 'The present writer knows no Jew of the Graeco-Roman diaspora with the name of John; whereas *e.g.*, Jude, Joseph, Jonathan, Samuel, Miriam, and Salome occur in Roman inscriptions' (*Introduction to the New Testament*, III, 1909, p. 433, n. 1). He proceeds to say, 'It was not until long after the time of Revelation that the custom arose among the Christians of calling themselves by the names of apostles.'

to choose from. We have no certain knowledge of any Christian John of this period other than the apostle, and John Mark. Even Dionysius, writing as early as the end of the third century, and trying to make a case for an author of Revelation other than John the apostle, can yet say no more than, 'I think that there was a certain other (John) among those that were in Asia, since it is said both that there were two tombs at Ephesus, and that each of the two is said to be John's.'[1] Notice the caution with which he puts the suggestion forward, 'I think... it is said....' Clearly Dionysius had no exact knowledge, and equally clearly he wanted to establish the point so that if he had had reliable information he would have brought it forward. E. Stauffer says that the evidence that there were two tombs in Ephesus bearing this name has been refuted by V. Schultze.[2]

The evidence that there were two Johns cannot be said to be really strong. Edwards says, 'The fact from which we start is that antiquity assigned the whole of the Johannine literature to one man. That judgment ought only to be disturbed on irrefutable grounds.'[3]

8. E. Stauffer sees in the liturgical interest common to the Fourth Gospel and the Revelation evidence for an affinity between them. He finds in this an argument for apostolic authorship for both.[4]

Stauffer has this to say on the matter of authorship: 'These three main Johannine writings are not just related in style, they are related in theology, too, and they form with II and III John an individual group of writings which stand out very clearly from the other literature of the primitive Church. In view of all this we have sufficient ground to ascribe these five writings to a common author of remarkable individuality and great significance, and to identify him as the apostle John.' Then he notes the possibility that disciples shared in the writing

---

[1] Eusebius, *H.E.* vii. 25, Loeb edn., II, p. 203.
[2] *Op. cit.*, pp. 262 f., n. 66. He gives the reference as *Kleinasien*, II, pp. 104 ff., 450.
[3] *Op. cit.*, p. 2
[4] *Op. cit.*, p 4:.

and concludes, 'So we have to sum up our position in the cautious thesis: the Johannine writings of the NT are to be ascribed to the apostle John or to his influence.'[1] Kümmel cites, as favouring apostolic authorship for the Gospel and Revelation, 'most of the Catholic scholars, Michaelis, Albertz, Hadorn, de Zwaan, Klijn, Feine-Behm, Guthrie, E. Stauffer'.[2]

9. A number of recent scholars accept the view that John the apostle was martyred early and that accordingly he cannot have been the author of Revelation (or the Gospel). I have discussed this view elsewhere and have endeavoured to show that the evidence in favour of this view is scanty.[3] It should be mentioned here for the sake of completeness but the idea has little to recommend it.

10. The statement that on the foundation stones of the heavenly city are written the names of 'the twelve apostles of the Lamb' (xxi. 14) is often adduced as incompatible with apostolic authorship. The allegation is often made very firmly, but it is difficult to see why. An apostle might well give this information.[4] Another subjective consideration is the contention that the writer shows no trace of having been an eyewitness of the earthly ministry of Jesus. This is scarcely a strong objection in a book so very much preoccupied with heaven.

IV. DATE

There appear to be two dates only for which any considerable arguments are available, in the time of the Emperor Domitian, or in or just after that of Nero. The early tradition of the church strongly favours the time of Domitian, i.e. somewhere about AD 90–95.[5]

---

[1] *Op. cit.*, p. 41.

[2] *Op. cit.*, p. 331.

[3] See *Studies in the Fourth Gospel*, 1969, pp. 280ff.

[4] An apostle must originally have been responsible for Lk. xxii. 30. Again, if the Pauline authorship of Ephesians be accepted, Paul can call himself an apostle and go on to speak of the church as built on the foundation of the apostles and prophets (Eph. i. 1, ii. 20; cf. iii. 5, iv. 11).

[5] Thus Irenaeus speaks of 'the apocalyptic vision' as 'seen no very long time since, but almost in our day, towards the end of Domitian's reign' (*Adv. Haer.* v. 30. 3, *ANF*, I, pp. 559 f.). Later tradition is of this type.

The principal reason for dating the book during this reign is the fact that it contains a number of indications that emperor-worship was practised, and this is thought to have become widespread in Domitian's day. These references are to the universal worship demanded by the beast, who is held to represent the Roman emperor (xiii. 4, 12, 15 f., xiv. 9, 11, xv. 2, xvi. 2, xix. 20, xx. 4). This point seems reasonably clear. It is difficult to think that these passages do not have the demand for worship of the emperor in mind.

But dating this accurately is more difficult. Thus Julius Caesar had been worshipped as a god during his lifetime, and, while Augustus was more cautious, there were temples in his honour in some of the provinces. Tiberius actively discouraged the practice, but Caligula went to the other extreme with the demand that his statue be worshipped (though there is not much evidence of any real attempt to enforce this). In any case his successor, Claudius, completely reversed this policy. Nero persecuted the Christians, but this was because he wanted a scapegoat for the great fire in Rome, not because he claimed to be divine. Neither in his reign nor in that of his immediate successors was emperor-worship set forward. Galba, Otho and Vitellius reigned so briefly that the question cannot be said to have been real for them, while Vespasian and Titus were practical men who did not concern themselves with being worshipped. It is true that, from the time of Nero on, the cult tended to grow in some areas and it is barely possible that the references in Revelation could be understood of some period under or after Nero.

But all are agreed that the significant advance in emperor-worship took place in the reign of Domitian (AD 81–96). Whereas the earlier emperors had at best accepted emperor-worship, and at worst actively discouraged it, Domitian seems really to have regarded himself as a god.[1] On the score of emperor-worship Domitian's reign is the most probable by far. It was Domitian above all who demanded worship from his subjects. A difficulty is that we do not know what method he adopted to bring this about. Specifically there is no record

[1] See Suetonius, *Domit.* 13.

of Domitian's having executed or imprisoned those who refused to worship him.[1]

Next we should consider the indications that Revelation was written in a time of persecution. There are some indications that persecution had already begun, for Antipas had been killed (ii. 13), and John himself appears to have been exiled to Patmos (i. 9). But there are more indications of approaching trouble, and the situation seems to be that what had already taken place was seen by John as the harbinger of worse to follow. Thus the church at Smyrna is about to suffer and her sufferings will include some imprisonment (ii. 10), and the church at Philadelphia is warned of 'the hour of trial (mg.), which shall come upon all the world, to try them that dwell upon the earth' (iii. 10). The visions have references to 'the souls of them that were slain for the word of God, and for the testimony which they held' (vi. 9), and to the woman 'drunken with the blood of the saints, and with the blood of the martyrs of Jesus' (xvii. 6; cf. xvi. 6, xviii. 24, xix. 2, xx. 4).

We may take it, then, that there had been some persecution of Christians, and that the indications were that much worse was in store. This, it is said, does not fit the time of Nero, for his outburst against the Christians appears to have been local and brief though fierce. It is said to accord much better with Domitian. But it is very difficult to find evidence that Domitian did in fact persecute outside Rome. There is evidence of his having certain people executed there, such as Flavius Clemens and his wife Domitilla. The reason given for this was 'atheism', which suggests to most students Christianity (it was a denial of the Roman gods, and Christians were often accused of this crime, their retention of belief in one God not being held sufficient to refute it). While later Christians sometimes speak of a persecution under Domitian[2] the evidence is not easy to

---

[1] It is perhaps worth noting that emperor-worship was not imposed by the emperors, at least before Domitian. It was the spontaneous response of the people in the provinces to the peace and good government they owed to the Romans. There was thus a popular demand for emperor-worship and the Christians would have found themselves very much out of step.

[2] E.g. Eusebius, *H.E.* iii. 18. 4, iii. 20. 5, Tertullian, *Apol.* v, *ANF*, III, p. 22.

find. Of course, if it be held on other grounds that this writing is to be dated during Domitian's reign, then it will certainly afford evidence of such persecution. But as far as establishing the date of the book goes, all that we can say from the evidence of persecution is that it accords with all that we know of Domitian that there should have been such persecution, and that there is no other period in the first century which fits nearly as well.

Again, it is urged that the book shows evidence of knowledge of the Nero *redivivus* myth (e.g. xvii. 8, 11). After Nero's death it was thought in some circles that he would return. At first this appears to have been a refusal to believe that he was actually dead.[1] Later it took the form of a belief that he would come to life again. This took time to develop and Domitian's reign is about as early as we can expect it.

A further indication is that the churches of Asia Minor seem to have a period of development behind them. This would scarcely have been possible at the time of the Neronic persecution, the only serious competitor in date to the Domitianic period. Thus we are told that the church in Laodicea was 'rich, and increased with goods' (iii. 17). But as the city was destroyed by an earthquake in AD 60/61 this must have been considerably later.[2] Again, the church at Smyrna seems not to have been in existence in the days of Paul.[3] All the churches in chapters ii and iii appear to have had a period of history. Especially is this the case with those of whom things could be said like 'thou hast left thy first love' (ii. 4), or 'thou hast a name that thou livest, and art dead' (iii. 1). Some have drawn a similar conclusion from the mention of the Nicolaitans. That they are referred to simply by name and with no reference to what they taught or did seems to indicate that

---

[1] This view is reflected in *Syb. Or.* v. 137 ff., where it was thought that Nero would reappear in Persia. A number of pretenders actually appeared

[2] Tacitus, *Ann.* xiv. 27.

[3] Polycarp writes to the Philippians, 'For concerning you he (Paul) boasts in all the Churches who then alone had known the Lord, for we had not yet known him' (xi. 3, Loeb trans.). As Polycarp was bishop of Smyrna his 'we' presumably means the church at Smyrna, and these words then indicate that the church was not in existence at the time in question.

they were an established group, perhaps even a sect or heresy. But this, too, would take time to develop.

The argument for a date in the time of Nero assumes that the reference to emperor-worship and to persecution will fit this reign. It is also thought that the 'number of the beast' is to be understood only by seeing the 666 as a reference to Nero (see the commentary on xiii. 18 for the reasons for this identification and also for the legitimate doubts that are raised). But the trouble is that the reference is by no means sure. Irenaeus, for example, discussed the passage, suggesting a number of views of what the 666 symbolizes, but he did not even include Nero in his list, let alone regard this as a likely conjecture.[1] Indeed, Zahn maintains that the view that Nero is in mind was not thought of by anyone until 1831 when Fritzsche put it forward.[2] The number of the beast cannot be said to give strong support.

Another passage which is said to support this dating is that which refers to seven kings of whom 'five are fallen, and one is' (xvii. 10). Counting from Augustus, Nero was the fifth emperor, and the argument runs that Revelation dates from the end of Nero's reign and the beginning of the following. This view runs into difficulties in determining who is the eighth king (xvii. 11). If we omit Galba, Otho, and Vitellius (none of whom was ever secure and whose reigns together occupied less than a year) we come to Domitian as the eighth. If we include them, it is Vitellius, but his reign was so short as to rule him out as a candidate for the eighth, who is called 'the beast that was, and is not' and is clearly cast for an important role.

Either way there are difficulties. Hort was impressed chiefly by two things. The first is the way the book fits in with the last days of Nero and the impression Nero made on his contemporaries: 'Nero affected the imagination of the world as Domitian, as far as we know, never did.' The second is that the book 'breathes the atmosphere of a time of wild com-

[1] *Adv. Haer.* v. 30. 3. He mentions Euanthas, Lateinos and Teitan and favours the last.
[2] *Op. cit.*, III, p. 447, n. 4.

motion'.[1] But there is evidence that the impression made by Nero was lasting. There is no reason for holding that it had faded away by the time of Domitian. And the second point is subjective. There is no valid reason for holding that it points to Nero rather than Domitian. The evidence for the Neronic date cannot be said to be conclusive.[2]

A further consideration, sometimes urged, is that if John the apostle wrote both the Fourth Gospel and Revelation then, in view of the linguistic differences between the two writings, there must be a wide divergence in dating. It is suggested accordingly that Revelation was written comparatively early, when the author's knowledge of Greek was very imperfect, and the Gospel some years later, when he had had time to become master of his new language.

But this view will scarcely stand. The date of John is far from certain and there are some grounds for holding that it is to be dated before the destruction of Jerusalem in AD 70. But the decisive thing is that the language of Revelation is not that of a raw beginner in Greek. It is not that the writer does not know the rules of Greek grammar, but that he decides for himself which rules he will keep. This view also disregards the possibility of the use of an amanuensis for the writing of the Gospel. If this was done (and it seems to me the only way in which common authorship of the two writings can be defended) nothing can be concluded from the standard of Greek as to the dates of the two writings.[3]

Some statements in the book are held to point to an early date. When, for example, the Seer is given a rod and told to measure the Temple (xi. 1) it seems a reasonable inference

---

[1] P. xxvi.

[2] R. M. Grant, however, after examining the evidence concludes, 'All we can say is that a situation between 68 and 70 is not excluded' (*A Historical Introduction to the New Testament*, 1963, p. 237).

[3] C. F. Burney thought that 'if the Gospel was written in Aramaic prior to the author's arrival in Ephesus somewhat late in his life, and he then adopted Greek owing to the exigencies of his new surroundings, such Greek as we find in the Apocalypse would not be surprising' (*The Aramaic Origin of the Fourth Gospel*, 1922, p. 149). The possibility cannot be ruled out, but few have been persuaded that the Fourth Gospel was, in fact, written in Aramaic.

that the Temple was standing at the time, so that the date will be before AD 70.[1]

Sometimes other dates are suggested. A few people have thought, for example, of a date in the time of Vespasian.[2] The principal reason is that Vespasian appears to be the emperor in mind in xvii. 10, which speaks of five kings as having fallen while 'one is'. This certainly looks like Vespasian, but does not preclude us from thinking of a vision originally seen in the reign of that emperor, and later incorporated into the book. But, while the evidence is far from being so conclusive that no other view is possible, on the whole it seems that a date in the time of Domitian, i.e. *c.* AD 90–95, best suits the facts.

V. SOURCES

A number of scholars have suggested that our author has made use of sources, sometimes a number of sources. Thus it is not uncommon to have it suggested that he has taken over a Jewish apocalypse or apocalypses. Sometimes this view arises from the contents of certain parts of Revelation which look like fragments of earlier writings. Sometimes scholars affirm that the way references to 'the Lamb' are brought in seems like an afterthought (e.g. xv. 3, xxi. 22 f.). They suggest that this is a way of making a Christian writing out of something that was not Christian before.

All such schemes seem to founder on the fact that the style of the whole book is so uniform. This does not mean that there are no differences, but that the differences are of a very minor character in comparison with the most unusual Greek which pervades the entire book. There was such a thing as the com-

---

[1] Zahn, however, maintains that the application to Jerusalem of the name Sodom in the same chapter (xi. 8) presupposes that the city had already been destroyed (*op. cit.*, p. 438).

[2] A. S. Peake cites Mommsen, J. V. Bartlet, and C. A. Scott (*op. cit.*' pp. 96 f.). In addition to the argument from xvii. 10 he thinks that 'the anticipation that Nero would return with the Parthians suits this period of Vespasian's reign (i.e. the latter part of the reign) far better than its beginning'. Against it he urges that 'it does not account so well as a later date for the reference to the eighth emperor, nor for the prominence given to the worship of the emperor, nor for the belief that Nero would return from the abyss, while it has no support whatever in tradition'.

mon stock of apocalyptic writings and there is no difficulty in holding that John made use of it. He may even have taken over sections of earlier writings which suited his purposes. But, if John did use sources, he made them so thoroughly his own that there is no chance of our separating them out now.

Attention is sometimes drawn to the repetition of themes or ideas. This can be demonstrated (e.g. the two accounts of the beast in chapters xiii, xvii). But this does not point to sources or diversity of authorship. Nor does the repetition of the sevenfold judgments, as in the seals, the trumpets and the bowls. It seems to be part of the method of our author to repeat his themes,[1] not exactly, it is true, but on another level like a spiral staircase. In this way the same ground is traversed, but other perspectives are revealed and fresh facets of the revelation are brought out.

It must also be borne in mind that apocalyptic was a peculiarly Jewish type of literature so that John would, in using this vehicle for his message, necessarily use forms with Jewish affinities. To show that part of the book contains Jewish ideas thus does not prove that it is a Jewish work adapted.[2] In any case it is unlikely that this book was written at one sitting. There is nothing improbable in the suggestion that the visions took place over a period of years. This would account for a certain lack of coherence. But the use of sources is not necessarily indicated.[3]

---

[1] This was noticed long ago by Victorinus of Pettau (who died under Diocletian, 284–305). Boismard cites him as saying that this book 'does not set forth a continuous series of future events, but repeats the same sequences of events under various forms' (*op. cit.*, p. 702).

[2] Cf. J. Moffatt, 'The criterion of Jewish or Christian is hazardous in a book which deals with eschatology, where no primitive Christian could work without drawing upon Jewish traditions, in themselves neither stereotyped nor homogeneous. Though a given passage may not be couched in Christian language, it does not necessarily come from a Jewish pen' (*An Introduction to the Literature of the New Testament*, 1927, p. 492).

[3] K. and S. Lake point out that 'by leaving out all the passages which have obviously Christian content, it is possible to arrive at an original Jewish source. But the question remains whether it is legitimate to excise those passages which are contrary to the hypothesis. Our own opinion is that it is not, and that the book was Christian from the beginning, though it is undoubtedly based on Jewish models' (*An Introduction to the New Testament*, 1938, p. 178).

ANALYSIS

I. PROLOGUE (i. 1–20).

   a. Introduction (i. 1–3).
   b. Salutation (i. 4–8).
   c. The first vision (i. 9–20).

II. THE LETTERS TO THE CHURCHES (ii. 1–iii. 22).

   a. To the church of Ephesus (ii. 1–7).
   b. To the church of Smyrna (ii. 8–11).
   c. To the church of Pergamum (ii. 12–17).
   d. To the church of Thyatira (ii. 18–29).
   e. To the church of Sardis (iii. 1–6).
   f. To the church of Philadelphia (iii. 7–13).
   g. To the church of Laodicea (iii. 14–22).

III. A VISION OF HEAVEN (iv. 1–11).

IV. THE SEVEN SEALS (v. 1–viii. 5).

   a. The unopened book (v. 1–5).
   b. The Lion of the tribe of Juda (v. 5–14).
   c. The first seal (vi. 1, 2).
   d. The second seal (vi. 3, 4).
   e. The third seal (vi. 5, 6).
   f. The fourth seal (vi. 7, 8).
   g. The fifth seal (vi. 9–11).
   h. The sixth seal (vi. 12–17).
   i. An interlude (vii. 1–17).
   j. The seventh seal (viii. 1–5).

V. THE SEVEN TRUMPETS (viii. 6–xi. 19).

   a. The first trumpet (viii. 6, 7).
   b. The second trumpet (viii. 8, 9).
   c. The third trumpet (viii. 10, 11).
   d. The fourth trumpet (viii. 12).
   e. The eagle (viii. 13).
   f. The fifth trumpet (ix. 1–12).
   g. The sixth trumpet (ix. 13–21).
   h. An interlude (x. 1–xi. 14).
   i. The seventh trumpet (xi. 15–19).

COMMENTARY

I. PROLOGUE (i. 1–20)

a. Introduction (i. 1–3)

1. The very first word of this book, *apokalupsis* (translated *The Revelation*), sets the stage. The word means an uncovering of something hidden, the making known of what man could not find out for himself. It makes plain that the book it introduces is not a book of human wisdom, nor for that matter a discussion of philosophical or theological problems. It is revelation. It is a setting forth of what God has made known. This revelation is the revelation *of Jesus Christ* which could mean either that the revelation was made by Jesus Christ or that it was made about Him or that it belongs to Him. In one way or another all three are true. But in view of the following *which God gave unto him* we should probably understand it to mean possession. It is His revelation and that of no-one else that we are to read. And it came from God the Father. It is not a human, or even an angelic production.

This revelation is concerned with prediction. It is expressly said that it is to show God's servants things which must happen soon. *Shortly* is not defined. We get the exact expression again in xxii. 6, and a similar one in ii. 16, iii. 11, xxii. 7, 12, 20. This could mean that the fulfilment is expected in the very near future. But we must also bear in mind that in the prophetic perspective the future is sometimes foreshortened. In other words the word may refer primarily to the certainty of the events in question. The Lord God has determined them and He will speedily bring them to pass. But speedily has a reference to His time not ours. With Him one day is as a thousand years and a thousand years as one day (2 Pet. iii. 8). It is also possible that the term should be understood as 'suddenly', i.e. not so much 'soon' as 'without delay when the time comes'.

The revelation was not made directly by God to John. God *sent* it, and *signified it by his angel* (cf. xxii. 6, 16). *Signified* is cognate with 'sign', and, though the point cannot be pressed, it is natural to associate this with the multiplicity of 'signs' narrated in the book. John describes himself as God's *servant*, i.e. 'slave', a designation which Paul uses quite often (Rom. i. 1, etc.).

2. John bore witness to the word of God. This may be a reference to some past occasion (the aorist indicates a specific occasion and not the general practice), but it is more likely to be something akin to an epistolary aorist and refer to this book. John is saying then that this book is his testimony to the word of God. With this he links *the testimony of Jesus Christ* (*testimony, marturia*, is cognate with *bare record, emarturēsen*). This could mean, 'the testimony about Jesus Christ', o*r*, 'the testimony borne by Jesus Christ'. It is likely to be the latter. Revelation is the record of what God has said to John through His angel and of what Jesus Christ has said to him. We should omit the *and* after *Jesus Christ*. The *things that he saw* are *the word* and *the testimony* previously mentioned, not an addition to them. *Saw* is peculiarly appropriate in a book like this where there are so many visions.

3. This is the first of seven beatitudes scattered through the book (i. 3, xiv. 13, xvi. 15, xix. 9, xx. 6, xxii. 7, 14). *Readeth* here means 'reads aloud', and in view of the context there is no real doubt but that reading in church is meant. This implies that John regards his book as holy Scripture. This is all the more likely in that he proceeds to call it a *prophecy* (even if we omit *this* with some good MSS there is no real doubt but that it is this book to which he is referring). This will also be the significance of the warning against meddling with its contents which he places at the end (xxii. 18 f.). It is for this reason that a blessing can be called down on those who read and hear the book. If the book were a merely human product this would be incongruous. As a divine revelation it is the most natural thing imaginable.

We should not understand *prophecy* to mean 'prediction'.

The word does allow for prediction (and there is certainly a liberal element of prediction in this book), but basically it points to divine origin. The prophet was a man who could say, 'Thus saith the Lord'. This book is from God. John proceeds to call not only for a hearing of it but for an observing of the things written in it. He does not wish merely to stimulate men's interest but to influence their actions. Scripture is a guide to conduct as well as the source of doctrine. For *at hand*, cf. xxii. 10 and the note on verse 1.

b. Salutation (i. 4–8)

The book of Revelation is cast into the form of a letter. Some have felt that this is artificial, but there is no real reason for doubt. It is addressed to seven churches in Asia Minor, and, while clearly it was meant from the beginning for a wider circle, it is equally clear that it was meant as a serious communication to these churches. For the usual epistolary form in the first century see the note on 1 Thessalonians i. 1.[1]

4. The address is to *the seven churches* of Asia, i.e. of the Roman province of that name, the western part of what we call Asia Minor. We do not know on what principle the seven were selected. There were certainly more than seven Christian churches in the region by the time this book was written (Acts xx. 5 ff.; Col. i. 2, iv. 13). John may have had some special relations with these seven. Again, if the seven named in verse 11 were visited in order, one would traverse a rough circle. This is a figure of completeness, and seven (a number of which our author is fond) is the number of perfection. For one so fond of symbolism such things can scarcely be without significance.

In the greeting, *grace* and *peace* (see the note on 1 Thes. i. 1) are said to be from *him which is, and which was, and which is to come* (cf. i. 8, iv. 8, xi. 17, xvi. 5). This most unusual expression clearly refers to God the Father. The Greek is not grammatical (*apo* is followed by a nominative, and *ēn* is preceded by an article), but it is an arresting way of stressing the changelessness and the eternity of God. The whole expression seems intended as a title. It is a name which expresses something of the character of God. Barclay comments: 'In the terrible days in which he was writing John stayed his heart on the changelessness of God, and used the defiance of grammar to underline his faith.'

The *seven Spirits* might conceivably refer to a group of angelic beings. But coming between references to the Father and the Son it is more probable that this is an unusual way of designating the Holy Spirit. John never uses the expression 'the Holy Spirit', but he uses the word *Spirit* in a variety of ways. 'The Spirit' is found in ii. 7, 17, etc., so he clearly knows of the Holy Spirit. *Seven Spirits* recurs in iii. 1, iv. 5, v. 6. On the whole it seems most probable that we should think of the number *seven* as signifying perfection or the like, and of the whole expression as pointing to the Holy Spirit. The number may be derived from Isaiah xi. 2f., and be meant to turn our thoughts to the seven modes of operation of the Spirit.

5. The third source of grace and peace is *Jesus Christ*, who is characterized as *the faithful witness* (cf. iii. 14, Ps. lxxxix. 37). John puts some emphasis on witness in verse 2 and this hammers in his point. He 'wants us to be in no doubt that what he reports is adequately attested. He goes on to speak of Jesus as *the first begotten of the dead, and the prince of the kings of the earth* (for the conjunction cf. Ps. lxxxix. 29). Jesus is a figure of majesty. But He is also revered for what He has done for men and John goes off into a doxology. He begins with Christ's love (the tense is really present, 'to him that loves us'), and then goes on to His redeeming activity. *Washed* should be 'loosed' (*lusanti* is read by the better MSS, and this would readily be corrupted into *lousanti* in view of the reference to blood). Christ has redeemed us from our sins and He did it at the cost of His own blood.

6. He has made us 'a kingdom' (so, rather than *kings*). The kingdom of God was stressed in the teaching of Jesus. It was

His main topic. Here we find that those who are Christ's constitute the kingdom. It is not like earthly kingdoms, a realm with known boundaries, population, etc. It consists of those people who have been loosed from their sins through Christ and who now live to do His service. The order is important. First comes the reference to His redeeming work, and only then that to the kingdom. As a result of what Christ has done for them, believers become other than what they were. They are made into the very kingdom of God. In apposition with 'kingdom' is the further expression, *priests unto God and his Father*. The kingdom consists of *priests*. Notice that it is ordinary Christians who are called *priests*, not some privileged hierarchy. Now the essential thing about a priest is that he mediates. He speaks to God on behalf of men and to men on behalf of God. Believers are assigned this responsible task by their God. They are to pray to God for the world. And they are to witness to the world of what God has done. They are to speak to the world in God's name the message of reconciliation (2 Cor. v. 20). There may also be the thought that priests offer sacrifice, for Christ's people make the sacrifice of themselves (Rom. xii. 1). Notice that God is characterized with respect to His relationship to Christ (*his* Father), rather than to us (not 'our Father'). To Christ, who has done so much for us, is ascribed *glory and dominion for ever and ever*. There are many such little expressions of praise in Revelation. John delights in his Lord, and loves to bring this out in doxologies and songs.

7. After the doxology comes a piece of eager looking forward to the coming of the Lord (cf. xxii. 20). John thinks of Him as coming *with clouds*, a description which recalls what is said of 'one like the Son of man' (Dn. vii. 13). Clouds are often mentioned in the Old Testament in connection with divine activity (e.g. Nu. xi. 25, Ps. civ. 3, Is. xix. 1), and we are to think here of a scene of divine majesty as the Lord Jesus returns to earth in triumph. This triumph will be open for all to see, and it is this reversal of things at the first coming on which John seizes. In language reminiscent of Zechariah xii.

10 he depicts the manifestation of the Lord to His foes, who will be disconcerted at this unexpected reversal of roles.

John's *Even so, Amen* (which combines the Greek and Hebrew forms of assent in a vigorous expression of approval) causes difficulty to some, coming as it does after *all kindreds of the earth shall wail because of him*. It is felt that this enthusiastic approval is rather less than Christian (and similar expressions recur throughout the book). But John is not being vindictive. When Christians suffer persecution the name of their God is reviled and their cause is despised. But this is not final. John records in vivid symbol the overthrow of the wicked and the vindication of God and of good. And this he does not as a mildly interested spectator. He is wholeheartedly committed to the service of God. He is eager that God's cause be seen to prosper. So he does not simply record that the wicked will in fact be overthrown. Their overthrow means the triumph of good and the vindication of Christians who had suffered so much. So John exults in it.

8. *The Lord* is most often used in the New Testament of Jesus, a usage which is found in Revelation (xi. 8, xxii. 20, etc.). But more often it refers in this book to the Father, as it does here. Revelation is concerned with the problems of power and this verse gives expression early in the book to the conviction that God is sovereign. *Alpha and Omega* are the first and last letters of the Greek alphabet, and mean much the same as the following *the beginning and the ending*. God was before all things, and nothing survives Him. His eternity is brought out also in *which is, and which was, and which is to come* (see on verse 4). The final expression, *the Almighty*, carries on the thought that none can resist the power of God, though we should bear in mind that the word denotes not so much the exercise of naked power as the all-embracing sovereignty which God exercises.

c. The first vision (i. 9–20)
John did not write this book of his own volition, but was instructed to do so. He tells us of this before getting down to

the matter of the book. We may profitably consider the vision in two stages, the first telling of the command to write and the second of how John saw the glorious Lord.

i. The command to write (i. 9-11). John begins by disclaiming any place of eminence. He is writing not because he is some superior person but because 'in the Spirit' he received a command to write.

9. John first underlines his lowliness, speaking of himself as *your brother*, and going on to remind his readers that he shared with them *in tribulation*. This word means sore trouble and in the Greek it is linked under one article with *the kingdom and patience* (this last means an active and manly endurance rather than a negative resignation; see note on ii. 2). The three in some sense belong together. The trials and the kingdom go together. John's further statement that he was *in the isle that is called Patmos, for the word of God* . . . probably signifies banishment, and in the case of one so insignificant as a Christian preacher, that would have meant hard labour in quarries or the like. Patmos is one of the Dodecanese Islands off the coast of Asia Minor. It is crescent-shaped and about eight miles by four miles.

10. *I was* (*egenomēn*) means 'I came to be' (as also in the previous verse). *In the Spirit* is an expression not uncommon in the New Testament, though elsewhere it is used of such things as prayer, love, or even baptism. The use here is peculiar to Revelation and is found again in iv. 2, xvii. 3, xxi. 10 (in each of which AV begins 'spirit' with a small 's'; the capital should be uniform). It may denote something like a trance. It is certainly a state in which the Seer is specially open to the Holy Spirit and ready to see visions.

This particular vision took place *on the Lord's day*. This is the only occasion in the New Testament when this day is mentioned, and is thus the first reference to a Christian Sunday (though the observance of the first day of the week as a day for Christian assembly and worship is found earlier, Jn. xx. 19, Acts xx. 7, 1 Cor. xvi. 2). Some have thought that we are to understand that John was at worship, but he gives no indication that he was with a company of worshippers. At any rate, on this day and in this state he first heard a voice, coming from behind him, a voice which he describes as *of a trumpet*. Trumpets are mentioned more often in Revelation than in all the rest of the New Testament put together, and they are usually associated with the last things.

11. The words *I am Alpha and Omega, the first and the last: and* are absent from the better MSS and have evidently been introduced into the text from verse 8. These terms can be used of Christ (verse 17, xxii. 13), but they are not so used here. John simply records the command to write what he sees and to send the resulting book to the seven churches. These are now definitely named, probably in the order in which they would be visited by a messenger taking the letters to them.

ii. The vision of the glorious Lord (i. 12–20). The placing of this vision of Christ right at the beginning of the book is significant. This book is an unveiling or revealing (see on verse 1). The Christians were a pitiably small remnant, persecuted by mighty foes. To all outward appearance their situation was hopeless. But it is only as Christ is seen for what He really is that anything else can be seen in its true perspective. So for these persecuted ones it was important that first of all the glory' and the majesty of the risen Lord be brought out. In doing this John persistently makes use of words and concepts associated in the Old Testament with God. He does not hesitate to employ divine attributes to describe the glorious Christ. And he does not do this and then forget it. The titles used of Christ in this vision are taken up and used elsewhere, notably in the addresses to the churches in chapters ii and iii (only that to the church of Laodicea is not drawn from this chapter).

12. The voice had come from behind the Seer so he turned to see who it was that spoke (*to see the voice* is a most unusual expression and does not appear to be paralleled; but the meaning is not in doubt). He saw seven golden 'lampstands' (so rather than *candlesticks*; *luchnia* denotes a stand on which a lamp, *luchnos*, or lamps might be stood or hung). Some have seen the origin of this in the Old Testament (Ex. xxv. 31, or 1 Ki. vii. 49, or Zc. iv. 2). But none of these passages gives us a picture of seven separate lampstands. Though John's language may have coincidences with these passages his thought is his own.

13. The lampstands are not important. They are no more than the setting for Him whom John describes as *one like unto the Son of man*. This last expression is not exactly the same in Greek as the one used so constantly by our Lord in the Gospels (there there are two articles, 'the Son of the man', but here none), and it seems to be based rather on Daniel vii. 13. There we read of a heavenly Being coming with the clouds and receiving a mighty dominion. Clearly John ascribed the highest place to Christ. The *garment down to the foot* is the mark of a personage of distinction. Some have argued from this robe and the following reference to being girded at the breasts that John thinks of Jesus as in priestly dress. Against this is the fact that others than priests wore long robes. Again, though priests did wear the girdle higher than others, in their case it was a woven sash and not a golden clasp, which was rather the mark of royalty. The clothing indicates that its wearer was important, but not necessarily that he was a priest.

14. The whiteness of Christ's hair reminds us that the hair of 'the Ancient of days' (i.e. God Himself) is likened to 'the pure wool' in Daniel vii. 9. Whiteness of hair conveys ideas like wisdom and the dignity of age. Here there is a double comparison to *wool* and to *snow* (wool, of course, is not necessarily white, but when pure wool is white it is very white). White hair by itself might leave us with the impression of calmness and dignity, but not of energy and spiritedness. This is rectified by the reference to the *eyes* which flashed like *a flame of fire* (cf. ii. 18, xix. 12, Dn. x. 6).

15. The *feet* are likened to *chalkolibanon*. This word is not found anywhere before this book, and neither here nor in its other occurrence in ii. 18 does the context make clear what it means. AV renders *fine brass*, taking its cue from the *chalko-* (though this properly denotes copper or bronze rather than brass; see note on 1 Cor. xiii. 1).[1] It seems probable that we should understand the term of some alloy of copper, but the evidence does not permit us to say with any certainty which particular alloy. *As if they burned in a furnace* strengthens the conviction that the term means something metallic. John next tells us that His voice was *as the sound of many waters*, a description applied by Ezekiel to the voice of God (Ezk. xliii. 2). Incidentally, this description is singularly appropriate for one living on the small island of Patmos and never out of the sound of the breakers.

16. The *seven stars* are explained in verse 20 as 'the angels of the seven churches'. Their situation *in his right hand* indicates favour and protection. This is all the more interesting in view of the strong criticisms to be urged in the next couple of chapters against some of them. They have their defects, but the strong Son of God has not abandoned them. Rather He holds them still in His hand. But the reference to the *sharp twoedged sword* which went *out of his mouth* is a reminder of the sterner side to His nature. The sword is a weapon of offence and points to decisive action against all those who oppose His will. Incidentally *HDB* comments on the imagery used here, 'This last image is not so strange as appears at first sight, for the short Roman sword was tongue-like in shape'[2] (cf. also Is. xlix. 2, Heb. iv. 12). John now goes on to the face, which he likens to the shining of the sun (cf. x. 1, Mt. xiii. 43) in its 'strength' (a distinctly unusual expression, but cf. Jdg. v. 31). The appearance of the Lord, then, is dazzling, and would be terrible for His foes.

17. Indeed, John, His servant, could not stand the sight, but *fell at his feet as dead*. The last two words show that this is not an Oriental prostration designed to show respect, but the physical effects of the tremendous vision. John was comforted by the Christ Himself, who put *his right hand* on him. We have

---

[1] Leon Morris, 1 *Corinthians* (*TNTC*), 1958.   [2] Art. 'Sword'.

already been told that Christ held the stars in this hand (16) and we are told so again (20). We should not preoccupy ourselves with the question of how He could do both these things with the one hand. John is talking in symbols and it is the symbolism that is important, not the possibility of our reconstructing the picture. At one and the same time Christ has the whole church in His hand, and He takes action for the needs of the individual. Both truths are important. John often uses pieces of imagery difficult to reconcile with each other (e.g. vi. 8; viii. 7 with ix. 4; viii. 12; xiv. 4; xvii. 1 with 3; xx. 3; xx. 13).

The words *Fear not* ('Stop being afraid') are familiar from the Gospels where Jesus spoke to several people in this way. *The first and the last* (used again of Christ in ii. 8, xxii. 13) means very much the same as 'Alpha and Omega' used of God in verse 8 (cf. Is. xliv. 6, xlviii. 12). It is another application of divine terms to Christ.

18. The bearing of the resurrection is now brought out. Christ's victory over death meant a great deal to the early Christians as we see from Acts, and the stress on the resurrection thus early in Revelation is quite in character. In this verse there is the thought of Christ's continuing life (cf. Jn. i. 4, xiv. 6, etc.). The same expression is used of the Father in Revelation iv. 10, x. 6 (cf. Dn. xii. 7), so that we have another example of the use of identical qualities to describe the Father and the Son.

Hell is the Greek *Hadēs*, the place of the departed spirits, and not 'Gehenna', the place of torment. It is used in this way in Acts ii. 27, 31. But in Revelation it is always linked with *death* and regarded as something of an enemy. Here Christ is said to have *the keys of hell and of death*. The *keys* symbolize authority. Christ has the power to send men to death and hell or to take men away from them. He is supreme, and a supremacy over the spirit world and over death itself is a supremacy such as the tyrants who persecuted John's readers never dreamed of.

19. Now the command to write (verse 11) is repeated and

enlarged. John is to include *the things which thou hast seen* (i.e. the vision of Christ; perhaps also the expression should be taken to mean 'the things you will have seen' for there are many other visions which are to be recorded), *and the things which are* (i.e. the true state of present events; we see this especially in the next two chapters where the condition of the seven churches is ruthlessly exposed), *and the things which shall be hereafter* (it was important that some indication be given of future events for the suffering saints; a good deal of this book is given over to what was to happen in days ahead).

20. For *mystery* see the notes on 1 Corinthians ii. 7, 2 Thessalonians ii. 7, *TNTC*. It does not mean what is 'mysterious' in our sense of the term, but something that men could never work out for themselves, but which has now been made known by God. It is often used of the content of the gospel message. Here it means that Christ makes known the meaning of certain symbols which men could not have worked out for themselves.

The *seven stars* are first explained as *the angels of the seven churches*. It is not clear what *angel* means here. The word means 'messenger' and can be used of human messengers (Lk. vii. 24, ix. 52). But it is much more often used of heavenly beings, God's 'messengers'. Indeed in Revelation, apart from the references in the first three chapters to the angels of the churches, there is no place where it does not refer to heavenly beings, and as the term is found sixty-seven times in all this consideration is important. Some have understood it to mean something like 'guardian angels' of the churches (cf. Mt. xviii. 10), but there is no evidence that churches have heavenly beings associated with them in this way. Moreover in the next couple of chapters the letters to the churches are in each case addressed to 'the angel' of the particular church, which is a strange way to treat a guardian angel. So some think of the expression as pointing to the essential 'spirit' of the churches. Thus Swete can say, 'In this symbolical book the angel of a Church may be simply an expression for its prevailing spirit, and thus be identified with the Church itself.'

Others prefer to think of some earthly representative of the churches. The great advantage of this view is that such a person is a much more natural recipient of a letter to the church than is any heavenly being. The disadvantage is in seeing who it could be. The messengers who took the letters to the churches are mentioned, but there seems no reason for addressing the letters to these 'postmen'. More is to be said for the view that the 'angels' are the bishops or pastors of the churches. This would be a good solution except that we do not know whether the churches had bishops or individual pastors as early as this. And if they did, why call them *angels*? There are difficulties in the way of all views, but perhaps fewest in that of seeing the *angels* as the spirits of the churches, standing for and symbolizing the churches. The *seven candlesticks* or, better, 'lampstands' are *the seven churches*, i.e. the actual existent churches. It is worth noting that the churches are no more than 'lampstands'. The light is Christ, and they are to show Him forth.

II. THE LETTERS TO THE CHURCHES (ii. 1–iii. 22)

Some interpreters (e.g. Kiddle) take the seven letters to the churches as purely a literary device. They see the message as addressed to the church at large, with the division into seven as purely artificial. Others take the churches to stand for periods in history, Ephesus representing the first century, Smyrna the period of persecution, Pergamum the age of Constantine, Thyatira the Middle Ages, Sardis the Reformation era, Philadelphia the time of the modern missionary movement, and Laodicea the apostasy of the last days (see Smith). Such views are unlikely. It seems much more probable that the letters are letters to real churches, all the more so since each of the messages has relevance to what we know of conditions in the city named. This does not mean that the letters originally circulated as individual units (though Charles takes this view). They were probably in this book from the first, and intended to be read by others than members of the churches named. John has addressed himself to the needs of the little churches but has dealt with topics which have relevance to God's people at all times and in all places. He is writing to the churches, but he is also addressing the church as a whole.

There is a general pattern to the letters which we may set out as follows:

1. A greeting: 'To the angel of the church that is in — '.
2. A title of the risen Christ, usually taken from the description in chapter i.
3. A section headed 'I know', introducing praise for what is good in the church's record (not in the case of Laodicea).
4. A criticism of the church (not in the case of Smyrna nor Philadelphia).
5. A warning.
6. An exhortation beginning, 'He that hath an ear — '.
7. A promise beginning with something like 'to him that overcometh will I give — '.

In the four last letters the order of 6 and 7 is reversed.

A further pattern is to be discerned in the sevenfold arrangement. Churches 1 and 7 are in grave danger, churches 2 and 6 are in excellent shape, churches 3, 4 and 5, are middling, neither very good nor very bad.

a. To the church of Ephesus (ii. 1-7)

Ephesus was the most important of the seven cities. Though Pergamum was the official capital of the province of Asia, Ephesus was its greatest city. It was an assize town and a seat of proconsular government (Acts xix. 38). When a new proconsul took up his appointment he had to enter his province at Ephesus. Situated near the mouth of the river Cayster, it was a great commercial centre (despite problems posed by the silting up of its harbour which have persisted so that the site is now several miles inland). Much of the trade of the East came to the Aegean via the port of Ephesus. The great road from the Euphrates terminated there, as did roads from the Cayster valley and the Maeander valley to the south.

Ephesus was an outstanding religious centre, the chief cult

being that of Artemis (cf. Acts xix. 24 ff.). The city had the
prized status of *neōkoros* (lit. 'Temple-sweeper'!) in connection
with the great temple which was one of the seven wonders of
the world. But religion and magic were hopelessly inter-
mingled, and magical arts were popular (cf. Acts xix. 19).
'Ephesian letters' were charms widely supposed to cure sickness
and to bring luck. Paul spent over two years in Ephesus establishing the church (Acts xix. 8, 10), to which the important
Epistle to the Ephesians was later sent. Timothy was resident
there for a time (1 Tim. i. 3), and tradition says that John
lived there in his old age.

1. The greeting is not actually to the church but to *the
angel of the church of Ephesus* (for *angel* see on i. 20). But there is
no doubt but that the message is meant for the church. The
message is from the risen Christ, described as holding *the
seven stars in his right hand* (cf. i. 16; the verb here is rather
stronger than 'had' in that passage and denotes a firm grip).
He is also said to be walking among the lampstands (in i. 13
there was no mention of walking, but cf. Lv. xxvi. 12). The
effect of this salutation is to give a picture of Christ as present
in the very midst of the churches, a Christ who is intimately
concerned with them and cares for them.

2. The exalted Christ knows what goes on among His
people. He selects three things: *thy works*, which is the general
term, *thy labour*, which means hard work (*kopos* signifies labour
to the point of weariness) and *thy patience*, better 'steadfastness' (cf. Barclay, 'the courageous gallantry which accepts
suffering and hardship and loss and turns them into grace and
glory').
The Ephesians' zeal for the right comes out further in their
inability to *bear them which are evil*. They have also tested out
men who claimed to be *apostles* and shown them up for what
they were. *Found them liars* shows that these men were not
merely deluded. They were deceivers. The term *apostle* of
course is not used here of the Twelve, but in the wider sense
(cf. 2 Cor. xi. 13). Paul had foretold that 'grievous wolves'
would trouble the Ephesian church (Acts xx. 29), and we see

59

here a fulfilment. Clearly the Ephesians did not take their faith lightly. They quite understood that it made demands on them, and they worked hard at being Christians. And they were not credulous. They tested and rejected false claims among professing Christians.

3. The better text reads here, 'And thou hast steadfastness, and hast borne for my name's sake'. The verb 'borne' is that used in the previous verse of their inability to bear evil men. But for Christ's sake they have 'borne'. *Thou hast not fainted* likewise takes up the word 'labour' of the previous verse, being the verb from the same root ('thou hast not grown weary of labour'). In these letters praise is regularly given where it fairly can to those churches which are to be rebuked for some failure. Thus there is more praise for Ephesus and Thyatira which are rebuked, than for Smyrna and Philadelphia which are not.

4. The condemnation of this church is expressed in one memorable phrase, *thou hast left thy first love*. It is not clear whether this is love for Christ ('you no longer love Me', Weymouth), or for one another ('you have given up loving one another', Moffatt), or for mankind at large. It may well be that a general attitude is meant which included all three ('you do not love as you did at first', Phillips). *Left* (*aphēkes*) is a strong term. We could translate it 'abandoned'. They had completely forsaken their first fine flush of enthusiastic love. They had yielded to the temptation, ever present to Christians, to put all their emphasis on sound teaching. In the process they lost love, without which all else is nothing.

5. There is nothing more to the accusation. But it is damning enough in all conscience. So Christ calls on them to come back. There are three steps. First He calls on them to *remember* their first state (there is a tragic air of completeness about the perfect, *pepiōkas, fallen*). It is possible to slip away gradually without realizing what is happening. A useful counter is to go back in thought to the first days. The Greek imperative is present, with a meaning like 'keep on remembering', 'hold in memory'. They had enjoyed a close walk with God. Let their

minds dwell on that. The second step is *repent* (the aorist
points to a sharp break with evil). Christians can never dally
with wrong. There must be a sharp break with it. But
Christianity is not basically negative and the third step is *do
the first works*, i.e. the works that had issued from the first love
just mentioned.

If they do not heed, dire consequences are sure and swift. *I
will come* is in fact in the present tense 'I am coming'. John
sees it before his eyes. If the church does not heed the injunction Christ will remove its lampstand, which appears to
signify the total destruction of the church. A church can
continue only for so long on a loveless course. Continuing on
that course means ceasing to be a church. Its lampstand is
removed. *Except thou repent* signifies that the judgment is not
irrevocable. If they repent they may yet be saved. But if not
there is no hope.

6. *But this thou hast,* says Christ, *that thou hatest the deeds of
the Nicolaitans, which I also hate.* While love is the typical
Christian attitude, love for the good carries with it a corresponding hatred for what is wrong. 'Neither doth he abhor
any thing that is evil' (Ps. xxxvi. 4, Prayer Book Version) is a
terrible condemnation. Notice that it is *the deeds* and not the
persons which are the objects of hatred.

Nothing is known about *the Nicolaitans* other than what is
recorded in Revelation. Irenaeus says that they owed their
origin to Nicolas, who was one of the Seven (Acts vi. 5).[1]
Clement of Alexandria defends Nicolas, saying that he was
misunderstood.[2] All here is conjecture. Victorinus of Pettau,
the first commentator on Revelation, refers to them as 'false
and troublesome men, who, as ministers under the name of
Nicolaus, had made for themselves a heresy, to the effect that
what had been offered to idols might be exorcised and eaten,
and that whoever should have committed fornication might
receive peace on the eighth day'.[3] But this, too, looks like

[1] *Adv. Haer.* i. 26. 3, iii. 10. 7.
[2] *Strom.* iii. 4. 25.
[3] *ANF*, VII, p. 346.

speculation. Etymologically the name combines 'victory' and 'people' and one could get roughly the same meaning from Balaam, from which it has been concluded that the Balaamites (verse 14) were at least similar. Since the practices of the Balaamites and of the followers of Jezebel (verse 20) are much the same, it appears that this group also was akin. It cannot be proved but it seems the most reasonable reading of the evidence that all three were connected, though not identical. This is not the enemy from outside openly seeking to destroy the faith. The false teachers claimed 'not that they were destroying Christianity, but that they were presenting an improved and modernized version of it' (Barclay). This is the insidious fifth column, destroying from within.

7. *He that hath an ear*, etc., occurs in each of the letters. It stresses the continuous activity of the Spirit and is a call to attention. There is a similarity to our Lord's formula (Mk. iv. 9, etc.) though He uses the plural, while the singular is found in Revelation. The expression is a personal challenge. The message is not only for those Asian Christians so long ago but for every one who 'has an ear'.

There is a little message to *him that overcometh* in each of the letters. Some have seen a reference to the Nicolaitans ('overcome' is *nikō*). But John is fond of this verb (he uses it seventeen times) and the connection is not necessary (though it may not be completely out of mind in this particular instance). Swete aptly says, 'The note of victory is dominant in St John, as that of faith in St Paul; or rather, faith presents itself to St John in the light of a victory'. To the man who perseveres through to final victory Christ says that He will give to eat of the tree of life (cf. xxii. 2, 14, 19). After Adam's sin the way to the tree of life was cut off and guarded by cherubim (Gn. iii. 24). Now it is given by Christ to His triumphant follower. But it is not to be taken for granted. Only some have the right to it (xxii. 14), and it may be taken away (xxii. 19). *The paradise of God* points to bliss in the presence of God Himself. *Paradise* is from the Persian, with a meaning like 'park'. It is used of bliss in the world to come.

b. To the church of Smyrna (ii. 8-11)

Smyrna was one of the greatest cities of the region, and indeed disputed with Ephesus for the title 'First (city) of Asia'. It enjoyed great natural advantages, including an excellent harbour at the head of a well protected gulf. It was thus the natural outlet for the trade of the rich valley of the Hermus and regions beyond. Smyrna was destroyed *c.* 580 BC, but *c.* 290 BC Lysimachus rebuilt it to a comprehensive plan. It was thus one of the very few planned cities of antiquity. Many writers comment on its beauty. It was one of the first cities to engage in worship of the Roman emperor and it won the honour of erecting a temple to him in the reign of Tiberius. Indeed there was a temple to the goddess of Rome as early as 195 BC.[1] Smyrna was a faithful ally of Rome in the days before Rome was acknowledged in the region, so its loyalty meant something.

8. The message is from *the first and the last* (cf. i. 17). As in i. 18 this is linked with a reference to the resurrection, very appropriate in a city which had died and now lived once more. In i. 18 the tense denotes continuity, whereas here the aorist tenses put the stress on the actual happenings, 'he became dead, and sprang to life again'.

9. Christ's knowledge of this church is concerned with the various kinds of trouble its members were undergoing. First is *tribulation (thlipsis)* which denotes serious trouble, the burden that crushes. Kiddle says, 'From this letter we can gain some idea of the unbounded fortitude of these early Christians. John assumes that the people of Smyrna (as typical of faithful Christians everywhere) share his own attitude to physical suffering: he speaks lightly of it, as one speaks of familiar things. Words so brief, spoken to men who might at any time go to their death, have in them a heroism which even now has power to stir the blood.'

Next comes *poverty.* John uses the strong word *ptōcheia*, which Trench distinguishes from *penia:* 'The *penēs* has nothing

[1] Tacitus, *Ann.* iv. 56. Barclay says this was the first in the world.

superfluous, the *ptōchos* nothing at all.'[1] The poverty of the
Smyrneans was extreme. Yet Christ can say *thou art rich*. There
is a richness in spiritual things which has nothing to do with
this world's wealth. Many think that the Smyrneans' poverty
was in part due to pillage of their goods by the Jews. Christians
seem often to have suffered at the hands of Jews or pagans.
Their religion was not legally permitted which made it easy
to take action against them. At a somewhat later time, when
Polycarp was martyred at Smyrna, the Jews' hostility to the
Christians came out in their zeal in setting forward the
execution. For example, though it was the sabbath, they
gathered wood for the fire in which the martyr was burnt.
Such hostility may well go back to the time when John wrote.

He goes on to refer to *the blasphemy of them which say they are
Jews, and are not* (cf. Rom. ii. 25, 28 f.). To be a Jew means
more than to possess outward membership of the race. These
men belong to *the synagogue of Satan*. This unusual expression
means that their assembly for worship does not gather together
God's people but Satan's, who is 'the accuser of our brethren'
(xii. 10).

10. The Smyrneans are not to be afraid, though suffering is
certain. Some will be imprisoned, and this is ascribed to *the
devil*. But God is supreme. Even through the devil and evil
men He works out His purposes. The imprisonment will be
that ye may be tried. The clear implication is that God will see
them through the test. This is so even if, as a number of
commentators think, prison was simply a place of confinement
while awaiting execution (against this view are passages like
Acts xvi. 23, 2 Cor. xi. 23).

The number *ten* may well point to the completion of their
suffering. Cf. D. T. Niles, 'It is only for a limited time that
you will have to endure, even though endurance will be tested
to the limit.' It certainly points to something more than three
and a half days, which is John's usual expression for a trial of
limited duration. Yet even ten has its limit. Not Satan but
God has the last word in this matter. In a memorable expres-

---

[1] *Synonyms of the New Testament*, 1880, p. 129.

sion the church is exhorted, *be thou faithful unto death, and I will give thee a crown of life* (cf. Jas. i. 12). Death, which men fear so much, is set in sharp antithesis to life, which alone matters. There is an article with *life* (though not with *death*). It is 'the' life, eternal life, that is in mind. *Crown (stephanos)* denotes a wreath or chaplet, and is to be distinguished from *diadēma*, which signifies a royal crown. The *stephanos* was the trophy awarded to the victor at the games, and the same word was used of the festive garland worn at banquets by all the guests. Here it is plainly the victory wreath, which would be specially appropriate in Smyrna, a city famous for its Games. The believer who remains faithful even when it means death will receive the trophy of victory. His *crown* is *life*.

11. For *he that hath an ear*, etc., see note on verse 7. The overcomer will not be harmed by *the second death* (explained in xx. 6, 14, xxi. 8 in terms of the lake of fire; it seems to mean eternal punishment: it is the negation of eternal life). *Not* is an emphatic double negative. The overcomer certainly will not be harmed. The emphasis would be welcome to those who faced the prospect of martyrdom.

c. To the church at Pergamum (ii. 12–17)

Pergamum was never important until it became the capital of the independent kingdom of the Attalids after Alexander the Great. Its last king willed it to Rome in 133 BC, when it became the capital of the Roman province of Asia. About fifteen miles inland, it did not have a good trading position. But, apart from its administrative importance, it was significant for its great library, said to have contained more than 200,000 parchment scrolls. Indeed, our word 'parchment' is derived from this name 'Pergamum'. It was an important religious centre. People came from all over the world to be healed by the god Asclepius, and Pergamum has been described as 'the Lourdes of the ancient world'. Zeus, Dionysos, and Athene also had notable temples in the city. Pergamum was a centre of Caesar-worship, and it had a temple dedicated to Rome and Augustus as early as 29 BC. It attained the coveted title *neōkoros*, 'Temple-sweeper', before either Smyrna or Ephesus, and took its devotion to emperor-worship seriously. In due course it added a second and a third temple in honour of the emperor. It was the principal centre of the imperial cult in this part of the world. But emperor-worship was not its sole religious activity. Behind the city was a great conical hill, the site of a multitude of heathen temples.

12. The greeting is from Him *which hath the sharp sword with two edges* (cf. i. 16), a sword which will be used (verse 16). In a city as devoted to the Romans as Pergamum, and the place of residence of the proconsul who possessed the power to put men to death and whose very symbol may be taken to be the sword (Rom. xiii. 4), it was a salutary reminder that there is a power greater than that of any earthly governor.

13. The verb *dwellest* (*katoikeis*) means that the Christians were not simply passing through Pergamum. They lived there. They had to face their difficulties to the end. *Satan's seat* (*thronos*) means 'Satan's throne'. Satan exercised sway there. Some think the allusion is to the serpent, the symbol of Asclepius, which was everywhere in Pergamum. While this emblem symbolized healing to the Pergamenes, it stood for evil for biblically instructed Christians (cf. xii. 9, xx. 2). Beckwith objects, however, that this kind of worship was very prominent in centres like Epidaurus. Pergamum had no mortgage on this kind of worship. A similar objection is urged against the suggestion that the great altar to Zeus is meant. This stood high on the Acropolis and dominated the city. But Zeus was highly honoured elsewhere. We have, however, already noticed that Pergamum did have pre-eminence in emperor-worship. Charles cites an inscription from Mytilene which shows that the city was the centre of the emperor cult for the whole province. And as this was a constant source of persecution to the Christians, we need not doubt that it was primarily in mind.

But the opposition had not led to any slackening of Christian zeal, and the exalted Lord can say, *thou holdest fast my name, and hast not denied my faith.* The reference to the one martyrdom,

that of *Antipas*, and the aorist tense in the verb *denied* point to
one definite crisis rather than a continuing persecution.
Nothing more is known of Antipas (though legend has it that
he was roasted in a brazen bull). But clearly he had remained
firm. He was *my faithful martyr.* The last word means literally
'witness' (as RSV), but came in time to mean those who wit-
nessed by their death. The addition *where Satan dwelleth*
stresses the significance of the evil one and his activity. Persecution does not take place simply at the behest of wicked
men.

14. We come now to the things that are amiss, of which
there are *a few.* They seem to be connected with false teaching.
Our knowledge is not such as to enable us to identify the error
with certainty. But *Balaam* (see on verse 6) was the man who,
after being prevented from cursing Israel, apparently advised
Balak, king of Moab, that the Israelites would forfeit God's
protection if he could induce them to worship idols (Nu.
xxxi. 16).

The incident at Baal-peor made a deep impression on
subsequent generations. It became proverbial for spiritual
declension. The allusion here is spelled out with the reference
to Balaam's teaching of Balak *to cast a stumblingblock before
the children of Israel.* The *stumblingblock (skandalon)* was the bait
stick of a trap, the stick which triggered off the trapping
mechanism when a bird perched on it. It is a vivid metaphor
for what entraps or troubles. Two points are singled out, the
eating of *things sacrificed unto idols* and the committing of *fornication.* It is possible that the former refers to the eating of
meat which had first been offered to idols and was then sold
on the open market (see *TNTC* on 1 Cor. viii), and the latter
to sexual sin in general. But it is more likely that both refer
to idolatrous practices. Feasting on sacrificial meat and
licentious conduct were usual accompaniments of the worship
of idols, both in Old and New Testament times.

15. *So (houtōs)* means 'in this fashion', i.e. that mentioned
in the previous verse. *Thou also* is emphatic *(kai su).* In addition
to others *you* have these false teachers. For the Nicolaitans

67

see note on verse 6. From the way this verse is connected with the preceding we should probably draw the inference that the Balaamite error was akin to that of the Nicolaitans (see on verse 6). But the language shows that they were not identical.

16. *Repent* is a sharp command, and the better MSS have 'therefore'. In view of the Lord's hatred for this kind of practice, *repent*. Evil must not be countenanced. *I will come* is another of John's vivid presents. He sees it happening even now. The alternative is to have Christ *fight against them*. The verb is confined to Revelation in the New Testament (apart from Jas. iv. 2). *The sword of my mouth* (cf. verse 12) is clearly the word Christ speaks. This word is either a comfort and a strength to us, or else it destroys us.

17. For *He that hath an ear*, etc., see note on verse 7. The overcomer is this time promised as food *the hidden manna*. There may be an allusion to the Jewish idea that when the Temple was destroyed the prophet Jeremiah hid the pot with manna that was in the Holy of Holies, and that when the Messiah came it would reappear. But more probably the meaning is simply that the believer who overcomes will receive celestial food not available to the world (cf. Jn. iv. 31–33).

With this is linked *a white stone* inscribed with *a new name*. This has puzzled commentators for centuries. At least seven suggestions have been made with some confidence. One arises from legal practice, where a member of a jury who was for acquittal handed in a white stone. A second view sees a reference to reckoning, since white stones were often used in calculations. A third idea is that the white stone is the symbol of a happy day (like our 'red-letter day'). A more prosaic suggestion is that the white stone represented a ticket to bread and circuses. Along somewhat the same lines is that which sees the stone as an amulet bringing good luck. A sixth suggestion arises from a rabbinic speculation that when the manna fell from heaven it was accompanied by precious stones (note that *manna* has just been mentioned). The seventh suggestion is that the reference is to a stone in the breastplate of the high priest with the name of one of the tribes written on it. A variant sees a reference to the Urim (Ex. xxviii. 30). Some of these may legitimately be criticized on the ground that either the stone is not white or it has no inscription. But none of them carries complete conviction. We simply do not know what the white stone signified, though clearly it did convey some assurance of blessing.

On the stone was *a new name written, which no man knoweth saving he that receiveth it.* For *new (kainon)* see note on v. 9. Some have thought that the *new name* is that of God or Christ. And indeed there is a reference to Christ as having a new name (iii. 12). But there is no indication that His name is secret, and it is the secret that is distinctive here. This must be understood in the light of ideas held in antiquity about the function of a name. With us a name is no more than a distinguishing mark, a label. But in antiquity the name was widely held to sum up what the man stood for. It represented his character. It stood for the whole man. Here then the new name represents a new character. The fact that no-one knows it would be a crippling disadvantage for us. In the modern world what is the use of a name which nobody knows? But for the men of antiquity the hidden name was precious. It meant that God had given to the overcomer a new character which no-one knew except himself. It was not public property. It was a little secret between him and his God.

d. To the church of Thyatira (ii. 18-29)

The longest of the seven letters is written to the church in the smallest and least important town! The values of God are not the values of men. Thyatira was situated between the Caicus and Hermus valleys. This was a good position for trading and the city appears to have been quite a commercial centre. There appear to have been a large number of trade guilds in Thyatira. In fact Sir William Ramsay says 'more trade-guilds are known in Thyatira than in any other Asian city. The inscriptions, though not specially numerous, mention the following: wool-workers, linen-workers, makers of outer garments, dyers, leather-workers, tanners, potters, bakers, slave-dealers and bronze-smiths.'[1] Over in Philippi we read of Lydia that she came from this city and was a 'seller of purple' (Acts xvi. 14). The town was famous for its wool dyeing, which may well explain this lady's occupation.

Unfortunately not very much is known about Thyatira, not nearly as much, for example, as is known about the other cities. This makes it difficult to be certain on some points and we must interpret this letter with due caution. The Christian church may have been small. At any rate no great record of achievement appears to be attributed to it.

18. This is the one letter which uses the title *the Son of God*, indeed the one place where it occurs in Revelation. The description emphasizes the majesty of His Person. His eyes and feet are as described in i. 14 f., but no other part of Him is mentioned. The eyes indicate that He sees all, and the feet that He will certainly and swiftly pursue all that is evil, and possibly also that He will tread it down.

19. The opening *thy works* is explained in a series of praiseworthy Christian qualities: *charity*, better 'love' (*agapē*), than which nothing is greater; *service*, for this is what the Master expects to find His servants doing; *faith*, for continuing trustful reliance on Christ is basic; and *patience* which is really 'steadfastness' (see on verse 2). The list ends as it had begun with *thy works*, and it is good to read, *the last to be more than the first*. There is progress in the life of this church. This is not something to be taken for granted. In fact the church at Ephesus has just been blamed for having slipped back (verse 4). There is much to commend at Thyatira.

20. But Christ must say, *Notwithstanding*. There are defects to offset the virtues. They are described in connection with a woman called *Jezebel*. We may assume that the name is symbolic. Certainly no Jew would have borne it in view of the evils practised by Ahab's wife. 'Jezebel' had become proverbial for wickedness. Some manuscripts add 'thy' to *woman*, which gives the meaning 'thy wife'. Some accordingly suggest that

---

[1] *The Letters to the Seven Churches of Asia*, 1904, pp. 324 f.

Jezebel was the wife of the bishop of the church. If this reading is correct the translation is in order. But it is difficult to see a bishop as early as the writing of this little letter (see note on i. 20), and in any case the reading should probably be rejected. Another suggestion is that the oracle Sambethe is meant (a female fortune-teller located at Thyatira). A strong objection to any such view is that *Jezebel* clearly professes the Christian faith.

She *calleth herself a prophetess.* But her teaching is false. Specifically she seduces the servants of God to immoral conduct and to eat idol meats (cf. verse 14). It seems that we have here the same kind of problem as that with which Paul deals in 1 Corinthians viii, probably in an exaggerated form, for there would have been strong pressure on the Thyatiran Christians. The strong trade guilds in this city would have made it very difficult for any Christian to earn his living without belonging to a guild. But membership involved attendance at guild banquets, and this in turn meant eating meat which had first been sacrificed to an idol. What was the Christian to do? If he did not conform he was out of a job. *Jezebel* apparently reasoned that an idol is of no consequence (cf. 1 Cor. viii. 4), and advised Christians to eat such meals. That these meals all too readily degenerated into sexual looseness made matters worse. But we can understand that some Christians would welcome a heresy of this type. It enabled them to maintain a Christian profession while countenancing and even engaging in immoral heathen revels. That *Jezebel* was a prophetess gave their course some standing.

We should not minimize the importance of the question at issue, nor the difficulty some first-century Christians must have had in seeing the right course. Nor should we dismiss the problem as only of academic interest since it does not concern us. Every generation of Christians must face the question, 'How far should I accept and adopt contemporary standards and practices?' On the one hand, the Christian must not deny his faith. On the other, he must not deny his membership of society. The cause of Christ is not served if Christians appear as a group of old-fashioned people trying to retreat from the real world. Christians in fact live in the same world as their neighbours, and face the same problems. They must find Christian solutions. The prophetess and her followers had apparently been so ready to conform to the practices of their heathen neighbours that they had lost sight of the essential Christian position. They had exalted expediency over principle. Had Christianity taken this way it must surely have become just another of the eastern cults which had their little day and perished. The risen Lord points to the very essence of Christian living when He urges high standards of moral conduct.

21. The Lord's judgments are not hasty. He gives time for repentance. But 'she does not will to repent' (so rather than *she repented not*). She persisted in her wrongdoing and ignored the invitation to repent.

22. The punishment scene is vivid, with its *behold*, and its present tense 'I cast' (so rather than *I will cast*). The *bed, klinē*, might be understood in more ways than one. Most take it to be a bed of sickness or pain, on which Farrer comments, 'The punishment fits the crime—she who profaned the bed of love is pinned to the bed of sickness.' This is probably the way to take it, though some have thought that the *klinē* was the couch on which she reclined at a meal (when she would be smitten as she engaged in idol-worship), and others that it is a funeral bier. *Them that commit adultery with her* will refer primarily to those who accepted her teaching (but since this involved sexual looseness the literal meaning is not far away). But *except they repent* still holds out the prospect of mercy. This is to be noted throughout this book. It is full of sore judgments, but always there is the prospect of deliverance for those who repent. They are called on to repent of 'her deeds' (so rather than *their deeds*). We get the force of this by comparing it with verse 26, where the word here translated *deeds* is rendered 'works'. They should do Christ's works, not those of Jezebel.

23. We would naturally take *her children* to mean her followers, except that they seem to have been dealt with already. Perhaps it refers to her most intimate disciples as against those whose adherence is not firm. Some have thought it is her literal children, but this seems less likely. These then will be killed *with death*, which probably means 'with pestilence' (as often in the LXX). This will have its effect on *all the churches*. From this judgment they will know that Christ *searcheth the reins and hearts* (cf. Je. xi. 20). The implication of *searcheth* is that nothing can be hid from him. Even secret things are known to Him. The *reins* are the kidneys, regarded as the seat of the emotions. In similar fashion the heart stands for the intellect. Each man will receive a recompense proportionate to his deeds. *Every one of you* (where we might have expected 'thee', in conformity with the address to 'the angel of the church', verse 18) makes it very personal.

24. There is now a message for true believers, those who have not been led astray by *this doctrine*. For them it is said they *have not known the depths of Satan, as they speak*. It is uncertain who this last *they* is. It may be the true believers or it may be the false teachers. If the former, the meaning will be that the heretics have claimed knowledge of 'the deep things' of God in a way which set them apart from lesser mortals. The orthodox are then saying that this 'deep' teaching is not heavenly. It is satanic, and the *depths* the heretics really know are the depths of Satan.

But it is more likely that the false teachers themselves made this claim. They may have meant something like Paul's 'we are not ignorant of his devices' (2 Cor. ii. 11), and have claimed superior power to overcome temptation. But in view of their conduct it seems probable that they held that to triumph over Satan it is necessary to know Satan's works. Curious as it seems to us, there were some (so far known to us at a rather later time than this) who seem to have held that the one important thing is to keep the soul pure whatever the body may do. They did not hesitate to engage in grossly sensual practices maintaining that these concerned only their bodies, but that their souls were pure. It could well be that we have here an early representative of this kind of teaching. For those who have repudiated the false teaching there is a

promise, *I will put upon you none other burden.* This raises the
question, 'Other than what?' The answer may be, 'Other than
the burden of Christian service already assumed.' The language
reminds us of the regulation in Acts xv. 28 f. Indeed Alford
says, 'To my mind the allusion to the apostolic decree is too
clear and prominent to allow of any other meaning coming
into question'.

25. This does not mean that life is easy. There is a necessary
task to be done. They are to *hold fast* ('take a firm grip on') the
thing (singular) that they already have, i.e. 'the sum total of
Christian doctrine and hope and privilege' (Alford). *Till I
come* turns their gaze to the glorious day when their Lord will
appear.

26, 27. To the usual *he that overcometh* there is linked *and
keepeth my works unto the end.* My works stands in contrast to 'her
works' (verse 22, where see note). It is a different quality
of life that is demanded from the Christian. *Unto the end*
reminds us that the Christian life is not a battle but a campaign.
Perseverance is important.

The reward for the overcomer is *power over the nations* (cf.
Ps. ii. 8), a dazzling prospect but one which demanded great
faith from a tiny church. With it is linked *he shall rule them with
a rod of iron* (presumably a staff tipped with iron). The verb
rendered *rule* literally means 'shepherd'. We usually think of
the shepherd in terms of kindness and tender care. But the
shepherd was an autocrat. His power over his flock was
absolute, and it is this aspect of the shepherd's life that is in
view. Shepherding with an iron rod might denote no more
than strength or firmness were it not linked with breaking to
pieces like clay vessels (cf. Ps. ii. 9, Je. li. 20). Further, it is
likened to the gift the Father gave the Son. This seems to
show that the overcomer will have a place in the final decisive
victory of Christ over the world forces opposed to God.

28. *I will give him the morning star* may be a further token of
triumph. Or it may be a symbol of the Christian's resurrection.
But, as Christ Himself is referred to as 'the bright and morning

star' (xxii. 16), it seems likely that it is the presence of the Lord that is meant. Even though this is an unusual way for Christ to refer to Himself this seems the best way of taking the words. The ultimate reward of the Christian is to be with his Lord.

29. This expression is repeated from verse 7, where see note.

e. To the church of Sardis (iii. 1–6)

Situated at the junction of five roads, and commanding the Hermus valley, Sardis was an active commercial city and very wealthy. It had been the capital of Croesus who was proverbial for his riches. The city's easy wealth seems to have made for slackness. It was captured by Cyrus the Persian (549 BC) and by Antiochus (218 BC), both times because of its slackness. The city was built on a hill so steep that its defences seemed impregnable. On both occasions enemy troops scaled the precipice by night and found that the over-confident Sardians had set no guard. A great earthquake in AD 17 made a profound impression. But the city was soon rebuilt, partly owing to generous aid from the emperor Tiberius.

The most important religion at Sardis was the worship of Cybele. John does not mention anything like the persecutions at Smyrna and Pergamum or the heresies of the Nicolaitans. It may be that this church had not suffered disturbance from without and that its troubles stemmed from its comparatively sheltered existence. The temptation for the sheltered is always to take things easy, and they readily become slack. It is worth noting that this church differs from those at Pergamum and Thyatira which also have mixed memberships. In those the faulty members are in a minority. But at Sardis they predominate. Only 'a few names' have not 'defiled their garments'.

1. *The seven Spirits of God* may denote the Holy Spirit (see on i. 4), and the form of expression seems to indicate that Christ bestows the gift of the Spirit. The *seven stars* are the 'angels' of the churches (i. 20) and they appear here in Christ's control. After this reminder of the dignity of the risen Christ there is a sharp condemnation of the church at Sardis. It has

75

a good reputation, *a name that thou livest*, but in fact it is *dead* (cf. 2 Tim. iii. 5, Jas. ii. 17). No condemnation could be sharper. Paul speaks of a very different attitude, 'as dying, and, behold, we live' (2 Cor. vi. 9).

2. *Be watchful* (cf. Rom. xiii. 11, 1 Cor. xvi. 13) must have come home with peculiar force to the church in a city which had twice been captured owing to its failure to watch. Lack of spiritual vigilance may likewise be costly. All was not yet lost for there are *things which remain*. But even these are *ready to die*. Unless an ember is fanned into flames it is lost. This church may have pleased men but it did not please God. Nothing it did was *perfect* (i.e. 'completed') *before God*. They did not bring their works to fulfilment. We may ask why both Jews and Romans apparently left this church undisturbed, unlike some of its neighbours. The answer may well be its lack of aggressive and positive Christianity. 'Content with mediocrity, lacking both the enthusiasm to entertain a heresy and the depth of conviction which provokes intolerance, it was too innocuous to be worth persecuting' (Caird).

3. *Remember (mnēmoneue)* is a present imperative with the meaning 'bear in mind' (rather than 'recall'). *How* refers to the manner of their hearing of the gospel, while *received* and *heard* both point to its derivative nature. *Hold fast* (present) enjoins a continuing activity, and *repent* (aorist) is urgent. If this church does not *watch*, Christ will come to it *as a thief*. This proverbial expression for unexpectedness (Mt. xxiv. 43, 1 Thes. v. 2, 2 Pet. iii. 10) is further emphasized with *thou shalt not know what hour I will come upon thee*. This is not a reference to the second coming. That will take place whether the men of Sardis are watchful or not. But Christ comes in many ways and this is clearly a limited coming in judgment on unrepentant Sardians. The fate of these unrepentant sinners is none the less fearsome because left undefined.

4. *Names*, of course, stands for the whole person (cf. Acts i. 15, Rev. xi. 13 where 'men' is literally 'names of men'). Defiling the garments is a piece of imagery whose general meaning is plain but whose detailed significance is not quite so clear. Moffatt, however, speaks of votive inscriptions in Asia Minor which show that dirty clothing was held to dishonour the deity, so that those who wore soiled garments were debarred from worshipping.

Walking with Christ *in white* has been understood by some as a reference to purity, by others to festivity, by others to victory. Beckwith sees it as 'a standing characteristic of the blessed and of heavenly beings'. All these views are possible, and examples can be adduced to support each. But, as Farrer points out, the parallel with the name left in the book of life in the next verse 'strongly suggests that the whites robes signify justification'. Those who have not defiled their garments, then, walk with Christ (contrast Jn. vi. 66) in accordance with their status as justified persons. *For they are worthy* does not mean that they have merited justification, but that they have done nothing to forfeit it.

5. Again we have a reference to *white raiment*, this time coupled with the thought that he who wears it will not have his name removed from *the book of life*, but will have Christ confess him before the Father and the angels. All these expressions help bring out the heavenly standing of those who belong to Christ. Christ's undertaking to *confess his name before my Father, and before his angels* means that in highest heaven this man has nothing to fear. When Jesus Christ vouches for a man he is accepted. There is a saying in the Gospels in which Jesus speaks about confessing before the angels him who confesses Him (Lk. xii. 8 f.). But that saying speaks also of Christ as denying him who denies Him as this one does not. The final chord struck in this message to the needy church of Sardis is one of hope and encouragement.

6. For *he that hath an ear*, etc., see note on ii. 7.

f. To the church of Philadelphia (iii. 7–13)

Philadelphia was founded *c.* 140 BC at the junction of the approaches to Mysia, Lydia and Phrygia. It was not unjustly called 'the gateway to the East'. Its founder, Attalus II Philadelphus of Pergamum, from whom the city derived its name, intended it to be a centre of missionary activity for the Hellenistic way of life. The city was prosperous, partly from its strategic situation, partly from the grape-growing that flourished in the vicinity. It was a centre of worship of the god Dionysos, but contained also temples to many other gods. Volcanic activity caused hot springs in the vicinity, but also earthquakes from time to time. Philadelphia suffered from the earthquake of 17 BC and received imperial assistance for rebuilding. The church was evidently small (verse 8), but of good quality. Its enemies came from outside, not inside, for there is no mention of heresy or factiousness. It had a good deal in common with that at Smyrna. Both receive no blame, only praise. Both suffered from those who called themselves Jews and were not, both were persecuted it would seem by the Romans, both are assured that the opposition is satanic, and both are promised a crown.

7. The church is greeted by One who is *holy* and *true* (epithets applied to God in vi. 10). *Holy* denotes connection with deity (cf. Is. xl. 25, Hab. iii. 3). It is used widely throughout the New Testament. *True (alēthinos)* is not often applied to people, either in the New Testament or elsewhere. It indicates that Christ is completely reliable.

This is the thought also in the rest of the verse. Christ has *the key of David* (cf. Is. xxii. 22). He *openeth, and no man shutteth; and shutteth, and no man openeth* (cf. Jb. xii. 14). This is the very opposite of caprice. He acts firmly and none can interfere. He does what He wills. Our writer does not tell us what it is that He shuts and opens. Some connect it with the Jews, who, they think, had excluded the Christians from their synagogues. They suggest that when Christ opens, the Jews cannot reverse it. More probably it is admission to the city of David, the heavenly Jerusalem, that is in mind, and this Christ alone gives or withholds.

8. The words *behold, I have set before thee an open door, and no man can shut it* are best taken as a parenthesis, and we should omit the indefinite article before *little strength*. The main thought is then 'I know your works, for you have little power and yet you have kept my word. . . '. This church had not embraced heretical teaching. Nor did it deny Christ's name. Evidently there had been persecution of some sort but the men of Philadelphia had stood firm. For those with little strength they had a noteworthy achievement.

In keeping with the description of Christ in verse 7 there is set before the church *an open door* (cf. Acts xiv. 27, 1 Cor. xvi. 9, 2 Cor. ii. 12), a door, which *no man can shut*. This may signify a door of missionary opportunity. The thought would then be that the reward of faithful service is greater opportunity for service. It is objected that this book does not elsewhere commend missionary activity and that the context requires the thought of reward. Accordingly some suggest that the open door leads into the Messianic glory or perhaps the Messianic community. Others think of the door as Christ Himself (as in Jn. x. 7, 9), others again of an opened door in contrast to the closed door of the synagogue, and yet others of the door of prayer. There is no lack of suggestions and a decision is not easy. Perhaps there is most to be said for the thought of entrance into the Messianic glory.

9. Instead of *I will make*, the best MSS read 'I give', but the construction is broken when the writer explains that those *of the synagogue of Satan* (see note on ii. 9) *lie* when they affirm themselves to be Jews. Christians are the true Jews (cf. Rom. ii. 28 f.) and Jewish persecutors of the church are not. In contrast to a Jewish expectation that the Gentiles would eventually submit to them (derived from Is. lx. 14, etc.) Christ says that these Jews will be made *to come and worship before thy feet*. It is to the church that all men, Jews included, must ultimately make their submission, for Christ is in it. They will also come to *know that I have loved thee*. The love of Christ for His own is not to be overlooked.

10. *Because* introduces the reason, but grammatically it might be the reason for the preceding or the following, i.e. it might be the reason for the triumph of the Philadelphians over them of Satan's synagogue, or for Christ's keeping them in the hour of temptation. There seems no way of deciding the point. *The word of my patience* (better, 'steadfastness'; see note on ii. 10) is a curious expression. It seems to mean 'the teaching which was exemplified in My steadfastness' (so Swete; cf. 2 Thes. iii. 5, Heb. xii. 1 f.). The same verb (*tēreō*) is used of Christ's keeping the Philadelphians as of their keeping His word. There is a justice about it all. He does what is right.

Keep thee from (ek) the hour of temptation might mean 'keep thee from undergoing the trial' or 'keep thee right through the trial'. The Greek is capable of either meaning. *Temptation* is better translated 'trial' (as mg.). It is a very thoroughgoing test, for it will *try them that dwell upon the earth*, which appears to mean all earth's inhabitants. John usually employs this expression to mean the heathen world (see note on vi. 10). Its use here accordingly may be another indication of compassion. The heathen are not simply judged and punished, but tested. God was giving them another opportunity.

11. The risen Lord speaks of His coming again. The present tense is vivid. The present imperative rendered *hold . . . fast* means 'keep a firm grip on', 'hold on to'. No-one, of course, can steal their crown. But they themselves can forfeit it, as Esau forfeited his place to Jacob, Reuben to Judah, Saul to David. To serve God is a high privilege. But it is a privilege which is withdrawn and given to another whenever a man fails to fulfil his task. *Crown* is *stephanos*, a 'garland' or 'wreath' (see note on ii. 10). It was often used of victory and this is clearly the allusion here.

12. The reward for *him that overcometh* is to be *a pillar* (cf. Je. i. 18, Gal. ii. 9, 1 Tim. iii. 15) *in the temple of my God* (the last two words receive emphasis from being repeated four times in this verse). This is, of course, symbolical and there is no contradiction with xxi. 22, which tells us that there will be no Temple in heaven. John is not in the slightest concerned to keep the details of one vision consistent with those of another. In each he is making a point with emphasis, and we should not try to dovetail one vision into the details of another. Here

his point is that the believer who overcomes will be permanently in the presence of God.

Charles sees as part of the background to this saying a custom
whereby 'the provincial priest of the imperial cultus at the
close of his year of office' used 'to erect his statue in the confines
of the temple, inscribing on it his own name and his father's'.
This may be so if *ep' auton*, rendered *upon him* (the believer) is
understood instead to mean 'upon it' (the pillar). This is
possible grammatically, but not necessary. In other parts of
this book we have the name written on the heads of the faithful
(xiv. 1, xxii. 4).

The triple name which follows is not that of the Trinity as
we might expect but that of the Father, the Son and the new
Jerusalem. *The name of my God* indicates that the overcomer
belongs to God. That of *the city of my God* signifies that he has
citizenship rights in the *new Jerusalem* (cf. Gal. iv. 26, Heb.
xi. 10, xii. 22, xiii. 14). *My new name* possibly refers to the new
state of affairs brought about by the consummation of redemption. Then Christ appears in a character in which He
could not appear until this consummation was reached. The
men of Philadelphia would appreciate references to a new
name more than most. While the name Philadelphia persisted,
twice the city had received a new name: that of Neocaesarea,
as a sign of gratitude for Tiberius' help in rebuilding after the
earthquake, and later Flavia, after the family name of the
emperor Vespasian.

13. For *he that hath an ear*, etc., see note on ii. 7.

g. To the church of Laodicea (iii. 14–22)

Laodicea, at the junction of the valley of the Lycus and the
Maeander and at the intersection of three important roads,
commanded the approaches to Phrygia. It was one of the
richest commercial centres in the world, so that we have here
a picture of the church in an affluent society. Laodicea was
noted for its banking and for its manufacture of clothing from
the local black wool. It was an assize town and boasted a
famous medical school.

An interesting feature of the city's religious life was a colony of over 7,000 adult male Jews. They had been granted the right to preserve their own customs. The Christian church had apparently been established by the preaching of Epaphras (Col. i. 7, iv. 12 f.). Paul wrote it a letter (Col. iv. 16) which has been lost (unless, as some hold, it is our Ephesians). In John's day the condition of the church in this city had deteriorated sadly. This church receives the severest condemnation of all the seven to whom letters are sent.

14. This is the one letter in which the titles of Christ are not drawn from the description in chapter i. They stress His faithfulness and His authority. The former will be in mind in *the Amen* (which reflects 'the God of truth', lit. 'the God of Amen', Is. lxv. 16), as well as in *the faithful and true witness* (cf. i. 5). This reliability stands in sharp contrast to the unfaithfulness of the Christians in this city.

The *beginning* (*archē*, cf. xxi. 6, xxii. 13) *of the creation of God* is better 'the moving cause of the creation of God' (Barclay). Christ is not saying that He was created first of all, but rather that He has the supreme authority over creation and that He is the origin of created being (cf. Jn. i. 3, Col. i. 15, 18). There are a number of resemblances in Colossians (which Paul had directed be read in Laodicea, Col. iv. 16) to expressions in this letter to Laodicea. It is a reasonable conclusion that the Laodicean church had copied and treasured Colossians and that John is appealing to their knowledge of it.

15. The *works* of this church are not described. They are simply summed up in the accusation that the church is *neither cold nor hot* (Paul uses a word cognate with *hot* in his exhortation to be 'fervent in spirit', Rom. xii. 11). Christ wishes the church were the one or the other. To prefer a rejection of the faith to the way the Laodiceans professed it is startling to say the least (cf. 2 Pet. ii. 21). But to profess Christianity while remaining untouched by its fire is a disaster. There is more hope for the openly antagonistic than for the coolly indifferent. 'There is no one farther from the truth in Christ than the one who makes an idle profession without real faith' (Walvoord). Their coolness was a denial of all that Christ stands for.

16. *Lukewarm* (*chliaros*, here only in biblical Greek) underlines the trouble, which is spelled out in the repetition of *neither cold nor hot*. *I will* is perhaps a little too definite for the Greek *mellō*, which Simcox sees as meaning 'I shall soon' or 'I am likely to', adding, 'The word used does not necessarily imply that the intention is final, and *v.* 19 shews that it is not.' A very strong warning is being given, but it is still a warning. *I will spue thee out of my mouth* expresses in the strongest possible fashion a vigorous repudiation of the Laodiceans. Lukewarmness is not to be endured. It is worth reflecting that the Ephesians were condemned for too great a zeal, coupled as it was with the absence of love, the Laodiceans for too little.

17. *Because* introduces a detailed account of the trouble. This church says (habitually, present tense), *I am rich, and increased with goods, and have need of nothing* (contrast this with the church at Smyrna which was poor materially but rich spiritually, ii. 9). Laodicea was a self-reliant city. It did indeed receive help from the government in AD 17, but when it was destroyed by the earthquake in AD 60, Tacitus could say the city 'without any relief from us, recovered itself by its own resources'.[1]

But this commendable attitude in material things can be a disaster if carried over into the spiritual realm. The Laodicean church saw itself as wealthy and did not discern its own poverty. *Thou* is emphatic and there is an article before *wretched*, which yields the meaning '*thou* art *the* wretched one'. Not simply 'a' wretched one, but 'the wretched one *par excellence*' (Charles). Where an unsatisfactory state of affairs is concerned this church leads all the rest. Christ speaks of its need of mercy (*miserable, eleeinos*), then describes it as *poor, and blind, and naked*. It is difficult not to think that this conjunction is a hit at Laodicea's banking, medical school, and clothing manufacturers. For *poor* (*ptōchos*) see note on ii. 9.

---

[1] *Ann.* xiv. 27 (cited from *The Modern Library* edn., 1942, p. 335).

18. For this threefold deficiency the remedy in each case is in Christ. From Him they should buy *gold tried in the fire* (cf. 1 Pet. i. 7), real wealth. *White raiment* should be seen against the city's reputation for making clothing from black wool. *The shame of thy nakedness* was in the ancient world the ultimate humiliation (cf. 2 Sa. x. 4, Is. xx. 4, Ezk. xvi. 37-9, Na. iii. 5, etc.), while contrariwise to be clothed in fine clothing was to receive honour (Gn. xli. 42, Est. vi. 6-11, Dn. v. 29). *Anoint thine eyes with eyesalve* may well allude to the fact that there was a world-famous remedy for sore eyes which came from Phrygia and which may have been especially associated with Laodicea. Christ alone gives real sight (cf. Jn. ix. 39).

19. *As many as* makes no exceptions. Chastening is the lot of all whom God loves (cf. Pr. iii. 12). On the use of the verb *love* Charles comments, 'It is a touching and unexpected manifestation of love to those who deserve it least among the Seven Churches.' The *I* is emphatic, for chastening comes not from hostile forces but from the Lord of the church Himself. This is the basis of an exhortation to a continuing state of zeal (*be zealous* is present continuous) and a decisive act of repentance (*repent* is aorist of once-for-all action).

20. *Behold* is vivid. John sees it before his very eyes. Christ is there now standing at the door. He is knocking, where the present tense signifies not a perfunctory rap, but a knocking continued in the hope of response. Up till this point the letter has been addressed to the church as a whole, but when Christ says *if any man . . .* He is appealing to the individual. Even if the church as a whole does not heed the warning the individual may. There is a note of tender pleading and probably also that of love (cf. Ct. v. 2). Christ promises to enter in to any man who opens the door. Not only that: *I . . . will sup* (*deipnēsō*) conveys the thought of familiar intercourse. The *deipnon* was the main meal of the day and was a leisurely affair, not a hurried snack. *And he with me* brings the believer into active fellowship. It is not really necessary for the sense, but it emphasizes the continuing fellowship. This is a remarkably tender appeal to a church far gone from its rightful state.

21. The *throne* signifies royal honour, and a place with Christ is the highest honour conceivable for a Christian. This is emphasized by likening it to the way Christ is enthroned with the Father (cf. xxii. 1, 3). *I also overcame* is important (cf. Jn. xvi. 33). Christ overcame by the way of the cross and this sets the pattern for His followers. They face grim days. But let them never forget that what seemed Christ's defeat was in fact His victory over the world. They need not fear if they are called upon to suffer, for in that way they too will conquer.

22. For *he that hath an ear*, etc., see note on ii. 7.

III. A VISION OF HEAVEN (iv. 1–11)

From the immediate concerns of the church on earth John switches his attention to heaven. 'The vision of the glorified Christ walking among the Churches on earth is followed by a vision of the Court of Heaven' (Swete). From this point onwards heavenly realities are right in the forefront. John begins with the vision of God Himself though he does not call it that.

1. *After this I looked* is a formula which, with slight variants, always in this book introduces a new vision (vii. 1, 9, xv. 5, xviii. 1; cf. xix. 1). *Behold* is a vivid touch. John sees the door before his very eyes and the door is *opened* (i.e. 'set open'; he does not see it opening). The way into heaven is open wide. A minor point is that John uses the singular 'heaven' and not the plural 'heavens' almost invariably (only in xii. 12 is there an exception in fifty-two examples of the term). The word must always be interpreted with care, for John uses it in different ways. Sometimes it is God's eternal dwelling place (iii. 12). But it can also be a heaven which will eventually be destroyed (xxi. 1), and even a place of conflict (xii. 7). Again, the same word can mean the sky (vi. 13). Here it is God's dwelling, but also the place where God chooses to reveal Himself, the place where heavenly realities are made plain.

The first voice is probably not to be understood in contrast with subsequent voices, for, apart from the 'thunderings and voices' which came from the throne (verse 5) there is no other voice mentioned until v. 2. It seems certain that the voice is that of the glorified Christ which was heard in i. 10. Both there and here it is likened to the sound of *a trumpet*. The voice called on John to come up to heaven (he has been on earth up till now). The Speaker further promises to show him *things which must be hereafter*. This contrasts with chapters i–iii, which have been concerned with the present (i.e. John's present) situation. The word *must* is important. The concern of this book is not with things which simply will happen, as though the future were of absorbing interest in itself. It is rather taken up with things which *must* happen, the outworking of the divine will. God is in supreme control. John is not writing about matters of chance, but about events which will certainly occur, for they are part of the divine plan.

2. Immediately John came to be *in the spirit* (for the expression see note on i. 10; here, as there, the word should have a capital, for it is the Holy Spirit, not John's human spirit, that is meant). The repetition of the expression shows that the condition it denotes was an intermittent state. John had evidently ceased to be 'in the Spirit', but now the state was resumed.

Again the vivid *behold* introduces the vision. John sees *a throne*. He is very interested in thrones, and specifically in the throne of God which he mentions in almost every chapter. He uses the word for *throne* forty-seven times out of total of sixty-two times in the New Testament. The emphasis he gives the term may be gauged from the fact that in Matthew, the book with the next highest number, the word occurs only four times. John's readers were familiar with earthly thrones, and they were troubled by all that Caesar's throne meant. John will not let them forget that there is a throne above every throne.

3. There is a description of One on a throne in Ezekiel i. 26 ff. (a passage to which this shows resemblances). But John's account is marked by greater reserve. He uses suggestion rather than description to convey the majesty and unfathomableness of God. In particular he makes a good deal of the worshipping host of heaven. God is usually made known to men by contact with those who know Him rather than by direct vision.

John likens Him on the throne to *a jasper and a sardine stone*. The lack of a scientific terminology among the ancients makes identification of precious and semi-precious stones a somewhat hazardous business. *Jasper* may be the same stone as the modern jasper, but some have thought it was green jade or green quartz (*NBD*). It has even been held to be diamond on the grounds that elsewhere it is said to be 'clear as crystal' (xxi. 11). It is agreed that *sardine stone* (or 'sardius') was a red stone, probably carnelian (rsv). Both were clearly costly, as was the emerald (the same three are linked by Plato, *Phaedo* 110E). There may be significance in the fact that the sardius and the jasper are the first and last of the twelve precious stones set in the high priest's breastplate, each being inscribed with the name of one of the tribes of Israel (Ex. xxviii. 17–21). Flashes of light from precious stones form an apt symbol of the divine presence, at once restrained as regards detail, but clear ás regards excellence.

Round about the throne was *a rainbow . . . in sight like unto an emerald*, 'a statement which teases the imagination out of all thought' (Caird). So difficult is this that some think of a halo rather than a rainbow (Phillips gets the best of both worlds with 'a halo like an emerald rainbow'!). Some see a reference to the bow of Ezekiel i. 28 and think of a means of concealing the Deity. It would then be part of John's restraint in depicting God. It is better, however, to take the word in its usual sense of *rainbow* and see a reference to the sign of God's covenant (Gn. ix. 16). The rainbow round the very throne of God then is a way of saying that the covenant is eternal. It will never be repudiated. The word rendered 'emerald' (*smaragdinō*) is of uncertain meaning, but J. L. Myres argues for a green stone.[1] I. H. Marshall thinks 'the green emerald is meant'.[2] If the colour green is significant it may, as many commentators think, point to the mercy of God.

[1] *EB*, 4804 f.
[2] *NBD*, p. 632.

4. Round God's *throne* were twenty-four other thrones (the word rendered *seats* is the plural of that translated *throne*), and on them twenty-four *elders*. These are probably a superior order of angels[1] (angels may be called 'elders', Is. xxiv. 23; AV renders 'ancients'). Some argue that the number twenty-four is to be seen as the sum of the twelve patriarchs of the Old Testament and of the twelve apostles of the New, who are thus seen to form a unity. The song of Moses and of the Lamb are indeed one (xv. 3). And, while the names of the patriarchs are on the gates of the new Jerusalem, those of the apostles are on its foundations (xxi. 12, 14). But a strong objection is that the redeemed do not sit on thrones until the final consummation.

Some, strangely as it seems to me, derive the elders from the twenty-four star-gods of the Babylonian pantheon (what is the Babylonian pantheon doing in John's heaven?). With more show of reason others see a reference to the courses of priests in David's organization for worship and the Levites who were responsible for the music at the Temple service (1 Ch. xxiv. 4, xxv. 9–31). On this view the *elders* represent the worship of heaven of which that on earth is at best a copy. Best is probably the view of Charles which sees in the *elders* angelic beings indeed, but angelic beings who are 'the heavenly representatives of the whole body of the faithful'. The thrones point to royal state and *white* is the colour of triumph. The *crowns of gold* also emphasize the high estate of these exalted beings (the Greek *stephanos* usually denotes a wreath of victory or festivity rather than a royal crown: see note on ii. 10; here, however, we must take the crowns in conjunction with the thrones).

5. When John says that *lightnings and thunderings and voices* came from *the throne* we should not understand him to mean that the throne itself originated these phenomena. We have already noticed the reserve with which he speaks of God and there can be no doubt that here *the throne* is a reverent way of referring to Him who sat on it. *Lightnings and thunderings* are awe-inspiring manifestations, and in this context *voices* is to be

[1] Cf. N. B. Stonehouse, *Paul before the Areopagus*, 1957, Chapter IV.

understood in the same way. Voices can be quiet and unobtrusive, but clearly John does not mean that kind of voice. Thunder is the voice of God in several Old Testament passages and we should understand all three terms in this way here (see viii. 5, xi. 19, xvi. 18 for this conjunction again).

Besides hearing the voice from the throne John sees *seven lamps of fire burning before the throne*. The present participle *burning* will denote a continuous state and the preposition *before* (*enōpion*) nearness to God. The seven fiery lamps are explained as *the seven Spirits of God*. As in i. 4, this expression is probably a way of referring to the Holy Spirit (see the notes there).

6. What was before the throne is not clear. Many think that John is speaking of an ocean in heaven above the firmament and refer to ancient cosmologies to prove the point. Others see a reference to the laver in Solomon's Temple, which was called a 'sea' (1 Ki. vii. 23). Such views give John's language a precision he himself does not give it, apparently of set purpose. He does not say *before the throne there was a sea* (as AV), but 'there was as it were a sea'. This is qualified by the adjective 'glassy' and likened to *crystal*.

Again John's reserve about heavenly things is to the fore. He is not giving an exact description but speaking in symbols. To estimate their significance we must bear in mind that modern ideas about glass did not apply in the first century. At that time glass was usually very dark, even opaque. Glass as clear as crystal would be enormously expensive. The Koran relates that when the Queen of Sheba came to visit Solomon she thought that a pavement of clear glass that he had set before his throne was water, and lifted up her skirt to pass through it (xxvii). The legend shows that clear glass was thought of as splendidly magnificent, as suitable paving for a royal court. This is part of the symbolism.

But there is dispute as to the rest. Thus Torrance can think of the *sea* as 'the sea of humanity in perfect harmony with God, without the ripple of trouble upon its many waters'. The trouble is that nothing prepares us for thinking of humanity as before God's throne. Caird, by contrast, sees it as 'the reservoir of evil out of which arises the monster (xiii. 1). It is the barrier which the redeemed must pass in a new Exodus, if they are to win access to the promised land (xv. 2–3). And in the new heaven and earth there is no more sea (xxi. 1).'

Now it is true that John can use the sea as a symbol of the maelstrom from which wickedness emerges and thus as having no place in the final scheme of things. But that does not mean that here 'as it were a glassy sea' has the same significance. Better is the position of Kiddle who discerns 'the appearance of some symbol conveying God's ineffable, absolute holiness— holiness in its original sense of *separateness*. Could any man born of woman cross this "sea of glass resembling crystal" into the presence of the Creator? As we read John's first vision of the heavenly court in chap. iv., we must have felt the utter impossibility of venturing near the haloed throne, whence issue "flashes of lightning, and loud blasts and peals of thunder." A shining ocean barred all approach.' John is emphasizing the majesty and the holiness of God.

John now speaks of four 'living ones' (*beasts* is an unfortunate translation; the Greek *zōon* emphasizes life). Their place is *in the midst of the throne* (ascribed to them here only) and *round about the throne* (a fairly common description). The former expression, which is elsewhere used of the Lamb (v. 6, vii. 17), will indicate close proximity. Perhaps also it means a place of honour, and again, conformity to the divine will. The latter signifies that they attend on God.

They are *full of eyes before and behind*, which signifies universal watchfulness. They are all-seeing, their eyes being both towards God and towards creation. Many scholars think these are the cherubim referred to in Ezekiel x. 2, 20. But there are not unimportant differences. The cherubim have four wings each, these six. They carry the throne of God, these are round it. They have four faces each, these have one. And there are other differences. We can safely say, in view of their closeness to the throne, that these are the most important of created beings, even that they stand in some way for the whole of creation. But it is hazardous to say more. They are important for they are close to God's throne (v. 6, xiv. 3). They constantly praise God (iv. 8, v. 8, 14, vii. 11, xix. 4). They are associated with the outpouring of the wrath of God (vi. 1–7, xv. 7).

7. Three of the living ones are said to be *like a lion . . . a calf . . .* and *a flying eagle,* while the other *had a face as a man* (cf. Ezk. i. 10, and the beasts of Dn. vii). There is a rabbinic saying in its present form dating from *c.* AD 300, but possibly much older: 'The mightiest among the birds is the eagle, the mightiest among the domestic animals is the bull, the mightiest among the wild beasts is the lion, and mightiest among all is man' (S Bk). This may give us the clue. As Swete puts it: 'The four forms suggest whatever is noblest, strongest, wisest, and swiftest in animate Nature. Nature, including Man, is represented before the Throne, taking its part in the fulfilment of the Divine Will, and the worship of the Divine Majesty.'

8. The living ones *had each of them six wings* (as did the seraphim in Is. vi. 2). A second time their eyes are mentioned: the all-seeing function is clearly important. The living ones praise God continually. Their song reminds us of that of the seraphim, 'Holy, holy, holy, is the Lord of hosts' (Is. vi. 3). The simple repetition is impressive. So is the fact that holiness comes first. John's readers lived in a world (as we do) where evil was rampant and apparently all-powerful. Goodness was weak and frustrated and ineffectual. But John's very first vision of heaven shows that these appearances are deceptive. God is holy. The word means primarily 'separate', and this separateness includes complete purity. Our God is good. And He is the *Lord God Almighty.* Real power is not with evil, but with God who is holy. Nor is this a passing phase. God is He who *was, and is, and is to come* (for the dramatic ungrammatical expression see on i. 4). God's power and eternal being ensure that His holiness will triumph over all evil.

9, 10. *When* (*hotan*) the living ones *give glory* seems to indicate that the song is intermittent. But only pedantic literalness will find a contradiction with the preceding verse. There John was making the point that in heaven God is worshipped unceasingly. Here he is saying that the worship offered by created beings (the 'living ones') is accompanied by that of the representatives of the people of God. The song gives *glory and honour and thanks* to God. It is difficult to see this in the words already quoted, so the meaning probably is that in heaven a variety of songs is sung.

God is referred to in terms of majesty (*the throne*) and eternity (*liveth for ever and ever*). The *elders* join in. They prostrate themselves before *him . . . on the throne*, worship the Eternal, and throw down their crowns before Him. All these are ways of giving Him the chief place. They themselves worship: they take the lowliest place. The throwing down of their crowns expresses the truth that He alone reigns. All other sovereignty must yield to His.

11. Their song begins *Thou art worthy*. In the most literal sense they worship (ascribe worthship). They salute God as 'Our Lord and God' (so rather than *O Lord*) and ascribe to Him worthiness to receive *glory and honour and power*. The first two are repeated from verse 9, but the 'thanks' of that verse are replaced with *power*. The reason is probably that creation, to which they immediately refer, is a work of power. God, they say, created all things. It was due to His will and to His will alone that they 'were' (not *are*), and that they *were created*. In view of the troubled state of the little church this is a noteworthy affirmation in the first heavenly vision. God has not abandoned the world, and it is indeed His world. He made all things and made them for His own purpose. John's readers must not think that evil is in control. Evil is real. But the divine purpose still stands.

IV. THE SEVEN SEALS (v. 1–viii. 5)

Chapter iv recorded a vision of God the Creator. Now comes a vision of God the Redeemer, the Lamb who has conquered through His death. The last chapter ended with a scene of worship of the Creator and this will end with the worship of the Redeemer. These two chapters are very important for an understanding of the message of the book. There are mysteries in life. Men feel themselves caught up in the world's evil and its misery, and they cannot break free. Some become rigid determinists, and we must all, at times, feel a sense of hopelessness and helplessness in the grip of forces stronger than we. The world's agony is real. And the world's inability to break free from the consequences of its guilt is real. This chapter with its seals which no man can break stresses man's inability. But it does not stop there. More important is the fact that through the Lamb the victory is won. The seals are opened and God's purpose is worked out.

This is the first of a series dealing with seven symbolic representations of plagues. Here it is seven seals; later we have seven trumpets and seven bowls with the seven last plagues. Some have held that the different groups denote separate and successive events. Since it is not possible to recognize any one series in the descriptions of the others this view must remain possible. But it is perhaps more likely that there is a unity. Kiddle aptly cites the reaction of Cortez and his men when from their peak in Darien they surveyed the Pacific (p. 296). Doubtless it was with 'a wild surmise', but doubtless also their gaze shifted, now taking in the immediate foreground, now the middle distance, but always returning to the great ocean which dominated the scene. For John the End is the significant thing. He does not take in the whole in any one vision or any one series of visions. He deals with different aspects, sometimes covering the same ground from different points of view and sometimes taking in different features of the landscape. Thus we may legitimately expect some things to recur in the visions, but always new details will make their appearance.

We should further notice that the events symbolized in this book often bear resemblance to those in the apocalyptic discourse of our Lord (Mt. xxiv, Mk. xiii, Lk. xxi), though Jesus does not use the same symbolism. But it is important that John is not composing freely. As the early church read his book it could recognize that he is dealing in another fashion with realities first spoken of by Christ Himself.

a. The unopened book (v. 1-4)

1. John saw a book on (not *in*; Gk. *epi*) *the right hand of him that sat on the throne*. This seems to mean that the book lay on the palm, not that it was held in the hand. *Book* here certainly means a scroll, which would be made up of sheets of papyrus joined edge to edge until the length required for the book was reached. The papyrus sheet in turn was made by placing thin strips of papyrus in two layers at right angles to one another. The two were joined by glue, Nile water, and pressure.[1] The side with the horizontal strips provided a better writing surface than that where they were vertical. Generally this side alone was used. But if space was important it was quite possible to write on the other side also. This was the case with the roll John saw, for it was written *within and on the backside*. The roll was full of writing, as full as it could possibly be. Some have identified the book with the Old Testament, others with Revelation itself. This approach is perverse. The book surely is that which contains the world's destiny, and its contents are revealed to us pictorially as the seals are broken. The book was *sealed with seven seals*, i.e. it was in seven parts, each of which was kept in place with an individual seal. It could thus be opened one section at a time as the seals were removed one by one.

2. John sees *a strong angel* (cf. x. 1, xviii. 21; the Greek is the same in all three). Probably the thought is that only one supremely strong could issue a challenge to all creation (in the next verse we see that his voice penetrates heaven and earth and what is under the earth). The angel looks for someone *worthy to open the book*. His concern is with worthiness, not naked power. The book records the judgments of God and these are moral. Knox translates, 'Who claims the right to open the book . . . ?' But this is not the thought. The angel is not concerned wth legal rights, but with goodness.

3. The Greek *oudeis edunato, no man . . . was able*, signifies complete impotence. The possibility is reduced to vanishing

---

[1] For the way rolls were constructed see Sir Frederic Kenyon, *Our Bible and the Ancient Manuscripts*, 1939, pp. 10 f.

point as region after region is found wanting. No angel in heaven, no saintly man on earth, no prophet in the realm of the departed was sufficient for this. Cf. Torrance, 'The secrets of the world belong to God and no man can pry into them. Who knows what a day or a night may bring forth? Who knows what this year holds in its dark unknown future? Even the strong angels of God are unable to open the book. Only God can unseal the seals and read the secrets of men.'

4. John *wept much* (his word denotes a noisy grief, a wailing), perhaps because he found it depressing that *no man was found worthy* for the task. More probably his distress was connected with the contents of the book. He had been promised that he would see things which would happen (iv. 1). Would he after all fail to see the revelation?

b. The Lion of the tribe of Juda (v. 5-14)
Now comes the answer. John finds that Christ, who is here called 'the Lion of the tribe of Juda', is worthy. But He is also spoken of as 'a Lamb as it had been slain'. The cross is central. It is as Christ crucified that He is worthy.

5. *One of the elders* comforts John. Often it is an angel who speaks with John (e.g. xi. 1, xxi. 9, xxii. 6), but an elder performs that function again in vii. 13. He tells John to 'stop wailing' for the seals will be opened. *The Lion of the Tribe of Juda* is an expression which occurs here only in the Bible. Judah is called 'a lion's whelp' (Gn. xlix. 9), and scions of the royal house of Judah are referred to in one passage in this way (Ezk. xix. 2, 3, 5, 6). But little use is made of the concept. Indeed the lion is Israel as a whole (Nu. xxiii. 24, xxiv. 9), or even the tribe of Gad (Dt. xxxiii. 20). It may even be used of heathen, as in Pharaoh's opinion of himself (Ezk. xxxii. 2). The lion is a symbol of the Messiah in 2 Esdras xii. 31 f., so it may well have been an accepted Messianic designation, at least in some circles.

The Root of David is another expression not found in the Old Testament. There are references to the root of Jesse (Is. xi. 1, 10, LXX), and in Ecclesiasticus we read that God gave 'unto

David a root out of him' (xlvii. 22). But these seem to denote
a 'shoot' rather than a 'root'. They refer to someone who has
sprung from David rather than one of his ancestors. John thus
means that Jesus was born of David's line (cf. Rev. xxii. 16).
He tells us that the Lion has *prevailed*. The word points to
Christ as completely triumphant, and the aorist tense of the
original may well indicate a victory once and for all.

6. John looked to see the Lion and he beheld—a Lamb!
This is the characteristic designation of Christ in this book,
and it is all the more striking in that the word for *lamb* (*arnion*)
is found twenty-nine times in Revelation and once only in the
rest of the New Testament (Jn. xxi. 15; there not with reference
to Christ). Elsewhere when Christ is called a Lamb the word
is *amnos* (Jn. i. 29, 36, Acts viii. 32, 1 Pet. i. 19). There is no
real difference of meaning, but the language of this book is
individual. It is striking and unexpected to have such an
animal chosen to symbolize Christ. Love points out that 'None
but an inspired composer of heavenly visions would ever have
thought of it. When earth-bound men want symbols of power
they conjure up mighty beasts and birds of prey. Russia
elevates the bear, Britain the lion, France the tiger, the United
States the spread eagle—all of them ravenous. It is only the
Kingdom of Heaven that would dare to use as its symbol of
might, not the Lion for which John was looking but the
helpless Lamb, and at that, a slain Lamb.'
This is true and important. Yet it should be added that it is
not the whole story. In the apocalypses a lamb might sometimes
be used to refer to a mighty conqueror, perhaps because such
symbolism would scarcely be expected by the uninitiated.
Thus in 1 *Enoch* xc. 9 the Maccabees are horned lambs (cf.
also *Test. Joseph* xix. 8 f.). We must also bear in mind that the
lamb was the typical sacrificial victim. It was not by any
means the only animal offered on the altars of antiquity, but
it was offered very often. When John speaks of the Lamb *as
it had been slain* there can be no doubt but that he is thinking
in terms of sacrifice. But he does not think of the Lamb as
'slain'. The Lamb is 'as though slain', for He is very much

alive. The Greek perfect tense here signifies that the Lamb was not only slain at a point of time, but that the efficacy of His death is still present in all its power.

The Lamb had seven horns. In the Old Testament the horn is frequently used as a symbol of strength (e.g. Dt. xxxiii. 17). Seven is the number of perfection and so the seven horns indicate the perfect might of the Lamb. He is completely adequate for any occasion. He also had *seven eyes*, which are explained as *the seven Spirits of God sent forth into all the earth* (cf. Zc. iv. 10). The expression may refer to the Holy Spirit (see note on i. 4). In this case the Spirit is closely associated with Christ (cf. 'the Spirit of Jesus', Acts xvi. 7, mg.). But there seems little reason for an allusion to the Holy Spirit here, and it is possible that the symbolism simply ascribes omniscience to the Lamb. The *seven eyes* on this view denote perfection of seeing. Nothing escapes Him. What John appears to be telling us, then, in his different symbols is that Christ, of the tribe of Judah and the line of David, is supremely powerful and all-knowing, and that He has won His victory by His atoning and sacrificial death. There is a striking combination of the thoughts of the utmost in power and the utmost in self-giving.

The Lamb is located *in the midst of the throne and of the four beasts, and in the midst of the elders.* The *throne* and the 'living ones' are linked, with another *in the midst* before the *elders.* John may mean that the Lamb was between the throne and the living ones on the one hand and the elders on the other (in verse 7 He 'came' to take the book). But perhaps more probably the two instances of *in the midst* are parallel. The Lamb is in the centre of all the beings named.

7. The Lamb *came and took the book out of the right hand of him that sat upon the throne.* Kiddle sees in this 'a thought impossible to visualize, but magnificent as a symbol of the death of Christ and its results. In his own way, John is expressing the perfect harmony between the will of God and the will of Christ'. This important point is made throughout the book.

8. The Lamb's action evokes a great outburst of praise and worship. Though the seven-sealed book is not yet opened all the hosts of heaven discern that it will be and in anticipation break out into a mighty chorus of praise. The four living ones and the twenty-four elders prostrate themselves before the Lamb. Each has a harp, an instrument which in this book is associated with the praise of God.

The Greek *phialē*, rendered *vial* in AV, means a 'broad, flat bowl or saucer' (LS). The word rendered *odours* more properly denotes 'incense' (as in viii. 3, 4), which is then described as *the prayers of saints* (cf. Ps. cxli. 2). On earth the saints are despised and accounted as of no importance. In heaven their prayers are precious, being brought into the very presence of God Himself, while the bowls in which they are offered are golden. John often brings out the reversal of values in heaven from those accepted by his earthly (and earthy!) contemporaries. It is worth noticing before we leave this verse that worship is reserved for God only (xxii. 9). That the Lamb is worshipped is evidence of His full divinity.

9, 10. *They sung a new song.* The word *ōdē* is 'the general word for a song, whether accompanied or unaccompanied, whether of praise or on any other subject'.[1] In the New Testament, however, it is always used of sacred song. That the song is *new* reminds us of the 'new song' in some Old Testament passages (Pss. xxxiii. 3, xl. 3, xcvi. 1, cxliv. 9, cxlix. 1, Is. xlii. 10), and later in this book (xiv. 3). The word *new* has a way of recurring in Revelation. It applies to the new name (ii. 17, iii. 12), to the new Jerusalem (iii. 12, xxi. 2), to the new heaven and the new earth (xxi. 1), and finally there is the resounding declaration that God makes all things new (xxi. 5). In so far as the Greek term *kainos* can be differentiated from the other word for new, *neos* (which does not occur in Revelation), it signifies 'fresh' as against 'recent'. It is concerned with quality rather than recency. The use of the term here raises the intriguing question of what is meant by a 'new' song in heaven. Are songs renewed there from time to time? This particular song arises from the opening of the seals as its first words show. The Lamb's saving work has created a new

[1] J. B. Lightfoot, *St. Paul's Epistles to the Colossians and to Philemon*, 1876, p. 225.

situation and this elicits a new outburst of praise. No song meant for another situation quite fits this. So the song is *new*. *Thou art worthy* takes up the word 'worthy' in verse 2. There the angel spoke of opening the book and loosing its seals: here the Lamb takes the book and opens the seals, but the meaning is the same. *Worthy* may be an acclamation taken from the secular world, as it does not appear to be used in religious texts.[1] It certainly ascribes excellence to the Lamb. His worthiness is now not reckoned in terms of His power or of the majesty of His Person, but of His death for men. *Thou wast slain, and hast redeemed us* points to the once-for-all action on Calvary (this is the most natural way of taking the Greek aorists). The verb *redeem (agorazō)* signifies simple purchase.[2] This is brought out further by the following *to God*, which indicates ownership. Redemption is not aimless. Sinners are purchased so that they may belong to God (cf. 1 Cor. vi. 19 f.). The purchase price is given: *thy blood*.

The universal scope of redemption receives mention with the piling up of expressions to show that the redeemed come not from any restricted group but from all over the world. John is fond of linking together *every kindred, and tongue, and people, and nation* (see vii. 9, xi. 9, xiii. 7—where 'people' is read in the better MSS after 'kindred' though omitted by AV—xiv. 6; and with a substitute for *kindred*, x. 11, xvii. 15). An interesting point of style is that his word order is not the same in any two examples. The expression reminds us of the 'people, nations, and languages' in a number of passages in Daniel (iii. 4, 7, 29, etc.). Some think John is quoting Daniel. But though our four terms are all found in either the LXX or Theodotion's translation, neither version has them all. Again, for the most part the Daniel references have three members, John's four. It is likely that John is using a phrase of his own, though one suggested by the language of Scripture.

The song goes on to record that the Lamb has made the redeemed 'a kingdom and priests' (for which see note on i. 6).

---

[1] So Gerhard Delling, *Worship in the New Testament*, 1962, pp. 68 f.

[2] For the concept of redemption see my *The Apostolic Preaching of the Cross*[3], 1965, Chapter I.

We should not miss *unto our God*. For the second time in the little song we are reminded that the redeemed belong to God. And in the same breath with this stress on their lowly place comes an indication of their high dignity with 'they (not *we*) reign (or possibly, shall reign) on the earth'. Theirs is to be a world-wide dominion (cf. Lk. xxii. 30). Some see a reference to a millenarian reign (xx. 4), but this is not necessary. The song looks for the vindication and ultimate triumph of the suffering saints of God. It is not concerned with specific details of how and when. We should probably read the present tense rather than the future. But the difference in this context is not great. The present perhaps gives a greater touch of certainty to the glorious day of triumph.

11. As John goes on with his songs we might have expected 'I heard', but he first says, *I beheld*. This is a book about visions, and there are continuing references to what is 'seen'. But he did also hear. Though there are many singers he speaks of *the voice*, which perhaps points to the unity of their song. The *angels* encircle the throne and the living ones and the elders. They are in an important place, but not the centre. Expression is piled on expression to bring out their number (cf. Dn.vii. 10). We should resist any temptation to multiply out the figures given in an attempt to reach a precise number. John is concerned simply to indicate that the number was vast. In fact what he means is 'innumerable'.

12. The words of the angels are introduced with *saying*, as in iv. 8, 10, v. 13, though all look like songs. Indeed, up till now the only specific reference to singing is in v. 9. But as the actual words of their song are there introduced with 'saying', it is plain that this verb is consistent with song as well as speech. The structure and content of the other passages mentioned show that they should likewise be understood as songs, as is the case with the present passage.[1] Like the preceding one this song begins with *Worthy*.

[1] B. F. C. Atkinson, however, sets before us an interesting point of view when he says, 'Angels cannot sing the new song, because they have never fallen or needed to be born again. As a matter of fact there is nothing in the Bible to tell us that angels can sing at all.'

For *the Lamb* and *was slain* see note on verse 6. A slight difference is that there the Lamb was 'as it had been slain' while here there is no 'as'. The fact of the slaying is allowed to stand out. The angels use seven expressions (the perfect number is probably significant) to indicate the wonder of the Lamb. The first four are qualities He possesses, the last three express the attitude of men to Him. Though there is no quotation there are resemblances to the praise of God in 1 Chronicles xxix. 10–12. Almost all the qualities here mentioned are ascribed to Christ elsewhere in the New Testament: *power* (1 Cor. i. 24), *riches* (2 Cor. viii. 9, Eph. iii. 8), *wisdom* (1 Cor. i. 24), *strength* (Eph. vi. 10, 2 Thes. i. 9), *honour* (Heb. ii. 9, cf. Phil. ii. 11), and *glory* (Jn. i. 14, Heb. ii. 9). *Blessing* is not specifically used of Him, but the corresponding verb is (Mk. xi. 9 f.).

13. Now the whole creation joins in the song. *Every creature* is explicit enough, but John spells it out in detail by mentioning specifically heaven, earth, the subterranean regions and the sea. *All that are in them* is redundant, for everything has been covered, but it serves to emphasize that all are included in the mighty chorus of praise. John's vision is not concerned with an obscure being of no importance. In the last resort there is no creature, wherever found, which does not recognize the superior worth of the Lamb.

The qualities selected for mention in this song are not the same as those mentioned in the preceding, and those retained are in a different order. The word for *power* is different (*kratos* here, but *ischus* there). In the former the whole seven are grouped under a single article in the Greek, whereas here each of the four has its own article to give separate emphasis. Here there is no mention of 'worthy', for it is not the achievement of redemption that is being hymned but the Persons themselves. But we should not unduly stress the niceties of what one song inserts and another omits. There is a certain exuberance about the songs which recks not of exact calculation. They simply represent the fervent outpouring of hearts full of adoration and love and praise for all that God has done through the Lamb. This song ends by linking *him that sitteth upon the throne* with *the Lamb*. The Two are joined in a way which is characteristic of this book (vi. 16, vii. 9, 10, 17, xiv. 1, 4, xxi. 22, 23, xxii. 1, 3). There cannot be the slightest doubt that the Lamb is to be reckoned with God and as God.

14. The four living ones add their *Amen*. They began the chorus of praise (iv. 8) and it is fitting that they should close it. The twenty-four *elders*, as they have done before, prostrate themselves in worship. It is not said whether they worship God or the Lamb (the better MSS end the verse at *worshipped*), and there is no need to. In this passage the Two are not differentiated.

c. The first seal (vi. 1, 2)

As we survey the picture revealed by the opening of the seals we may be a little surprised. The picture is a grim one, but it is not particularly new. War, bloody conquest, famine and pestilence are found in many apocalypses. We begin to wonder why John wept at the prospect of such well-known contents remaining undisclosed (v. 4). But there is something new here, and that is the place of the church. The martyrs are singled out in verses 9 ff., and chapter vii is given over to the great multitude of the redeemed. John sees God as in control of the whole process and God is concerned for His people. So, though apocalyptic judgments be loosed against all mankind, God's people need never be dismayed. They will be preserved no matter what the tribulation. That is the precious new revelation.

The first four seals form a unity. They show us the self-defeating character of sin. When the spirit of self-aggrandisement and conquest is abroad all God need do is let events take their course and sinners will inevitably be punished. In the wake of conquest come war and famine and pestilence. This is not the whole story and other aspects are brought out later (as in the first four trumpets which show that God is not inactive: He sends His judgments on sinful men). But this is the aspect with which John is concerned here. After the first four seals comes a group of two dealing with things in heaven rather than on earth. The final seal stands apart from all the rest. It is kept back until viii. 1 and ushers in the next series of visions. We shall find this pattern of four, two and one repeated with the trumpets and the bowls.

1. The vision is introduced with *I saw*. Revelation is full of the things John saw. *The Lamb* Himself opened one of the seals to introduce the first judgment. It may well be that we are to understand Christ's saving work for men as including an element of judgment: 'From the Death on the Cross flow whelming tides of divine Wrath. The mystery of Redemption is, we say, as yet only partially disclosed' (Kiddle). Christ's death was not only salvation from sin, but condemnation of sin. One of the living ones spoke in a voice appropriately enough likened to *thunder*. He spoke the one word *Come*. The words *and see* are not in the best MSS and must be rejected. They give the impression that the command was addressed to John, whereas it was really to the horseman of the vision. It calls him into action.

2. *I saw, and behold* is a frequent formula with John (iv. 1, vi. 5, 8, vii. 9, xiv. 1, 14, xix. 11; despite the small changes in AV, the Greek is identical). NEB brings out something of its vividness with, 'And there before my eyes was a white horse'. It might have been expected that when the book was opened John would have read it or heard someone else reading it. But instead he sees its content in a series of visions. The first four are of horses with colours like those in Zechariah vi. 1 ff., though there the horses were drawing chariots, and here they are ridden by horsemen. Indeed the riders are more important than the horses.

The first *horse* is *white* and his rider carries *a bow*. Later John sees a rider on a white horse who is called 'The Word of God' (xix. 11 ff.), from which a number of commentators conclude that it is Christ who is meant here. But there is no point of similarity apart from the colour of the horse, and this seems insufficient. Everything in this chapter points to the seals as unfolding a series of disasters. And Christ would surely not appear merely as one of the 'Four Horsemen of the Apocalypse'. This man is a victorious warrior for he carries *a bow* and is given *a crown* (*stephanos*, see on ii. 10; it is to be distinguished from *diadēma*, a royal crown, used, e.g., in xix. 12). Cf. Weymouth, 'a victor's wreath'. White was often associated with victory (Charles cites a number of triumphant warriors who rode white horses). He went forth not only *conquering*, but *to conquer*. The expression indicates purpose. Conquest was his whole aim. We should not overlook the fact that the crown *was given unto him*. Doubtless he thought of his own might as producing the victory. But John is sure of the sovereignty of God. The conqueror has only what God allows him to have.

Some see in the horseman a symbol of the victorious progress of the gospel. But there is nothing to indicate this. The four horsemen must surely be taken together, and they all indicate destruction, horror, terror. This one surely stands for war, triumphant war of conquest. Others try to give the horseman a precise historical identification, usually the Parthian king Vologäses who won a notable victory over the Romans in AD 62. But it is more than difficult to see why the Seer, writing at the end of the first century, should think of this battle as something revealed by the opening of a sealed book. It is true that Parthian prowess with the bow was proverbial (and still is—witness our expression 'Parthian shot'). But we need more than a mention of a bow to see an allusion to a specific Parthian king. It is more likely that we should take the symbolism from the Old Testament. Cyrus makes his enemies 'as driven stubble to his bow' (Is. xli. 2), and the overthrow of both Elam and Babylon is described in similar terms (Je. xlix. 35, li. 3, 56). Sometimes God destroys bows, i.e. breaks military power (Ps. xlvi. 9, Ezk. xxxix. 3, Ho. i. 5). The same imagery may be used for the cessation of war (Zc. ix. 10). A bow may even be associated with God Himself, when He is depicted as a triumphant warrior (La. ii. 4, iii. 12, Hab. iii. 9).

The opening of the first seal, then, sees a warlike conqueror on his way. The bow was not a typical Roman weapon, so it points beyond the Empire. John's mind is on more than the

Parthian king or the Roman emperor. He is saying that any nation that embarks on a career of conquest unleashes bloodshed and famine and destruction. He is saying that this will be so till the end of time and, indeed, especially in the last days. 'The lust of conquest which makes great Empires . . . was the first and most momentous of the precursors of the final revelation' (Swete).

d. The second seal (vi. 3, 4)

3. John does not explain whom he means by *he*. But clearly it is the Lamb who had opened the previous seal. That had been called simply 'one of the seals', but this is definitely named *the second*. This is the practice now throughout the series. The second living one summoned the second horseman with the same invitation that the first had given earlier.

4. There came out (from where?) a *horse that was red*. To its rider certain power *was given*. Again we see the divine sovereignty. God uses human history for history's judgment. In this way He works out His purpose. The *power* given was that *to take peace from the earth*. As distinct from the wars of conquest denoted by the first rider, this will point to civil war. Barclay says that between 67 and 37 BC 100,000 men perished in rebellions in Palestine, while the revolt in Britain in AD 61, associated with Queen Boadicea, saw the deaths of 150,000. It is such happenings which form a sombre background to Revelation. Notice that, while to this rider *there was given . . . a great sword*, he is not said to kill anyone. Men kill one another. He takes peace away and men proceed to do all the damage. The word rendered *kill* is not the usual one, and has a meaning like 'slaughter' (NEB) or 'butcher' (Berkeley).

e. The third seal (vi. 5, 6)

5. The same formula as before leads to a summons by the third living one to the third horseman. This time John sees *a black horse* (cf. Zc. vi. 2, 6), which symbolizes famine. The rider carried *a pair of balances*, unusual equipment for a horseman. It will probably refer to the weighing of bread in famine (grain would be measured by volume). Ezekiel speaks of eating food 'by weight' (Ezk. iv. 9 ff.), and again the Lord says, 'When I have broken the staff of your bread, . . . they shall deliver you your bread again by weight' (Lv. xxvi. 26).

6. John heard not *a voice* but 'as a voice', his characteristic reserve coming out in the expression. He does not say who spoke, but as the sound came from the midst of the four living ones the voice must be that of a divine Person.

A *measure* (*choinix*) was about a litre (1½ to 2 pints). The *penny* or *denarius* was a day's wage for an unskilled worker (Mt. xx. 2). Charles cites Herodotus and others to show that a *choinix* of wheat was the daily ration for a man. This price then means that the full day's wage would be expended on one day's ration. As, however, a labourer would buy barley rather than wheat and there were *three measures of barley for a penny*, our text envisages a little as being available for his dependants. It is a famine price but not a starvation price. *Hurt* is a curious verb to be used of *the oil and the wine*. But the meaning appears to be that there will be abundance of oil and wine coupled with scarcity of bread. The necessities of life for the poor will be in short supply, while the luxuries of the rich will not cease. Charles tells of a time when Domitian, in an effort to stimulate the growing of cereals, ordered that no new vineyards be planted in Italy and that half the vineyards in the provinces be destroyed. This provoked such an outcry that the edict was repealed. It is this kind of thing that John has in mind. Some see a reference to the Old Testament habit of linking corn, oil, and wine as man's basic needs. When one is harmed and the others not, then partial provision at any rate is made. All this adds up to a famine which is not yet a disaster. It is in the nature of a warning. Things are difficult, but the end is not yet.

f. The fourth seal (vi. 7, 8)

7. The fourth horseman is summoned in the same way as the first three. There is a tiny variant in that this time John hears *the voice* of the living one. But the meaning is the same.

8. There emerges a *pale horse*. The Greek *chlōros* (from which we get our word 'chlorine') denotes 'yellowish green' (AG), and is thus a curious colour for a horse. Simcox suggests that it may refer to the bare skin of a 'mangy' horse. While each of the preceding riders had an emblem (a bow, a sword, a balance) Death needs no such sign. For *Hell* (*Hadēs*), see the note on i. 18. Death and Hades are commonly linked in this book. There is no horse for Hades, but we should not look for too great consistency on points of detail (see on i. 17). As Swete puts it, 'whether on the same or another horse or on foot the writer does not stop to say or even to think', It is enough to mention the presence of Hades without particularizing its method of locomotion.

Once more we read that *power was given*. God is supreme and the little church is reminded that even Death and Hades exercise only the power that He gives them. But the power given on this occasion is awe-inspiring. A quarter of earth's population is slain in the ways mentioned. For *sword* see note on i. 16. *Death* in this context will signify 'pestilence' (as often in LXX). The four agents of death are the same as those sent by God in Ezekiel xiv. 21.

Swete sums up the meaning of the first four seals: 'The first group of seal-openings, now completed, describes the condition of the Empire as it revealed itself to the mind of the Seer. He saw a vast world-wide power, outwardly victorious and eager for fresh conquests, yet full of the elements of unrest, danger, and misery; war, scarcity, pestilence, mortality in all its forms, abroad or ready to shew themselves. This series of pictures repeats itself in history, and the militarism and lust of conquest, which it represents both in their attractive and repellent aspects, are among the forces set loose by the hand of Christ to prepare the way for His coming and the final publication of the secrets of the Sealed Book.'

g. The fifth seal (vi. 9–11)

The first four seals have had to do with happenings on earth. Now we are transported to heaven.

9. This time there is no living one to say 'Come'. But the opening of the seal ushers in the vision. John saw the souls of the martyrs *under the altar* (for the altar see viii. 3, 5, ix. 13, xi. 1, xiv. 18, xvi. 7). Some have argued for two altars in heaven, but there is no evidence. The sacrifice that puts away sins has already been offered, and there is room only for the altar of incense, which typifies homage and the offering of prayer. The association with it of the souls of the martyrs may be meant to indicate that the martyrs have offered up their lives as a sacrifice to God. Christina Rossetti reminds us that the sword 'has had its will of many a martyr, and yet has despatched him to glory'. John's words are a reminder that throughout history there has been a persistent hostility towards deeply-committed Christians on the part of those wielding power. It is manifest today as at other periods, and it will be so to the end of time.

The situation *under the altar* is unusual. There are Jewish references to those buried in Israel as though under the altar, but none is cited to souls under the altar. It seems to be a place of privilege, probably also of safety in God's keeping. John may also mean that when the martyrs sacrificed their lives for God (cf. Rom. xii. 1, Phil. ii. 17) the most significant part of what happened took place in heaven.

For *slain* see note on 'kill' in verse 4 (it is the same verb); for *the word of God* and for *the testimony* see on i. 2. *Which they held* probably refers to the testimony which Christ gave to them (cf. Jn. iii. 32) rather than to the testimony they bore to Him. They were dedicated, committed men, and they retained their concern for the testimony rather than hold fast to life itself.

10. They uttered a loud cry for vengeance. They address God as *Lord* (*ho Despotēs*; the term is applied to God in Lk. ii. 29, Acts iv. 24, and to Christ in 2 Pet. ii. 1, Jude 4; the reference could be to either in 2 Tim. ii. 21). The term is the word for a master of slaves and thus emphasizes God's absolute power. But though His sovereignty is thus in mind He is not thought of as simply a powerful Despot. He is *holy and true* (cf. iii. 7). The expression stresses God's goodness and reliability. This line of thought continues when we come to the verbs *judge and avenge* (cf. xix. 2, which is almost the answer to this prayer) for both had to do with justice. While the martyrs clearly do not wish their persecutors to remain untroubled they are asking not for indiscriminate revenge, but for justice.

Them that dwell on the earth recurs in Revelation and it always seems to refer to unregenerate mankind as a whole (iii. 10, viii. 13, xi. 10, xiii. 8, 14, xvii. 8, the Greek being identical in all these places; cf. also xiii. 12, xvii. 2 where it differs but slightly). There is another prayer for vengeance in Luke xviii. 7, this time by the living (cf. Rom. xii. 19). In both passages there is the recognition that the Christian should not pursue personal vengeance. Retribution is a divine prerogative. Some suggest that the prayer of the martyrs here is less Christian than, say, Stephen's prayer for his killers (Acts vii. 60). But we must see it in the light of John's interest in the theology of power. The cry is intelligible only on the basis that the supreme power in the world is God's power, and that He exercises it in a moral way.

11. Some have seen in the *white robes* a reference to justification (as in xix. 8). The robes are *given*, for men do not justify themselves. God justifies them. Perhaps more probable is the view that (just as was the case with the white horse in verse 2) white is to be regarded as the colour of victory. The martyrs appeared to have been defeated by their enemies. Actually they were given the victory by God. As in verse 6, there is a speech without the speaker being named. But clearly the words are authoritative. The martyrs are to *rest yet for a little season*. The verb *rest* (*anapauomai*) may mean 'desist from their cry' (cf. Goodspeed, 'be quiet a little while longer'), or 'rest in blessedness' (cf. xiv. 13). Both may be in mind, but there is surely more of an emphasis on the latter.

The end will not come until *their brethren, that should be killed as they were, should be fulfilled*. God has determined who are to be martyrs, and He waits until His plan for them is accomplished. The problem of God's failure to punish sin here and now was one which exercised the first Christians. They found part of the answer in the cross. The cross does not mean the abolition of judgment. It means that men will be judged by their attitude to the sacrificial love of God shown on Calvary. But the cross shows that God has no truck with evil. Finally it will be totally overthrown. God waits till the number of the martyrs is complete. But then the destruction of evil is certain. It is not a question of 'Whether?' but of 'When?'.

h. The sixth seal (vi. 12–17)

We have already seen that there are resemblances in this section to the apocalyptic discourse in the Synoptic Gospels. Particularly is this the case with the sixth seal. The importance of this is that when John's picture of a ruined universe was brought before his readers this was not some strange new teaching. It was 'a restatement of beliefs already held on supreme authority. What the faithful Witness at one time had said on earth, He now repeats from heaven' (Kiddle).

12. The opening of the sixth seal brings about a variety of cosmic activities. The language is reminiscent of Joel ii. 31 (see also *Assump. Moses* x. 5; it is typical apocalyptic language).

13. *Untimely figs* are late figs. A brisk wind would readily make them drop from the tree. John uses this as a simile for the way the stars would fall from heaven at the catastrophe. We could take this to refer to a shower of meteorites except that it must be taken with the following verse. In the apocalyptic literature generally the regularity of the heavenly bodies is often referred to (1 *Enoch* ii. 1, xli. 5, lxix. 16, 20 f., *Test. Naph.* iii. 2, *Ps. Sol.* xviii. 11–14). The thought of the end of the world is accordingly often thought of as accompanied or even ushered in by irregularities of various kinds (1 *Enoch* lxxx. 4 ff., *Syb. Or.* iii. 801 f., 4 *Ezra* v. 4 f.).

14. In the first century most people appear to have thought of heaven as a solid vault. John uses this conception to express the completeness of the cosmic disaster. Heaven is thought of as rolled up like a scroll (cf. Is. xxxiv. 4, and for later literature,

Syb. Or. iii. 82), and taken out of the way. On earth *every mountain and island* was shaken out of its place. In vivid and forceful language John is describing the complete break-up of this cosmic system. Yet he can scarcely mean this to be taken literally, for if so men would not be in a position to hide themselves, as in the next verse.

15. Fear fell on all earth's inhabitants, as well it might. John lists seven classes, a favourite number. He concentrates attention on the great and powerful, though *every bondman* shows that the lowly are not forgotten. But the emphasis is on the fact that no matter how we understand greatness, even the greatest will not be immune. They all hide themselves in caves and rocks (cf. Is. ii. 10, 18 f.).

16. *And said* is really a vivid present. John hears them speaking to the hills and rocks. The plea to *the mountains* to fall on them shows that the calamity with which they are confronted is so great that anything is preferable to facing it (cf. Ho. x. 8). *The wrath of the Lamb* is an expressive phrase, found only here. 'Who ever heard of a lamb being angry? What a terrible thought—the gentlest of all God's creatures angry! It is the wrath of love, the wrath of sacrificial love which, having done the absolute utmost for us and our salvation, tells us as nothing else could the certainty with which evil awaits its doom at the hand of God' (Torrance). This book has a good deal to say about wrath. *Orgē* is used here and in vi. 17, xi. 18, xiv. 10, xvi. 19, xix. 15, and *thumos* is found ten times. John is in no doubt but that the divine wrath is a grim reality. Men must reckon with it in the end. NEB renders 'vengeance' here and in most places. This is no improvement, and looks like an attempt to rewrite the Seer rather than translate him.

17. The description of the last day as *the great day of his wrath* is noteworthy. So far-reaching is the divine wrath that the last day can be described in terms of it. It is the day of reckoning for all evildoers. The language is reminiscent of a number of Old Testament passages (e.g. Joel ii. 11, 31, Zp. i. 14, 18, ii. 2). *Who shall be able to stand?* highlights the impotence of all mankind in that day. It is probably meant also as a contrast to the later statement that 'a great multitude . . . stood before the throne, and before the Lamb' (vii. 9). In the same way the statement about the mountains moving (verse 14) is probably meant in the light of prophecy: 'For the mountains shall depart, and the hills be removed; but my kindness shall not depart from thee, neither shall the covenant of my peace be removed, saith the Lord that hath mercy on thee' (Is. liv. 10). In no place in this section is John trying to terrify the saints. He is using familiar apocalyptic imagery to reassure them, and to give them the certainty that their God is over all. God is bringing His purposes to pass, and He will do so though it means that this world order, and indeed this whole mighty universe, pass away.

i. An interlude (vii. 1–17)

i. The sealing of the servants of God (vii. 1–8). The sixth seal has been opened, but before coming to the seventh there is an interlude (a device which John sometimes adopts elsewhere). Here we find that the servants of God are under His special care (He has 'sealed' them). There are some great difficulties here. Specifically, commentators differ as to whether the 144,000 and the great multitude later in the chapter are the same or different groups, whether the former refers to literal or spiritual Israel, and whether either or both refer to the martyrs. There is little evidence to decide these points and we must be guided by our understanding of the book as a whole.

1. John saw *four angels standing on the four corners of the earth.* We should understand this not so much as a statement of John's view of the shape of the earth as a way of saying that the angels overshadow the whole earth. None of it is beyond their control. Their function is to hold back *the four winds of the earth.* John takes no notice of intervening winds, but we should not interpret this with pedantic literalness. The meaning is plain enough. The angels are preventing harmful winds from blowing on *the earth,* on *the sea,* and on *any tree.* Trees seems a curious inclusion in this list. Perhaps they symbolize what is living, and in any case they would suffer most from a great wind.

The four winds may be another way of referring to the four horsemen of the first four seals. Zechariah's four horsemen are explicitly interpreted as 'the four winds of the heavens' (Zc. vi. 5, mg.; cf. also Ps. lxviii. 33, Is. xix. 1, lxvi. 15, etc.). Whereas Zecharaiah speaks of 'winds of heaven', thus stressing their subjection to God supreme in heaven, John refers to *winds of the earth*, for their destructive activity is connected with the earth. Winds are a natural symbol of destruction (cf. Je. iv. 11 f., xlix. 36, li. 1 f.). The vision, then, takes us back in time. It answers the question, 'What is the fate of believers during the terrible happenings just described?'

2. John sees *another angel ascending from the east*. This may be meant as the source of blessing (the place where light originates). It is not impossible that John recalls that it was from the east that wise men came with the news that the Christ had been born (Mt. ii. 1 f.). Victorinus curiously speaks of this angel as Elijah, but there seems little to be said for this ancient interpretation. The angel had *the seal of the living God*. The seal was basically a mark of ownership (important in an age when many could not read). Here it marks the men sealed as God's and thus preserves them from a destruction that will fall on others (cf. Ezk. ix. 1 ff., and for a slightly different thought, Ex. xii. 23). God's own bear His mark elsewhere in this book (ix. 4, xiv. 1, xxii. 4), and the wicked are also marked (xiii. 16 f., xiv. 9, xvi. 2, xix. 20, xx. 4). This angel shouts to the other four who are characterized by their ability to hurt earth and sea.

3. He commands them not to hurt earth, sea, or trees, *till we have sealed the servants of our God in their foreheads*. *Servants* (*doulous*) means 'slaves'. The word stresses utter devotion. There is no indication of a limit and apparently all God's servants are sealed. This restraint of the forces of destruction is important, and Torrance sees it as 'the great master-thought that informs this Book'. It means that 'every moment on the

earth is made to serve the redeeming purpose of God for mankind. The four winds from the four corners of the earth cannot
blow and vent their rage as they like, but only as they are
made to serve the Church of Jesus Christ.'

4. John hears the number of the sealed (the perfect *esphra-
gismenōn* may mean 'sealed permanently'; God does not go
back on His choice). The number 144,000 is the multiple of
the square of twelve (the number of Israel) and the square of
ten (the number of perfection). It thus indicates completeness,
the perfect total of Israel. Some take this to mean the literal,
physical Israel, so that a perfect number of Israelites will be
found among the redeemed. A strong objection is that in this
case Israel is sealed for protection but a mighty multitude from
all nations (verse 9) is saved without this sealing. Surely both
would be sealed if they are different groups. Others think of
the church as Israel. The church can be referred to as 'the
twelve tribes' (Jas. i. 1; cf. Mt. xix. 28, Lk. xxii. 30), and this
is probably the thought when a letter is sent to 'the Dispersion'
(1 Pet. i. 1, mg.). The Christian appears to be the true Jew
(Rom. ii. 29) and the church 'the Israel of God' (Gal. vi. 16).
Descriptions of the old Israel are piled up and applied to the
church (1 Pet. ii. 9 f.; cf. Eph. i. 11, 14). It is the church which
is God's 'peculiar people' (Tit. ii. 14), and Christ's own who
are 'Abraham's seed' (Gal. iii. 29) and 'the circumcision'
(Phil. iii. 3). Many hold that 'Israel after the flesh' (1 Cor.
x. 18) implies an 'Israel after the Spirit'.

The view is thus widespread. Nor is it alien to John. He
expresses it by implication when he speaks of those 'which say
they are Jews, and are not, but are the synagogue of Satan'
(ii. 9; cf. iii. 9). He regards the new Jerusalem as the spiritual
home of Christians (xxi. 2, etc.), and it has on its gates the
names of the twelve tribes (xxi. 12). There is thus good reason
for seeing a reference here to the church as the true Israel.
Here it is the church, sealed in view of the coming trials;
later in the chapter it is the church triumphant and at peace.
Some, it is true, see a reference to the martyrs who are preserved from famine, pestilence, etc., for a greater destiny is

reserved for them. But the view does not seem adequately based and no convincing reason is put forward to support it.

5-8. It is not really necessary to list the tribes. But doing this puts some stress on the inclusion of all God's people. There are 12,000 from each tribe except Dan, which is omitted. The twelve are then made up by including Manasseh as well as Joseph. This is rather curious, for Manasseh is included in Joseph. If there are two Joseph tribes we expect Ephraim and Manasseh. Some scholars see a copyist's error, 'Dan' being read as 'Man' and subsequently taken as an abbreviation for 'Manasseh'. This seems unlikely and it is more probable that Dan was omitted because of its association with idolatry,[1] or because the antichrist would arise from this tribe.[2]

The order of the tribes has aroused comment, for it differs from every other order known to us. It must be significant that Judah comes first, for this is the royal tribe, the tribe from which came the Messiah, 'the Lion of the tribe of Juda' (v. 5). But apart from this we should probably not concern ourselves with the order. As G. B. Gray long ago pointed out, in about twenty lists in the Old Testament there are eighteen different orders.[3]

ii. The great multitude (vii. 9-17). John proceeds to paint an unforgettable picture of a vast crowd of people from every nation on earth but now in the bliss of heaven. They are free from pain and anxiety and sorrow.

9. John's *lo* after *I beheld* adds a touch of vividness. He saw it all before him. The *great multitude* was so large that no-one

---

[1] Cf. Jdg. xviii. 30, 1 Ki. xii. 19. Rabbinic writers stressed this. Thus R. Johanan said that Abraham prophetically 'saw his descendants who would practise idolatry in Dan' (*Sanh.* 96a).

[2] This view is put forward by Irenaeus (*Adv. Haer.* v. 30. 2), who bases it on the words, 'The snorting of his horses was heard from Dan' (Je. viii. 16). Swete cites Hippolytus: 'As the Christ was born of the tribe of Judah so the Antichrist will be born of the tribe of Dan' (*De Ant.* 14). Satan is said to be this tribe's prince (*Test. Dan* v. 6). Dan's bad reputation may be quite old, for this tribe (along with Zebulun) is omitted from the genealogies in the early chapters of 1 Chronicles.

[3] *The Expositor*, VI, v, 1902, pp. 225-240.

was able to count it. The definite number in verse 4 pointed to completion: none was missing. The great throng here shows the impossibility of counting up the number of the redeemed. They came from *all nations, and kindreds, and people, and tongues* (see note on v. 9). He piles one expression on another to indicate the crowd's universality. Incidentally this is a further indication that spiritual rather than physical Israel is referred to in the earlier part of the chapter, for otherwise the crowd would be the Gentiles only, not all the nations. The vast throng stands *before the throne, and before the Lamb*. Once again Christ is accorded a place with the Father.

The redeemed are dressed in *white robes*. The Greek noun *stolas* signifies long robes, and is much more appropriate to glorious garments than to workaday clothing. The white robes probably point us to justification. The saved stand before God perfect in the righteousness which Christ supplies. White is also the colour of victory and *palms*, too, were often emblems of triumph. This stress on triumph leads some to hold that the white-clad throng are the martyrs. Against this, there is no indication in the narrative such as we get elsewhere, e.g. the reference to those who 'were slain for the word of God' (vi. 9), or to those who 'were beheaded for the witness of Jesus' (xx. 4). Moreover it was not their death but Christ's that won the triumph. Victory comes through His saving work and it is He who provides the white robe of justification. For men confronted with tyrants who put their trust in sword and bow, it is good to be reminded that final triumph comes through quiet trust in Christ.

10. *With a loud voice* the multitude ascribes (*cried* is really a vivid present) salvation to God and the Lamb (see note on v. 13). Both are in mind, not one. And as God is He who *sitteth upon the throne* it is God as sovereign of whom John is thinking. Salvation then comes from the sovereign act of God in Christ.

11, 12. This concerns *all the angels* as well as men. They were standing round the throne and therefore round the elders and the living ones. But at the cry of the redeemed they prostrated themselves and worshipped. They first said *Amen*, which is their assent to the cry of the multitude. It further shows that this act of worship is called into existence by the angels' joy at God's saving act. They proceed to ascribe seven qualities to God, each being preceded by an article in the Greek (a construction difficult to bring out in English). It is 'the' blessing, etc. and not 'a' blessing, etc. which they have in mind, i.e. the blessing above all others. The list is the same as that in v. 12 (where see note) except that *thanksgiving* replaces 'riches'. *For ever and ever* is a sonorous conclusion which puts all this into the realm of eternal verities. The angels end, as they had begun, with *Amen*, affirming the reliability of it all.

13. *One of the elders* (cf. v. 5) now *answered* John. The verb is curious, for John had asked nothing and is in fact told nothing, for the verb introduces an inquiry. It is equivalent to 'said'. The elder draws attention to the white-robed throng and asks where they came from.

14. John throws the ball back to the elder with his *Sir, thou knowest* (the emphatic *su, thou,* implies 'It is you who know'). The elder explains that the multitudes are those who are coming (present tense) *out of the great tribulation*. The article in the Greek may indicate the great trouble at the end of things (cf. iii. 10). But it is in any case likely that it also refers to tribulation in general, for not all will undergo the great tribulation. Cf. Niles, 'The great tribulation! That certainly meant the persecution in which we were caught. But it also meant that constant tribulation of life which was the result of evil's warring against God. Out of that tribulation, and because of it, come the host of the redeemed.'

The elder further informs John that these triumphant ones *have washed their robes, and made them white in the blood of the Lamb* (both verbs are aorists, in each case indicating once-for-all action). 'Whitened in the blood' is a striking paradox and we should not let our familiarity with hymns which have borrowed it dull its splendour (for the thought, cf. Ex. xix. 10, 14, Is. i. 18, 1 Cor. vi. 11, Heb. ix. 14). The complete efficacy of Christ's atoning death is being strongly asserted. It is on the grounds of His death for men that they are able to stand before the throne properly clothed. This is a further indication that the throng comprises all the saved and not simply the martyrs or some other group. For all are saved in this way and no other.

15. It is for this reason (*therefore*) that they are before God's throne. They serve Him by day and by night (cf. 1 Ch. ix. 33). John does not envisage heaven as the scene of holy inactivity. The *temple* (*naos* properly signifies 'sanctuary') raises problems, particularly in view of the later statement that in the final state of things there will be no Temple (xxi. 22). Probably the whole of heaven is being regarded as a sanctuary in which all God's people are priests (i. 6, v. 10) and enjoy the immediate presence of God. *He that sitteth on the throne* (i.e. God in His aspect as King) *shall dwell among them*. The verb *skēnōsei* evokes memories of the Tabernacle (*skēnē*) in the wilderness. We might translate 'He will make His Shekinah to dwell with them', where 'Shekinah' is taken (as it often was among the Jews of the time) to mean the immediate presence of God. We might have expected a present tense, but John uses the future as he points to the glorious prospect ahead.

16. The bliss of the saved is conveyed in a series of negatives (mostly from Is. xlix. 10). They will know no unsatisfied desire. They will not hunger. They will not thirst. They will suffer neither sunstroke nor burning heat (*kauma*; cf. Ps. cxxi. 6). Typical physical ills are taken as symbols. Whatever the torment they will be free from it.

17. The reason? The Lamb. He is *in the midst of the throne* (i.e. closely related to God in royal state), and He will *lead them unto living fountains of waters*. The verb *poimanei* ('lead') is normally associated with a shepherd, and is a striking word to use of a Lamb. It marks a complete reversal of roles. So does John make his point that Christ in His sacrifice of Himself makes provision for the needs of His people. *Living fountains of waters* shows that the absence of thirst in verse 16 meant the absence of unsatisfied desire. It did not mean satiety. The saved will always thirst for God and that thirst will be satisfied. Finally God will wipe away every tear (the word is singular) from their eyes (cf. Is. xxv. 8). God's people are delivered from every ill. They enjoy warm fellowship with Him. His tender concern makes complete provision for their every need.

j. The seventh seal (viii. 1–5)
John now returns to the seals. The final seal is opened. There is an impressive silence, which we cannot but think portends the End. But instead it begins a new series of visions heralded by angels with trumpets. This is typical of John's method. He goes over the ground again and again, each time teaching us something new. There is more to the End than we can readily take in. Every series of visions brings out new facets of it.

1. The sixth seal was opened as far back as vi. 12, so there has been quite an interval. At the opening of the seventh *there was silence in heaven about the space of half an hour.* Clearly it was a solemn and impressive moment. It is possible that the silence is connected with the offering of the prayers of the saints (verses 3 ff.) just as in vii. 3 certain plagues were held back until the servants of God were sealed. The saints appear insignificant to men at large. But in the sight of God they matter. Even great cosmic cataclysms are held back on their account. And the praises of the angels give way to silence so that the saints may be heard. It is also possible that we should think of the silence as resulting from a sense of awe at the presence of God (cf. Hab. ii. 20). He is about to launch severe judgments on men. All heaven remains silent.

2. The vision introduced by the opening of the seventh seal was that of *the seven angels which stood before God.* The definite article shows that a certain defined group is in mind. This may be the seven who 'present the prayers of the saints, and go in before the glory of the Holy One' (Tobit xii. 15). Their names are given as Uriel, Raphael, Raguel, Michael, Saraqael, Gabriel and Remiel (1 *Enoch* xx. 1 ff.). John has other references to seven angels (verse 6, xv. 1, 6 ff., xvi. 1, xvii. 1, xxi. 9). But after this chapter they all refer to the angels who had the seven bowls introducing the seven last plagues, and it is uncertain whether they are the same seven. Standing before God and serving God mean much the same thing (cf. 1 Ki. xvii. 1, xviii. 15, 2 Ki. iii. 14, v. 16; it is interesting that RSV translates the last two with 'whom I serve' instead of 'before whom I stand' though the Hebrew is the same). To these angels are now given *seven trumpets* ('war horns', Schonfield). Trumpets are often associated with the end-time in apocalyptic writings (cf. Mt. xxiv. 31, 1 Cor. xv. 52, 1 Thes. iv. 16).

3. Before the angels blow their trumpets the prayers of the saints are offered. This is not an unrelated parenthesis. John means us to see that the prayers of God's people are supremely important. Even the cataclysmic judgments which follow are held up until these prayers have been offered. Indeed in a sense it is these prayers that set the judgments in motion (verse 5).

John not infrequently brings a new angel on the scene with the formula *another angel*. We have no means of identifying this one. Nor do we know who gave him *much incense*. The incense is closely connected with *the prayers of all saints*, though it is not identical with them as it was in v. 8. It is offered with them, which we may take to symbolize the unity of the worship of heaven and earth. The use of the *golden* censer and of the *altar* of like material point us to the value of the prayers. Some hold that we should translate *tais proseuchais* 'for the prayers' rather than 'with the prayers'. Their thought is that the prayers of men are imperfect, but when they have been 'censed' they ascend to God. It may be freely granted that men's prayers are at best imperfect but it is not a scriptural idea that an angel renders them fit to ascend to God. *With the prayers* is correct. A surprising number of translators render *dōsei* (AV *offer*) by 'mingle' (RSV, Goodspeed, C. Williams, Amplified, Twentieth Century), a rendering not easy to defend. The word means 'give' and is rightly rendered *offer* (AV, NEB, Knox, Schonfield, etc.). For *altar* see on vi. 9. That it is *golden* and thus valuable and that it is *before the throne* are ways of stressing the importance and value of the prayers of the saints.

4. The incense and the prayers went up before God. Notice that they went up *out of the angel's hand*. This is probably a way of saying that heaven and earth are one in this matter. Prayer is not the lonely venture it so often feels. There is heavenly assistance and our prayers do reach God. It may be significant that there is mention of an altar in connection with this, for it signifies that there is something sacrificial in true prayer. We should not think of the angel as a mediator. Angels are 'fellowservants' (xix. 10, xxii. 9). But we are Christians only because of Christ's sacrifice, and all our service (and our praying) is to be sacrificial.

5. It is not easy to see how the angel *took the censer* when he already had it (verse 3). Perhaps the thought is that earlier he had it for purposes of intercession. Now he took it for purposes of judgment. He *filled it with fire of the altar, and cast it into the earth*. The result was *voices, and thunderings, and lightnings, and an earthquake* (see on iv. 5). The fire comes from the very altar on which the prayers of the saints have been offered. This surely means that the prayers of God's people play a necessary part in ushering in the judgments of God. 'What are the real master-powers behind the world and what are the deeper secrets of our destiny? Here is the astonishing answer: the prayer of the saints and the fire of God. That means that more potent, more powerful than all the dark and mighty powers let loose in the world, more powerful than anything else, is the power of prayer set ablaze by the fire of God and cast upon the earth' (Torrance).

V. THE SEVEN TRUMPETS (viii. 6–xi. 19)

For the relation between the trumpets and the other series, see the note at the head of chapter v. As with the seals there is a distinction between the first four and the last three. Here the four are largely concerned with the forces of nature and the last three with men. More exactly the division is four, two, and one. The last is singled out for emphasis by an interlude between the sixth and the seventh. The division between the four and the three is underlined by an eagle flying in mid-heaven and uttering a triple 'woe' on account of the plagues to follow.

The trumpet judgments do not concern the church as such. They are God's judgments on the world. A good deal of Revelation is taken up with this kind of thing. Human wickedness does not go unnoticed in heaven. God has His own way and His own time for dealing with it. John uses a good deal of conventional apocalyptic in this section to emphasize that God is really in control and that He does what He wills. We must bear in mind further that, whereas the seals drew our attention to judgment as following more or less inevitably on the sins of men, the trumpets rather direct our attention to the divine activity. God moves against sin. We should also bear in mind that these are not the final judgments. In each case a third only is affected, and this serves as a warning. Indeed, the sound of the trumpet is essentially to give warning (Ezk. xxxiii. 3).

a. The first trumpet (viii. 6, 7)

6. We return now to the trumpets introduced in verse 2. The angels got ready to blow them, though what is involved in *prepared themselves* is not said.

7. The first trumpet was the signal for widespread destruction, brought about by *hail and fire*, the latter being most naturally understood of some electrical phenomenon accompanying a thunderstorm such as lightning or fireball (cf. Ex. ix. 24). *Mingled with blood* may give us the colour (cf. Joel ii. 30), or it may indicate the kind of destruction brought about by the lightning. Blood was shed. Some have thought of blood-red rain such as has been attested in the Mediterranean region as a result of the air being thick with fine red particles of sand blown in from the Sahara. But this scarcely seems adequate.

John speaks of widespread devastation among *trees* and *grass*. *The third part* stands for a significant proportion but not the majority. The whole earth is not destroyed, but enough to give serious warning. Some find a difficulty in that in ix. 4

neither grass nor green growth is to be destroyed, and ask how this could possibly be if *all green grass* had already been destroyed. The answer might be, in the first instance, that this verse does not appear to mean that all the grass on earth is destroyed. Throughout this section John is concerned with plagues which affect one third. His meaning here is surely that all the grass in the one third of the earth mentioned was burnt up. But in the second instance it is a great mistake to read this fiery, passionate and poetic spirit as though he were composing a pedantic piece of scientific prose. He is painting vivid pictures and it does not matter in the slightest that the details do not harmonize readily (see on i. 17). John does not tell us who it was who cast the fire and hail upon the earth. We should understand some heavenly being, but precisely which does not matter. What matters is that God sends His plagues on evil men. This is true throughout the ages and it will be so till the End.

b. The second trumpet (viii. 8, 9)

8. In response to the second angel's trumpet comes something which is not described exactly. It is not a burning mountain but like one ('what I can only call a great mountain', Barclay). As with the previous phenomena it is not said who *cast* it *into the sea*. We must understand once more that it is a divine visitation, but that the precise agent is unimportant. Whereas the first trumpet had been concerned with the land this one deals rather with the sea, *the third part* of which *became blood*. This may be meant to remind us of Exodus vii. 20 f. Indeed the plagues of Egypt are recalled by quite a few expressions in this section of the book. We are perhaps meant also to remember the words of the psalmist: 'Therefore will not we fear, though the earth be removed, and though the mountains be carried into the midst of the sea' (Ps. xlvi. 2). The throwing down of mountains is indeed a terror to the wicked. But God's people have nothing to fear from God's judgments on the godless.

9. Whatever it was that happened in the waters destroyed one third of all marine life. This is not pollution of the water on a grand scale because one third of the ships were destroyed. John is not describing natural happenings but a divine intervention.

c. The third trumpet (viii. 10, 11)

10. From the water of the sea attention is switched to the waters on the land. The third trumpet brought about the fall from heaven of *a great star* like a blazing torch. Again a *third part* is affected, this time a third of *the rivers* and *the fountains of waters*. This is an unusual happening and Charles finds no parallel in Jewish apocalyptic. John may be thinking in part of the frequent worship of river deities and the like. All such spirits are impotent before the judgments of Almighty God. But the main thrust of the passage is concerned with the effects on men. John's prime concern is with the punishment of ungodly men.

11. The name of the star is *Wormwood*, a very bitter substance. One third of the waters *became wormwood* with the result that *many men died*. Wormwood as we know it is not poisonous. John may have in mind another substance resembling it in some ways. Some suggest that he is taking the bitterness of the taste as in itself suggesting poison.

d. The fourth trumpet (viii. 12)

12. The sounding of the fourth trumpet was followed by effects in the heavenly luminaries (cf. the ninth plague in Egypt which was concerned with darkness). Sun, moon and stars were all *smitten*. The proportion of one third is retained, though exactly what happened is not easy to say. The first part of the verse appears to mean that one third of all three failed, so that there was one third less light at any time. The latter part seems to mean that one third of the time there was no light at all by day or by night. But perhaps John is not greatly concerned with consistency. He is making the point vigorously that one third of all light was gone. Again, some see a contradiction with v. 13 where 'the stars of heaven fell

unto the earth'. That verse, however, does not mean that all
the stars, without exception, fell. There is no contradiction.
But in any case we must insist that difficulty in harmonizing
details should never worry us in this book. John is painting
pictures, not writing scientific prose (see further on i. 17).

e. The eagle (viii. 13)

13. This verse marks an interlude in the sequence of trumpets.
John saw and heard (cf. v. 11, vi. 1) an eagle. There seems no
doubt that the true text reads 'one eagle' and not *an angel*. The
force of the 'one' may be 'one solitary eagle' (Barclay), 'a lone
eagle' (Schonfield). The eagle, a bird of prey, is often a sign
of disaster (cf. Mt. xxiv. 28, and for its use in apocalyptic cf.
2 *Bar.* lxxvii. 19 ff.). The eagle was in full flight in *the midst of
heaven*, an expression which indicates the highest point of
heaven, the place the sun reaches at meridian. From this
vantage-point the eagle proclaims a threefold *woe* to *the in-
habiters of the earth* (the expression is identical with that translated 'them that dwell on the earth' in vi. 10, where see note).
The triple *woe* is connected with the trumpets which are yet
to sound. The first *woe* is proclaimed as past in ix. 12, and the
second in xi. 14. But the third is not specifically mentioned.
It may be the descent of Satan in xii. 12. The solemn words
of the eagle show that the plagues to come are worse than those
already experienced. There is a deepening of intensity.

f. The fifth trumpet (ix. 1-12)

As with the last three seals, with the last three trumpets we
move into the realm of spirit. But whereas the seals were concerned with heaven and heavenly realities the trumpets tell
of the abyss and the demons. These visions are described in
much greater detail than the first four. The symbolism of the
locusts is horrible and strange. It is not surprising that it has
been interpreted in a variety of ways. It is unwise to be dogmatic, but the most probable understanding of it refers it to the
preaching of the gospel. When men fail to respond to God's
gracious invitation and set themselves in opposition to His
purposes, then they become the prey of horrifying demonic

forces. They suffer the consequences of their choice. They are not defeating God. His sovereignty is clear to John. God is not mocked. Even in the demonic horrors He works out His purpose. But men must abide the results of their choice. This is so now and it will be so in the last days.

Torrance sees the passage like this: 'St. John's vision likens the Word of God to a star that falls out of Heaven and opens the bottomless pit of human nature. . . . Preach the Gospel and keep on preaching it, and either men are ashamed and converted or the bottomless pit is opened. Surely that is what has happened in the western world, in civilised Europe, as well as in the land of the Mau Mau, for example. The Cross of Jesus Christ has provoked such a reaction against it that all the latent evil in men has been pushed to the surface in unbelievable wickedness and bloodshed. The very bottomless pit has been opened in our midst, so that heaven and earth have been darkened with its fumes and the whole atmosphere of the world has been poisoned.' This, I think, is true. There are possibilities of evil always latent in men and in the modern world all too often we see them realized.

But John is saying more than this. There are evil forces other than those latent in men, and those other forces, demonic forces, have scope when men turn away from God. 'Such a picture etches forever on the soul one of the most terrible truths of life. It is this: whenever men go beyond their own humanity in committing their crimes, whenever they become so debased that they let themselves be possessed by a force of evil greater than human nature itself could conjure up, then human sin becomes inhuman, men are the offspring of beasts, and judgment lashes the soul with its most unspeakable terrors' (Love).

There is another thought here, namely that God uses the evil results of men's sins to call them to repentance. From verse 20 we see that repentance is in mind. John sees the release of the demonic forces from one point of view as the results of men's sin. But from another it is God's chastening, and God's chastening is not aimless. Rightly received it should lead men to amendment. John sees God, not the demons, as in control.

1. When *the fifth angel sounded* John saw a star fallen to the earth (so rather than *fall*, as the tense is perfect; cf. Moffatt, 'a Star which had dropped'). Unlike the star in viii. 10 this one was in some sense a person. Angels were sometimes called stars (cf. i. 20) and it seems likely that this star was an angel. Some take 'fallen' very literally and think of a 'fallen angel'. But this is probably reading too much into it. On the basis of certain apocryphal passages Charles argues that when the imagery is that of a star there is not much difference between falling (1 *Enoch* lxxxvi. 1, lxxxviii. 1) and descending (1 *Enoch* lxxxvi. 3). So this verse will mean much the same as xx. 1. The most diverse indentifications of the star-angel are given. He might be Nero (Weymouth), a fallen angel (Simcox, Love), an evil spirit (Kiddle), or even Satan himself (Hendriksen, Atkinson; Swete thinks 'possibly Satan'). On the other hand he is seen as the Word of God (Torrance), an angel, possibly Uriel (Charles), our Lord Himself (Berkeley). With the experts so divided it is unwise to be dogmatic. John does not identify him and we simply do not have enough information to supply the lack.

To *him* a key was given. Some have held that the *him* means *the fifth angel*. This is grammatically possible, but it is quite out of keeping with John's method. The function of *the fifth angel*, like that of the other six, was to blow the trumpet, nothing more. *Him* refers to the star angel. *Was given* is another way in which God's sovereignty is brought out. The star-angel had no independent authority. The *key of the bottomless pit* is that of 'the shaft of the abyss' (NEB). The abyss is seen as a great pit with a narrow opening at the top, but broadening out further down. The narrow opening, 'the shaft', is locked, but its key is now given to the star. The abyss is seen as the place to which the demons in the Gadarene swine expected they might be sent (Lk. viii. 31), while in Paul's one use of the term it is the abode of the dead (Rom. x. 7). All the other examples of the word are in Revelation (ix. 1, 2, 11, xi. 7, xvii. 8, xx. 1, 3). Here it is a place inhabited by spirits, and firmly under God's control (the key is 'given' in this verse, and that seems implied in xx. 1). It is not the place of punishment, for that is described as a lake of fire (xx. 10, 14 f.). Charles speaks of the abyss in this book as 'the *preliminary* place of punishment'. But the idea of punishment does not seem to be implied in any passage where the term is used. It is the place of incarceration of Satan (xx. 1 ff.), but torment is not implied. It is inhabited by beings hostile to God, but they are subject to His control.

2. The star-angel opened the shaft. *Smoke* came out *as the smoke of a great furnace* (cf. Gn. xix. 28, Ex. xix. 18). *The sun and the air were darkened.* In viii. 12 one third of the light was taken away, but there is no equivalent estimate of the effects here. The point is rather that so great was the quantity of smoke that even the light of the sun was blotted out. *The air* (mentioned again in xvi. 17) was held to be the abode of demons (cf. Eph. ii. 2), though the thought is not stressed here.

3. *Out of the smoke* came *locusts*. It is not a cloud of locusts, but they came from it. Locusts formed the eighth plague in Egypt (Ex. x. 12 ff.), and a plague of locusts is behind the little book of Joel.[1] To them *was given* (notice this verb again; the forces of evil have no independent authority) *power* (i.e. authority) like that of *the scorpions of the earth*.

4. *It was commanded* the locusts, but there is no indication of the speaker. This is a device John uses often. It indicates that the command had divine sanction, coming ultimately from God, but it shows that it is unimportant who actually said the words. The content of the command was that the locusts were not to harm vegetation. This is described under three headings. First is *the grass of the earth* (for the view that there is a conflict with viii. 7 see note on that passage). Next is *any green thing*, which will denote plant life between grass and trees, which are specified in the first and third groups. Finally is *neither any tree*. This spells a total prohibition of action against any form of plant life, the natural food of the locust. Instead

---

[1] There is a valuable discussion of the types of locust known in Palestine in an Excursus appended to S. R. Driver's commentary on Joel in the *Cambridge Bible for Schools and Colleges*.

they are to hurt those men who were not sealed (vii. 3 ff.). Like the other plagues in this series this is directed against the godless. Those who belong to God are not included in the commission given the locusts. The demonic world has no power against them.

5. Once again *it was given* reminds us of the limitations on the power of evil. The demons can exercise only that power that is given them. On ·this occasion they have power to torment, but they are not permitted to kill. The period of *five months* assigned to their *torment* accords with the fact that it is *as the torment of a scorpion*. The bite of the scorpion, though painful, is rarely fatal. The time mentioned may be due to the fact that the natural locust has a life span of about this period. Or the thought may be that of incompleteness. It lasted but five-twelfths of the year (cf. the use of one third in earlier plagues). S Bk draws attention to the frequent use of the number five, as five sparrows (Lk. xii. 6), five in a house (Lk. xii. 52), five yoke of oxen (Lk. xiv. 19), five talents (Mt. xxv. 15), two groups of five virgins (Mt. xxv. 2), five days (perhaps meaning 'a few days', Acts xx. 6, xxiv. 1), five husbands (Jn. iv. 18), five brothers of the rich man (Lk. xvi. 28), five barley loaves (Mt. xiv. 17), Paul's five beatings (2 Cor. xi. 24). Some of these examples are certainly not arbitrary. For example, if the market rate for sparrows was five for two farthings, then no other number was possible. But some of the other examples are certainly such as to leave the impression that sometimes 'five' was used in the sense 'a few'. If that is the meaning here the torment was of limited, but undefined duration.

6. Men will be in considerable torment. *Men* (*hoi anthrōpoi*, i.e. mankind at large) will seek out death, but not find it. The statement is given emphasis by being repeated in another form. Men *shall desire to die, and death shall flee from them* (actually this last verb is present tense, 'death keeps running from them'). There is an interesting contrast with Paul, whose personal preference was for death, which he regarded as a gain, but who accepted life (Phil. i. 23 f.).

7. A description of the locusts shows them to have been of fearsome appearance. They are likened to horses, as in Joel ii. 4 (a number of points in this description recall that in Joel). There are probably two points in this comparison: the shape of the locust's head is not unlike that of the horse (as has often been pointed out), and the compact ranks of the locusts seem rather like cavalry lines. The comparison might be held to indicate that these locusts were of abnormal size, but there is nothing else to indicate this in the entire description. As in Joel the appearance and not the size is in mind. They had on their heads *as it were crowns like gold*. John does not say that they had crowns (as he does in other connections, e.g. iv. 4, vi. 2), but what looked like crowns. Some explain this by referring to the natural appearance of certain types of locust. This is probably misguided. John is not describing the appearance of any naturally occurring insect, but of certain demons. Thus he goes on, *their faces were as the faces of men*. This is not part of natural history.

8. Their hair was long, *as the hair of women*. Many commentators see a reference to the antennae of the locusts, but this seems far-fetched. Their teeth were like those of lions (cf. Joel i. 6). We should think not of size. but of ferociousness. They were very destructive.

9. The scales covering their bodies were like *breastplates of iron*, i.e. they were well protected. Enemies so covered are difficult to destroy. The word *thōrax* signifies 'breastplate', as AV, but here it applies to bodily covering in general. The number of these fearsome creatures is indicated by the noise made by their wings, *as the sound of chariots of many horses running to battle*.

10. John now uses the present tense, 'they have' (not *had*, as AV), though previously he has used the past. The scene becomes increasingly vivid to him. He sees the locusts with tails like scorpions, complete with stings. It was doubtless this which gave them power to hurt men for the five-month period already mentioned. The repetition of this period from verse 5 indicates that it is significant.

11. The locusts are not a leaderless rabble. In contrast to natural locusts (cf. Pr. xxx. 27) they have (present tense again) a king. He is first called 'the angel of the abyss' (so rather than *bottomless pit*; see note on verse 1), an expression which does not appear to occur anywhere else, though we read of Satan's angels (Mt. xxv. 41, 2 Cor. xii. 7, Rev. xii. 9). S Bk draws attention to the positions ascribed to Uriel (as having authority over Tartarus) and Jeremiel (as presiding over the abyss and Hades), in Jewish thought. But the present passage is not concerned with a good angel, carrying out God's commands. It is the leader of the demonic hordes. His name is given in two languages. *Abaddon* transliterates a Hebrew word with the meaning 'destruction' (Jb. xxvi. 6, xxviii. 22, Ps. lxxxviii. 11, Pr. xv. 11). The Greek equivalent is given as *Apollyon*, which means 'Destroyer'. It is possible that this name is used rather than one of the other possible equivalents in order to convey a derogatory allusion to the god Apollo. What the Greeks worshipped as a god was no more than a demon.

12. The eagle had announced that there would be woe to the inhabitants of the earth on account of the last three trumpets (viii. 13). So significant is this that the events in question are now characterized as *woes* rather than described with reference to the trumpets. The first is past. It is out of the way. But mankind's troubles are not over. *Behold* and the present tense in *come* make the scene vivid. Two more woes are yet to come.

g. The sixth trumpet (ix. 13-21)

The fifth trumpet had unleashed forces of destruction which were likened to locusts. Those set loose by the sounding of the sixth trumpet are in the form of angels and are much more deadly. Whereas the locusts tortured, the angels and their hosts killed. As before, a third must be taken as indicating a large number, but not a majority. It is a warning to the rest to repent, but John sadly records that they did not. The vision is to be interpreted along the lines of the preceding vision, but everything is greatly intensified. Instead of torment there is death, and instead of locusts a huge army of fiery horsemen on strange steeds.

In this vision there is some emphasis on the failure of men to repent. God does indeed send His judgments upon wicked men. But His aim is not to hurt. There is a purpose of love behind the judgments. They are to show men the seriousness and the ill desert of sin, so that they may repent, and turn to God and be saved. Yet when they do nothing of the sort they need not think that they have triumphed over God. He is in supreme command. They may resist His will, but it is to their own hurt.

There is a further point to be borne in mind. John was not writing to or for the pagan world. He was writing for the Christian church. Believers must live in this world, not an imaginary world of their own choosing. John is making plain to a little group of persecuted believers that they must not expect to live in a world that understood them and welcomed their witness. No matter how severe the judgments of God on it, the world continues with its idolatries and its manifold sins. Believers must not delude themselves. This world that John depicts, with sinful men resisting God to the limit no matter how much they hurt themselves in the process, is the world believers must live in. There is no other.

13, 14. When *the sixth angel sounded* there was no setting in motion of forces of destruction, as in the case of the blowing of the previous trumpets. This time John simply *heard a voice* (lit. 'one voice'; cf. Berkeley, 'a solitary voice'). It came from the *horns of the golden altar* (see note on vi. 9). In vi. 10 the martyrs cried to God from under the altar, and in viii. 3–5 prayer was offered on it and judgment released as the result. It is likely that the prayers of God's people are still in mind. After all, this whole series of judgments was precipitated by those prayers and it would be appropriate to recall them again. If so, this further judgment is brought on by those prayers. John does not want us to forget that prayer is a mighty force. The altar is specifically said to be *before God*. As usual, John does not say whose voice it was, but this may be meant to indicate that it was a divine voice or at least that it came with divine approval. It may of course have come from the angel associated with the altar (viii. 3 ff.).

The voice addressed itself to *the sixth angel*, identified as him *which had the trumpet*. These last words might be taken as the first part of the address, 'Thou that hast the trumpet, loose . . .'. But this is not the kind of Greek which John normally uses and AV is probably correct. The command was that the angel should loose four angels who were bound at the Euphrates. The definite article, *the* four angels, shows that a specific group is meant. But this four at the Euphrates is not attested elsewhere. Their location prevents us from identifying them with the four angels of vii. 1 (though some do in fact hold to this identification). The fact that they have been *bound* appears to show that they are not good angels going forth voluntarily to do God's will. They are evil beings who have been restrained until now. This fits in with the general pattern, that this section of the book deals with the demonic. There are many references to angels of punishment in books like 1 *Enoch* (xl. 7, liii. 3, lvi. 1, lxii. 11, etc.). But these are not the same. We can say no more than that they are evil angels who cannot act until God permits them.

The *Euphrates* is described as *the great river*, as often in the Old Testament (Gn. xv. 18, Dt. i. 7, Jos. i. 4; cf. Rev. xvi. 12). There it is regarded as the ideal limit of the promised land. These angels of wrath accordingly come from just outside. In the first century people would have thought of the Parthians, the world's most dreaded cavalry, for they came from this region and filled men with foreboding.

15. The angels were loosed, presumably by the sixth angel, though that is not specifically mentioned. They had been prepared for this time and John specifies it in detail, hour, day, month and year. There are examples in the Old Testament of the specification of the time by day, month, and year (e.g. Nu. i. 1, Hg. ii. 10), but none includes also the hour (the hour is mentioned in the apocryphal 2 *Enoch* xxxiii. 2, but there it is in 'a time of not-counting'!). The Greek has 'the hour' (not *an hour*) and, while the article is not repeated it should be understood to apply to the others in the series. It is clear that John is speaking of a divine plan. God has a purpose and it is worked out. It is a purpose of judgment and on this occasion *the third part of men* were slain. As before, one third will signify a large number, but not the majority. It is not the blotting out of sinful mankind, but a very stern and severe warning. The four angels are loosed to do the killing, but the part they play is not said. We hear next of a mighty army of horsemen, but it appears that it is the horses who actually slay the men (verse 18). The natural interpretation is that the angels are the leaders. They direct the mighty host in order to bring about the intended result.

16. The number of men in 'their squadrons of cavalry' (NEB) is given as two hundred million (cf. Ps. lxviii. 17). *I heard the number of them* shows that an exact figure is meant and not simply a very large number as in v. 11. John had to be told the number, for such a mighty horde was beyond counting.

17. John reminds us that all this was seen *in the vision*. This may be a way of reminding us that there is a strong symbolic element in what he is saying. *Breastplates of fire, and of jacinth, and brimstone* should probably be taken as a reference to colour rather than to material. *Fire* will mean reddish; *jacinth* (cf. xxi. 20) 'appears to denote a dusky blue colour as of sulphurous smoke' (MM). This takes it as akin to sapphire. Some think it the colour of a reddish orange gem, but in view of the fact that in this context *fire* is reddish, it is more likely that blue is meant. *Brimstone* we now commonly call sulphur. The meaning might be that the breastplates were tri-coloured or that some were red, others blue, and others yellow. John proceeds to liken *the heads of the horses* to *the heads of lions*. The ferocity and destructiveness of the animals are stressed. Their fearsome nature is further seen in the fact that from their mouths issued *fire and smoke and brimstone*.

18. The fire, the smoke and the brimstone are regarded as three separate plagues (the better MSS read 'by these three plagues', as RSV, rather than *by these three*). Between them they killed *the third part of men* (for this proportion see on verse 15). *Which issued out of their mouths* keeps before the reader the fact that this was not a natural phenomenon but a demonic visitation.

19. These fearsome horses have power to harm at either end: in their mouths as before mentioned and in their tails. It now appears that these latter are like snakes with heads with which *they do hurt*. The deadliness of the tails links this vision with the preceding. It is the same type of thing, only more severe. The mention of snakes evokes associations with the demonic, for demons and serpents were widely linked in antiquity. Some see a reference to the habit the Parthians had of twisting their horses' tails so that they looked like snakes. They recall also the Parthian skill in shooting arrows behind them as they rode. Such facts may have helped to shape John's imagery, but it is not this he is describing. He sees demonic forces.

20. John turns his attention from the plagues and those who suffered in them to *the rest of the men which were not killed by these plagues*. They might have been expected to take warning from what had happened and become devout servants of God. But they did not repent. They did not cease from their idolatry. John spells this out. He refers first of all to their worshipping of *devils* (cf. 1 Cor. x. 20 for the conjunction of idols and demons). The idols, as not uncommonly in Scripture, are characterized by their material and by their inability to see, hear, or walk (cf. Pss. cxv. 4 ff., cxxxv. 15 ff., Dn. v. 23). In this way he underlines the folly of those who refuse the call to repentance. Their preference is for impotent deities.

21. From their gods John turns to their sins. There are several lists of this sort in the New Testament (cf. Mk. vii. 21 f., Gal. v. 19 ff., Rev. xxi. 8, xxii. 15), but none appears to have this particular group of four vices. *Sorceries* is understood by some in the sense 'poisonings' (e.g. Ferrar Fenton). But there seems no good reason. The word denotes the use of drugs or enchantments and may occasionally denote poisoning, but 'sorceries' is much more likely here.[1] *Fornication* is singular (as it usually is in the New Testament), the others plural. This does not mean that this kind of sin was less frequent than the others. It simply sums up many acts in one. The term, as usually, will stand for sexual sin in general and not specifically fornication.

h. An interlude (x. 1–xi. 14)

As in the case of the seals, there is an interlude between the sixth and the seventh trumpets. In both cases the effect is to set off the seventh visitation as particularly important. We are all keyed up for the climax but it does not come. We are kept in suspense. This is not simply a literary device. It is part of life. Men cannot predict how God's judgments will operate. They take unexpected courses. There are delays which give opportunity for repentance.

This interlude centres on an open book, which is surely the Word of God (x. 2). This is to be eaten by John after which he is to prophesy about 'many peoples, and nations, and tongues, and kings' (x. 11). This will mean that the Word of God is to be preached everywhere before the End comes (cf. Mk. xiii. 10). John has dealt with the fate of sinners during the days leading up to the climax. Before dealing with that climax he turns his attention to the church. It has duties to perform and troubles to undergo. He warns it.

i. The little book and the seven thunders (x. 1–4). Some

of the things spoken of in the book are more mysterious than others. With the seven thunders we come to something so secret that it may not be revealed.

1. Again we have *another angel* (cf. viii. 3), and again an angel is described as strong (cf. v. 2, xviii. 21). John saw him in the act of coming down (present participle) from heaven (cf. xviii. 1, xx. 1). The direction perhaps indicates that John is now on earth (cf. also verses 4, 8), whereas previously he has been writing from the perspective of heaven (e.g. ix. 13).

---

[1] See also J. B. Lightfoot, *Saint Paul's Epistle to the Galatians*, 1902, p. 211.

Up till now little has been said about the appearance of angels, the attention being rather on what they did and said. But the appearance of this one is described fairly fully. Each of the points mentioned has elsewhere some connection with God or with Christ, and so this angel is clearly important. Some have gone further and identified him with Christ. This, however, is not justified. Christ is never called an angel in this book, and this angel is not accorded divine honours. He is not worshipped, for example. The swearing of an oath (verse 6) does not look like an action of the Christ. The angel was dressed in *a cloud* (cf. Ps. civ. 3 for the clouds as God's chariot), his hat was the *rainbow* (cf. the rainbow round the throne, iv. 3), *his face* was like *the sun* (cf. i. 16), and *his feet* (clearly 'legs' is the meaning: LS notes a meaning of *pous* for 'the leg with the foot') were like *pillars of fire* (a pillar of fire was the symbol of God's presence with His people in the wilderness, Ex. xiii. 21 f.). Several commentators see the rainbow as produced by the sunshine of the angel's face falling on the cloud.

2. The strong angel of v. 2 was associated with a book, that one being written inside and out. It was called a *biblion*. This one *had in his hand* a *biblaridion, a little book*. This particular word for a small book is not previously attested. Since we have no usage to guide us we do not know whether the diminutive termination is to be taken seriously or not. The distinction between a 'book' and a 'little book' is apt not to be so very marked when it is merely a question of the length of a roll. If the present word has diminutive force the significance will be that the *little book* contained part only of the revelation of God's purpose. It is in the angel's hand and it is *open*. The perfect participle rendered *open* carries the suggestion of permanence. The book is not concealed and it is not likely to be. The angel *set his right foot upon the sea, and his left foot on the earth*. The reason for the choice of foot is not apparent, but the fact of treading on both land and sea probably indicates mastery over both (cf. Ps. lx. 8). He treads the sea as easily as the land. It also means that his message is a universal message. It concerns all whether on land or sea.

His posture is also an indication of gigantic size. The believer is expected to discern the implication of this. The world despised him as a member of a little, insignificant church. It held all that he stood for as of no account. But his faith was based on the Word of God. And the Word of God is in the hand of this colossal figure, who, though dimly seen through the enveloping cloud, spans both land and sea. The Word of God is supremely significant. It is not puny and insignificant. It towers above all the affairs of men.

3. The previous strong angel cried out with a loud voice (v. 2), and so does this one. His voice is likened to that of a lion roaring (actually the verb *mukaomai* is mostly used of the bellowing of oxen, but the use of its cognate noun for the roar of lions is attested and *roareth* is clearly the right translation here). *Seven thunders*; better 'the seven thunders' as RSV. The article points to a definite group of seven thunders but it has not been identified. An interesting suggestion refers the words to Psalm xxix, which speaks of a thunderstorm and uses the expression 'the voice of the Lord' seven times. But if the reference is to some such definite group we have no means of identifying it with certainty.

4. The seven thunders not only *uttered their voices*, but produced words, or at any rate sounds with meaning. John was about to add their content to his memoirs, but was forbidden. The voice which forbade him is anonymous, but it was divine in origin (*from heaven*). *Seal* (*sphragizō*) in the sense 'keep hidden' is found in the New Testament only here and in xxii. 10. Sealing was common in the ancient world, but mostly as a means of identification or as a means of certifying and authenticating. In apocalyptic, however, it does seem to mean 'keep hidden' (cf. Dn. xii. 4). Charles speaks of it as a technical term in this sense. But its use here for 'sealing' something unwritten seems unparalleled. The meaning is clear, however. And it is reinforced by the following *write them not* (there is some emphasis on *them*: contrast the command to write, i. 19).

Human nature being what it is there has been a good deal of speculation as to what the thunders portended. Some have

thought that they represent a series of judgments on unbelievers, and that, as enough of judgment has already been
disclosed through the seals and the trumpets, they are sealed
up fast. To write more would be unnecessary, especially as
the subject of the book is now to be the church rather than the
world. But such an explanation makes the thunders completely
inexplicable. Why would God make a revelation that was
unnecessary? It is better to think of the thunders as conveying
a revelation to John himself (clearly he understood them),
but which he could not pass on. Paul speaks of such experiences
(2 Cor. xii. 4). Not all the counsel of God is open to every
man. It is good to be reminded that there are parts of it which
the more spiritual can take in but which are beyond ordinary
people like ourselves. A further value of our knowledge that
the thunders are sealed is that it is a warning against the kind
of date-fixing which has characterized some schemes of
prophecy based on this book. On John's own showing we do
not have all the information. God has kept some things back
from us. Let us beware of proceeding as though all has been
revealed.

ii. The angel's oath (x. 5–7). The angel solemnly proclaims the imminence of the fulfilment of what he calls 'the
mystery of God' (verse 7). This stands for the whole purpose
of God (see note) and conveys to John's readers the assurance
that there is an answer to the perplexities of history. The
mystery of God will be finished. Prophecy will be fulfilled.
The angel solemnly confirms this with an oath.

5. *The angel* is identified with him of verse 1 by the fact that
he stands on the sea and the earth. It is the same one. He
now swore a solemn oath. He lifted up his hand to heaven, a
common accompaniment of oaths in antiquity (cf. Gn. xiv.
22, Dt. xxxii. 40, Dn. xii. 7).

6. The oath is made very solemn by the prolonged description of God. The angel singles out His eternity and His
activities in creation. This is to bring out the point that what
the angel is about to speak of is not some panic device to which

a surprised God must resort in reaction to the machinations of evil men and evil spirits. He is supreme over time and over creation. He fulfils what He plans. 'The last days, no less than the first, are in His hands' (Kiddle). The content of the oath is that *that there should be time no longer*. This translation has been made the basis of a view that in the next life there will be no such thing as time. Men will live in a great eternal present. Time will give way to eternity. Whatever be the truth of this view, it is not what the angel is saying at this point. The meaning is, as AV mg. and most modern translations, 'that there should be no more delay'. The angel is solemnly swearing that the events of which he speaks will take place certainly and speedily when the seventh angel blows his trumpet.

Charles thinks that John had in mind the reference to 'a time, times, and an half' (Dn. xii. 7; cf. Dn. vii. 25), words which refer to the period of the antichrist's power, and which is already present in the visions of Daniel. Here, however, it is still future and is to be introduced by the seventh angel (verse 7). This is possible, all the more so since the angel is speaking from the standpoint of the future. He is speaking between the sixth and the seventh trumpets. From that vantage-point he assures John that when the necessary conditions have been fulfilled there will be no delay. The End will come. The fact that the seventh trumpet does not sound until xi. 15 is no contradiction. The intervening sections do not describe a series of happenings intervening chronologically between the sixth and seventh trumpets. Rather they represent a parenthesis in which the task of the church throughout the ages comes before us.

7. *But* is the strong adversative *alla* and signifies 'but, on the contrary'. This strengthens the view that 'delay' rather than 'time' is meant at the end of the previous verse. The time is defined more exactly as *in the days of the voice of the seventh angel, when he shall begin to sound*. For *mystery* see on i. 20. The term is not uncommon in the New Testament and the very expression we have here occurs elsewhere (1 Cor. ii. 1 (cf. RSV mg.), Col. ii. 2; the plural without the article in 1 Cor. iv. 1, cf.

also Eph. i. 9). Moffatt translates it here 'the secret purpose of God'. The word is usually associated with the gospel and this may be in mind when John uses the verb *euēngelisen*, here translated *declared*, and which usually means 'preach the gospel'. There is that about the gospel which is not accessible to the mind of men. Left to ourselves we would never have worked out that God would save men in this way. It has to be revealed.

The good news was proclaimed to *his servants the prophets* (cf. Am. iii. 7). It is possible that we should understand *prophets* here to mean the New Testament prophets as well as those of the old dispensation. God has one purpose through the ages and it reaches its climax at this point. From the very beginning God has planned to bring His people to salvation, and thus His whole purpose is coming to its culmination. It involves the judgment of evil, but also the deliverance and vindication of the people of God. John's readers are to reflect that the mighty world forces they saw, far from being triumphant, are about to be overthrown decisively. A purpose that God has planned before the world and has matured throughout all ages will not lightly be jettisoned. *The mystery of God* will indeed be finished.

iii. The little book (x. 8–11). John takes the scroll from the angel's hand and eats it. This gives him the message he must use in prophesying to many peoples. Charles regards the contents of the little book as 'a *proleptic* vision of the reign of the Antichrist' (on verse 1). It is not necessary to be so specific. It is the Word of God to John. But since he does not specify to what it refers with any precision we are on dubious ground when we attempt to improve on him.

8. John now heard again *the voice which I heard from heaven* (verse 4). Once again there is no indication of the speaker, but we must take it as authoritative. The voice instructs the Seer to take the book from the angel, who is described for the third time in terms of the place where his feet rested. Clearly his position on both land and sea is regarded as important.

The word for *little book* is *biblion* whereas both before and after it is *biblaridion* (verses 2, 9, 10). There appears to be no difference in meaning, and it is not clear why John should use *biblion* just this once. The book is again said to be 'opened'. This is important. The revelation is not hidden.

9. So John went to the angel and asked him for the little book. The angel said, *Take it, and eat it up.* This last verb, *kataphage*, means 'devour it', 'eat it down', i.e. 'make its contents completely your own', 'take them into your innermost being'. The angel proceeds to assure John that *it shall make thy belly bitter, but it shall be in thy mouth sweet as honey.* Both Jeremiah and Ezekiel had similar experiences. Jeremiah ate God's words and they became joy and delight (Je. xv. 16). Ezekiel was commanded to eat a scroll and as he did so it was sweet as honey in his mouth (Ezk. iii. 1–3). Neither, however, reports John's experience of bitterness in the belly. Being God's Word it is necessarily sweet to any believer (cf. Pss. xix. 9 f., cxix. 103). But because the book contains stern denunciations and tells of woes on evildoers it is also bitter. We should not miss the point that it is the belly of John, the firm believer in Jesus Christ, which is made bitter. As verse 11 makes clear, the scroll is concerned with the message he must proclaim. The true preacher of God's Word will faithfully proclaim the denunciations of the wicked it contains. But he does not do this with fierce glee. The more his heart is filled with the love of God the more certain it is that the telling forth of 'woes' will be a bitter experience.

Some interpretations miss this. Thus Hendriksen understands the bitterness to refer to the persecutions the believer must undergo. While it is true that suffering is inevitably the lot of the faithful disciple that scarcely meets the present case. Here the bitterness is internal, something within the believer. It is not external like the persecutions which come from without. Again, Kepler misinterprets John when he says, 'The book is "bitter" because its message foretells persecution and death; but when the message is digested, it is "sweet as honey," since the rewards of the "New Jerusalem" await those martyred for their faith.' The fact is that the sweetness is in the mouth, and the bitterness after the message is digested. Kepler has reversed John's sequence. The wickedness of man grieved God at His heart (Gn. vi. 6), and the true preacher of God's Word enters to some degree into this suffering.

10. Now we have the fulfilment of the angel's words. It is worth noticing that twice John was told to 'take' the roll. He asked the angel to 'give' it to him. But the angel told him to 'take' it. And in the end he did 'take' it. The revelation of God is something the messenger of God must take for himself. He cannot be passive. So John took the roll and devoured it. He found it in his mouth *sweet as honey*. But it made his stomach bitter.

11. *He said* in the better mss is 'they say', which is curious. Up till now there has usually been one single speaker. The plural subject is not identified. It may be the equivalent of the passive, as rsv's 'I was told'.

Again is also a little strange, for up till now John has not so much prophesied as heard and seen things. But he has also recorded his visions, and throughout it has been clear that he will proclaim the things he has seen. He has spoken of his book as a prophecy (i. 3), so he can be said in a measure to have prophesied already in what he has recorded. But now he is called upon to prophesy again, and to do it on a larger scale, *before many peoples, and nations, and tongues, and kings* (for this expression see on v. 9; this is the only one of the seven similar expressions which includes *kings*). The word of John is concerned not with any one group of people, be it church, nation, or empire, but with many. This has had a striking fulfilment through the centuries. The reference to *kings* is appropriate as reminding us that the word of God through His prophets is superior to even the highest among men (cf. Je. i. 10).

iv. The two witnesses (xi. 1-14). In this section John refers to the tremendous opposition faced by the people of God

143

throughout the centuries and especially in the last days. He speaks of two witnesses who bear unflinching testimony to the Word of God. And of the terrible figure of the antichrist. We see something of the nature of the conflict between the antichrist and the people of God and John gives us a glimpse of the triumph of the latter.

The chapter is extraordinarily difficult to interpret, and the most diverse solutions have been proposed. Some see it as irrelevant. It is on their view an interpolation or at best a digression in which John makes use of some material he happens to have at his disposal, but which does not fit in well with his main theme. It is not uncommon to find verses 1 f., and 3–13 regarded as originally two distinct Jewish works, the one composed in the expectation that the Temple would be preserved though Jerusalem would be destroyed in the war of AD 66–70, and the other presuming that Jerusalem itself would stand. Why John should take over prophecies which had proved false is not explained. At the other extreme Kiddle thinks that in many respects this is the key to John's main theme. It seems to me that this view is more likely to be correct than the former. Even if John did take over this chapter from some earlier source (which is far from having been proved) we must assume that it expressed his meaning when he incorporated it.

It seems to me important that the whole section (verses 1–13) is to be taken symbolically. It is plain enough that the sanctuary of verse 1 is symbolical, but most expositors proceed to take the witnesses and the holy city literally. Then difficulties multiply. They are fewer when we see all as symbolism and a coherent pattern emerges. John has already used the lampstand symbol and explained that it refers to churches (i. 20). Thus it seems best to take the witnesses as symbolizing the witnessing church or some part of it. Since John has spoken of seven churches only two of which are not blameworthy (Smyrna and Philadelphia), it is tempting to think of the two witnesses as standing for that part of the church which is completely faithful even unto death, i.e. the martyrs. It is possible that part of the significance of the number 'two' is that in the law the testimony of two witnesses is required in important matters (Dt. xvii. 6). God has provided all the witness that is needed.

Kiddle speaks of 'a brilliant reinterpretation of another familiar apocalyptic theme'. Elijah was expected before the End to preach repentance to the Gentiles, sometimes in company with Moses or Enoch. John sees the task as too great for any two men, but 'the martyrs, John believes, will be endowed with a spirit of prophecy no less powerfully than the greatest prophets of old. The opposition they must face will be equally fierce—it will come from the same source. Their need for supernatural protection will be equally great. Therefore they shall be equipped with the same powers as Moses and Elijah' (pp. 183 f.).

The great city (verse 8) is often identified with Jerusalem. But the very verse which allows us to do this calls the same city Sodom and Egypt. 'The great city' recurs in xvi. 19, xvii. 18, xviii. 10, 16, 18, 19, 21. It is better to think of it as the earthly city in opposition to the heavenly city of chapters xxi, xxii. It is man in organized community and opposed to God. It is another name for this world as a worldly system.

What John is doing then is outlining the function of the witnessing church. Its lot will be hard, but its eventual triumph is sure. This is a heartening message for his troubled readers.

1. It is not said who gave John *a reed* but the divine authority is clearly behind it. *Kalamos* may be used of a reed swaying in the wind (Lk. vii. 24), but clearly here something stiffer is meant by *a reed like unto a rod*. The better MSS omit *the angel stood*, so that the speaker is not named.

John is told to *measure the temple of God* (cf. Ezk. xl. 3 ff.). Measuring may be either for destruction or preservation (2 Sa. viii. 2). The command represents something new. Hitherto John has been a spectator of visions (with an indication in x. 11 that he is to prophesy). Now he will take an active part. He is to measure *the temple*, or rather, sanctuary (*naos*) and the altar and the worshippers. There are references to a sanctuary in heaven (vii. 15, xi. 19). But as John's standpoint when last mentioned was on earth, and as the courtyard of this sanctuary is to be trodden by Gentiles (verse 2), it is better to think of a sanctuary on earth. If a material building were in mind the Temple at Jerusalem is most probable. But it is more likely that John is referring to the church, elsewhere described as God's sanctuary (1 Cor. iii. 16, 2 Cor. vi. 16, Eph. ii. 21).

The altar is the most important part of the equipment of the Temple and it is a reminder of the sacrificial nature of Christian service. *Them that worship* stands for the people of God in their capacity as a worshipping community. It is not clear how they are to be measured with a reed. Moffatt's 'numbering the worshippers' probably gives the sense of it. The meaning apparently is that what is measured at God's command is under the direct control and care of God. The church will be protected in the coming disaster (cf. the sealing of vii. 3). This does not mean that none will perish. There will be martyrs. But the church will not be destroyed.

2. The outer courtyard is not to be measured *for it is given unto the Gentiles*. This is not easy to interpret. The starting-point for John's imagery is the Jerusalem Temple, where the outer court might be used by Gentiles, but the inner courts, including the sanctuary, by Israelites only. The church, the true Israel, is the sanctuary in the vision. John may mean that there is to be a reversal: Judaism is now the outer court and it is to be under the control of the Gentiles. More likely he is dividing mankind into Christians and Gentiles (cf. 1 Cor. v. 1, 1 Thes. iv. 5).

Further, he seems to be using 'the temple', *the court which is without the temple* and *the holy city* as symbols of the church under different aspects. To *the Gentiles* there *is given* power over the church in some of its aspects. Notice *is given*. Neither the Gentiles nor anyone else can exercise any power other than that which *is given*. They trample *the holy city* for *forty and two months* (for trampling a holy place cf. Is. lxiii. 18, Dn. viii. 13, Zc. xii. 3 LXX, Lk. xxi. 24). Though they are not permitted to destroy the church, the Gentiles are permitted for a limited time to oppress it. The distinction between the sanctuary and the outer courts shows that there is a limit on the extent to which the Gentiles can do their trampling, and the time stated puts a limit on the period.

Forty and two months (again in xiii. 5) is the same period as 1,260 days (xi. 3, xii. 6), or 'a time, and times, and half a time' (xii. 14, Dn. vii. 25, xii. 7; 'a time'=one year, 'times'= two years, 'half a time'=six months). That is to say, the same length of time as in Daniel is allowed for the treading down of the holy city by the Gentiles, the prophesying of the two witnesses, the woman's stay in the wilderness, and the beast's exercise of authority. This is the period during which Antiochus Epiphanes tyrannized in Jerusalem, a time of unbelievable horror for the pious Jew, but a time which came to its end. So John will mean his readers to discern that the trial of the people of God will be of measurable duration and that they will be delivered out of it. Perhaps we should also notice that forty-two is the number of the encampments of Israel in the wilderness (Nu. xxxiii. 5 ff.). As John uses a good deal of symbolism from the deliverance from Egypt (see note on xii. 3) it is possible that some of the time periods• contain an oblique reference to the wilderness story.

3. Without warning, *my two witnesses* make their appearance. As a result of the divine gift they *shall prophesy* for 1,260 days (for the period see on verse 2). Their identity is not completely clear. Some think of Moses and Elijah, who would suit verses 5 f. very well. They are referred to in an oracle of hope at the end of the Old Testament (Mal. iv. 4 f.), and they appeared on the Mount of Transfiguration (Mt. xvii. 3). Other suggestions are Elijah and Elisha, Enoch and Elijah (who both ascended to heaven supernaturally), the Law and the Prophets, the Law and the gospel, the Old Testament and the New. There is no shortage of suggestions. The context seems to demand something directly associated with the church, and in view of verse 7 perhaps we should think particularly of the martyrs.

The number *two* may stand for adequacy of testimony (as in Dt. xvii. 6). Or it may derive from the two faithful churches in chapters ii–iii, and point to that section of the church which is faithful unto death, the martyrs. The clothing of the witnesses is *sackcloth*, which points to mourning. They are prophesying doom and their attitude accordingly is sad and penitent. The church is a powerful church only when it is a penitent church. A comfortable, easy-minded church has no power to stir the world either to salvation or to opposition.

4. The witnesses are described as *the two olive trees*, as in Zechariah iv. 3. In both places they indicate a plentiful supply of oil. In Zechariah the oil and the Spirit are connected, so that the message is 'not by might, nor by power, but by my spirit, saith the Lord of hosts' (Zc. iv. 6), a message very appropriate to John's situation. Zechariah's olive trees are described as 'the two anointed ones, that stand by the Lord of the whole earth' (Zc. iv. 14) which closely resembles John's words. John then is referring to their dependence on the Spirit of God and their closeness to God.

He goes on to refer to them as 'lampstands' (so rather than *candlesticks*, see note on i. 12). Zechariah speaks of one lampstand, but John's symbolism this time is probably the same as that in his first two chapters, where he uses 'lampstand' six times, each time referring to the churches. The witnesses are collective rather than individual and stand for the church. But as there are seven lampstands in i. 13 and but two here, it is only part of the church that is meant. The combination of the word 'witnesses' (*martures*) and the death of the two point irresistibly to the martyrs. We should not overlook the reference to *the God of the earth*. John never forgets that God is a great God with dominion over all the earth.

5. No-one can harm God's witnesses before their mission has been accomplished. Those who try succeed only in bringing destruction upon themselves. The *fire* is to be taken figuratively. The witnesses are not concerned with the physical destruction of their enemies. They are concerned with a message (which has a fiery aspect, Je. v. 14). It is probably not out of mind that Elijah was vindicated by a God who answered 'by fire' (1 Ki. xviii. 24, 38). *Devoureth* (*katesthiei*) signifies total destruction. The word of the faithful witness is a consuming fire. *Must . . . be killed* shows that the death is inevitable. *Must (dei)* points to a compelling divine necessity.

6. *In the days of their prophecy* the witnesses have a privileged position. They can prevent rain (cf. Elijah, 1 Ki. xvii. 1, Jas. v. 17). Their powers are connected with water again when it is said that they can turn *waters* into *blood* (cf. viii. 8, Ex. vii. 20, 1 Sa. iv. 8). Their third power is *to smite the earth with all plagues, as often as they will.* There are other references to the power given to the servants of God, a power limited only by lack of faith (e.g. Mk. xi. 23, Jn. xv. 7). John may well have in mind here that the faithful performance of the church's duty is itself one of the ways in which the judgments of God are set in motion against an evil world (cf. viii. 5). His imagery here expresses the truth that God's servants in the new dispensation have just as great resources as did Moses and Elijah in the old.

7. But there is a limit to their exercise of power. When *their testimony* is concluded their invulnerability goes. *Finished (telesōsin)* means that the testimony has reached its end or aim *(telos)*. The witnesses are not cut short. They accomplish their task. Then they are opposed by *the beast.* It is not 'a' beast, but *the* beast, an evil being who is prominent throughout the second part of this book. He comes *out of the bottomless pit* (the 'abyss'; see note on ix. 1), which indicates his connection with the forces of evil. The two witnesses are evidently regarded not as individuals but as a mighty host. For it is not said simply that the beast will kill them or the like, but that he will *make war* with them (cf. Dn. vii. 21). In this war he will be victorious, with fatal consequences for the witnesses. When Christ's martyrs have completed their task they are removed from the scene. The words have relevance to every persecution the church has suffered, though especially to that in the last days. Hendriksen, commenting on verse 8, sees this illustrated by conditions in countries (such as Russia) where the church is seriously restricted: 'Thus, just before the second coming, the corpse of the Church, whose public and official testimony has been silenced and smothered by the world, lies on the great city's High Street.'

8. *Bodies* is actually singular, 'body', which may point to a close unity between the two. There is no verb in this part of the sentence and we must supply one (AV supplies *shall lie*). The meaning apparently is that they are killed in the street and their bodies allowed to lie there. The city is identified in two ways. First it *spiritually is called Sodom and Egypt*. The two names are proverbial for wickedness and oppression (for Sodom, Is. i. 9 f., Ezk. xvi. 46, 55; Egypt is the place where Israel was a slave; Sodom and Egypt are linked in Wisdom xix. 14 f., and Egypt is a name for persecuting nations in *Gn. Rabbah* xvi. 4). They also both felt the judgment of God. Despite its might Sodom was destroyed. And despite its might Egypt was 'ruined' by the plagues God sent (Ex. x. 7). Secondly, the city is the place *where also our Lord was crucified*. Some conclude that Jerusalem is in mind. But if the passage is symbolical, as I have maintained, it is unlikely that any one earthly city is meant. The 'great city' is every city and no city. It is civilized man in organized community.

9. *They of* (partitive *ek*) denotes part of the groups, while *people and kindreds and tongues and nations* (see note on v. 9) is very comprehensive. John is speaking of representatives of all mankind which is another indication that it is not one earthly city that he has in mind. The *dead bodies* were apparently left where they fell for three and a half days (cf. the three and a half years, verse 3). The triumph is short-lived. No reason is given for the refusal of burial. But among the Jews proper burial was important. To refuse it was to heap shame on the deceased. In this case it is also probably an expression of triumph. The persecutors always rejoice in the discomfiture of the Christians.

10. For *they that dwell upon the earth* see note on vi. 10. Mankind in general *shall rejoice*. The coming of the beast sees wickedness triumphant and that on an unprecedented scale. The reason for the joy of the world is that the witnesses, now described as *these two prophets*, had *tormented* them. The faithful preaching of the gospel is never soothing to the impenitent, so that the removal of an outstanding preacher is commonly a matter of rejoicing for those whose consciences he has troubled. This provokes Torrance into some searching questions: 'Why does the Church of Jesus Christ today sit so easy to her surroundings? Why do Christian people live such comfortable and such undisturbed lives in this evil and disturbed world? Surely it is because we are not true to the Word of God.'

11. Now the three and a half days are ended. The witnesses come to life again because *the spirit of life from God entered into them* (cf. Ezk. xxxvii. 10). There is a change to the past tense, which now becomes the characteristic tense. The time has not changed, but John sees these events as so certain that he can speak of them in the past. The witnesses stood up and *great fear fell upon them which saw them*. History has often seen the church oppressed to the very verge of extinction, but it has always seen it rise again from that verge of death. Each such resurrection strikes consternation into the hearts of her oppressors.

12. *They* will refer to the two witnesses, but it is not clear whether the voice was heard by anyone else. As so often in this book there was *a great voice from heaven*, but with no indication of the speaker. The voice called them up into heaven whither they *ascended . . . in a cloud*. In the fullest sense this is to be fulfilled in the rapture Paul describes (1 Thes. iv. 17). 'But meanwhile it has been partly anticipated in the sight of the world by the tribute paid to the victims of a persecution, sometimes within a few years after their dishonour and death . . . paganism saw the men it had hated and killed called up to heaven before its eyes' (Swete).

13. The removal of the two is accompanied by a *great earthquake*. One tenth of the city collapsed. This is the only mention of this proportion in the whole book. One third and one quarter are much more common. It perhaps indicates a significant, but not a crippling proportion. The number of the dead is given as *seven thousand*. Kiddle thinks that this is another way of saying one tenth, on the grounds that 70,000 is the number that represents mankind in general. But it still remains curious that on this occasion John has given us a fixed number, whereas previously he has always spoken of a proportion, mostly one third. The effect of all this was that *the remnant were affrighted.* But they not only gave way to fear, they also *gave glory to the God of heaven.* This is a new note, for John has not hitherto spoken of sinners as being other than hardened by the judgments of God (e.g. ix. 21). But these happenings were so striking and so clearly from God that even sinful men could not forbear from ascribing glory to Him. This is more than the attitude of vi. 15 ff., which recognized indeed God's judgment but sought only to escape.

14. The completion of the first woe had been signalled in ix. 12. The end of the second is now recorded in similar fashion. But this time there is an added note that the third *cometh quickly* (cf. x. 6 f.).

i. The seventh trumpet (xi. 15-19)

When the seventh seal was opened we expected the climactic judgment. Instead there was half an hour of silence in heaven, out of which came the seven trumpets. Now as the trumpets reach their climax we are still kept in suspense. There is a difference in that this time there are 'great voices' instead of silence. But we do not reach the final judgment or anything like it. Instead we have a chorus of heavenly voices praising God. It is true that the voices announce the climax, but there is no mention of this actually taking place. In fact just as the seven seals led into the seven trumpets so the trumpets lead into the next series of visions, the seven significant signs. Once again John has brought us to the verge of the final judgment. Once again he breaks off to unfold further teaching in a new series of visions.

15. There has been quite a long interval since the sixth angel blew his trumpet (ix. 13). Now *the seventh angel sounded.* This evoked not some sore judgment, but *great voices in heaven.* As is so often the case these speakers are not identified, but plainly they are the heavenly host. They proclaim the replacement of *the kingdoms of this world* by that of our Lord, and of his Christ (cf. Ps. ii. 2). Actually *kingdoms* should be 'kingdom'. The thought is not that of a multitude of earthly kingdoms, but of secular power considered as a unit. Perhaps, too, the beast is held to have established universal dominion. In the New Testament as a whole *our Lord* usually refers to Christ, but in Revelation it is more often used of the Father (see note on i. 8). The choice of language here may be affected by the fact that the words represent the homage of men at large rather than of the church. For those who see no need of redemption 'the Lord' is God the Father, while the Lord of the church is 'the Lord's Christ' (so Swete). The use of the past tense arises because the event is certain. It is as good as having occurred. Moreover this is no temporary phenomenon. God will reign *for ever and ever*.

16. The twenty-four elders were last mentioned between the sixth and seventh seals (vii. 11). As the proclamation of the establishment of the kingdom is made they prostrate themselves in worship.

17. The elders utter a thanksgiving to God whom they characterize in terms of His power and eternity. For *Almighty* see on i. 8, and for *which art, and wast* on i. 4. *Art to come* is lacking in the better MSS, for the coming is no longer future. This is the time of consummation. There is a variation in the tenses of the Greek verbs which may be significant. The first, *thou hast taken*, is perfect, which may be meant to indicate that God has taken the power permanently. It is all the more likely that this is the correct understanding in that the following verbs are all aorist, so that this one perfect stands out. *Hast reigned* will point to the crisis. God has decisively dethroned evil and entered on His reign.

18. The nations *were angry* (cf. Pss. ii. 1, xcviii. 1 LXX), but God's anger 'came' (cf. vi. 17). The punishment fits the crime. God's wrath is not irrational, but the fitting reaction to the conduct of *the nations*. *Time* (*kairos*) has about it the air of 'the right time'. Judgment does not take place until the time is ripe. God will requite both good and bad. *Reward* is rather 'what is due' (*misthos*). There is a recognition of merit. God's *servants* are divided into three groups, *the prophets, the saints*, and *them that fear thy name*, the chief effect of which is to make the expression comprehensive. *Small and great* is a common expression in this book (xiii. 16, xix. 5, 18, xx. 12). That God will *destroy them which destroy the earth* means once again that the punishment fits the crime. There is nothing arbitrary about the judgments of God (cf. 1 Cor. iii. 17).

19. God's 'sanctuary' (*naos*) was now opened, to disclose *the ark of his testament* (better 'covenant'). In the Old Testament this was the very symbol of God's presence. It is not known what became of it after Josiah told the Levites to put it in the Temple (2 Ch. xxxv. 3). Jeremiah looked for a time when the people would know God so intimately that they would not miss the ark (Je. iii. 15 ff.). In view of this attitude it is all the more curious that a legend grew up that Jeremiah hid the ark (together with the Tabernacle and the altar of incense) in a place which no man can find 'until God gather the people again together' (2 Macc. ii. 4–8). But the legend betokens an interest in the ark which we see also in the present passage. Here, however, it is not the earthly ark but its heavenly prototype. Its disclosure, taken with the opening of the sanctuary, will indicate that the way into God's presence is open wide (cf. Heb. x. 19). In the earthly sanctuary the veil permanently covered the ark, thus making it clear that men had no rights of access (cf. Heb. ix. 8). But Christ in His work for men has changed all that and now the way is wide open.

The reference to the 'covenant' is also important. The covenant is eternal. God has worked out His purpose throughout history and now at the climax the symbol of His covenant faithfulness is publicly disclosed. This is a tremendous moment. Not surprisingly it is the occasion for unusual celestial phenomena, *lightnings, and voices, and thunderings, and an earthquake, and great hail* (see on iv. 5, though the phenomena here are fuller).

VI. SEVEN SIGNIFICANT SIGNS (xii. 1–xiv. 20)

The seven trumpets followed immediately on the opening of the seventh seal, and indeed the seventh seal leads into the trumpets. We might expect that similarly the seventh trumpet will lead into the seven last plagues. This proves not to be the case however. In between comes another series of visions, which we may call 'seven significant signs'. In them there is no common factor like seals or trumpets or bowls. But there are seven of them and it seems that John means us to take them as another of his series.

This group of visions is connected with the troubles of the church. It is, of course, true that the whole of Revelation is written to a church which faced persecution, and that whatever else it may be meant to do, every section of the book is designed to help harassed believers. But especially is this so with the section to which we now come. It stresses the important truth that God has decisively defeated the devil. Satan opposed Christ from the beginning and tried to destroy Him, but without avail. The evil one has been cast out of heaven. His power on earth is, to be sure, terrifyingly real to believers. But this is not because he is triumphant. It is because he knows that he is beaten and has but a short time. Let the church then take heart. She will have her martyrs, but ultimate triumph is sure. All this is clear. Yet we should add that no part of the book is more difficult to interpret in detail. While we may speak with some confidence of the main thrust of the visions the significance of many of the details eludes us. We must not expect too much.

Some commentators discern references to a number of pagan myths in chapters xii–xiv. None of the parallels is very exact but it is just possible that John has taken some of his material from such myths. If so, his purpose will be to show that the true answer to men's problems is in Christ, not in paganism. 'The *true* mother of the incarnate Son of God is the messianic people—not Leto, nor any other goddess of pagan veneration. And the true Son of God is Christ, not Apollo; it is Christ whose witness and warfare will result in the dragon's ultimate defeat—He and His loyal servants are the true actors in the great struggle between light and darkness' (Kiddle).

But John's imagery is to be understood from its use in Revelation, not from the imagery of the myths. The 'woman clothed with the sun', for example, is to be understood in contrast to 'the great whore' (xvii. 1). Any lesson we can learn by thinking of a pagan sun-goddess is purely incidental. John is an artist in words with a divinely-given message. We must not degrade him to the level of a copyist of ill-digested pagan myths. Moreover it is plain from his whole book that he abominated paganism. It is thus most unlikely that he would borrow significantly from that source, or that pagan religion will give us the key to his ideas. We must let his own usage be our guide.

a. The woman clothed with the sun (xii. 1-6)

1. The word *wonder* translates *sēmeion*, a word often used in the Fourth Gospel of Jesus' miracles (it is usually rendered 'sign'). Here it seems to refer to a significant person rather than to a significant happening (so also in verse 3, xv. 1). *In heaven* should perhaps be rather 'in the sky', and so again in verse 3. The action John is describing appears to take place on earth, but he sees the actors in the sky first of all. He sees *a woman clothed with the sun, and the moon under her feet, and upon her head a crown of twelve stars* (cf. Ct. vi. 10). In this symbolism we must discern Israel, the chosen people of God. 'She comes standing upon the Old Testament revelation of reflected light and clothed with the New Testament revelation which is as the sun shining in his strength' (Torrance). The *twelve stars* will be the twelve patriarchs or the tribes which descended from them. The symbolism is that of Joseph's dream (Gn. xxxvii. 9; cf. also *Test. Naph.* v. 3 f.). In view of this Old Testament symbolism it is unnecessary to see a reference to pagan mythology.

2. The figure of Israel as a travailing woman is found several times (Is. lxvi. 7 f., Mi. iv. 10, v. 3, etc.). Especially important are some words of Isaiah:

'Like a woman with child,
  who writhes and cries out in her pangs,
  when she is near her time,
so were we because of thee, O Lord;
  we were with child, we writhed,
  we have as it were brought forth wind.
We have wrought no deliverance in the earth,
  and the inhabitants of the world have not fallen'
                        (Is. xxvi. 17, 18 RSV).

The old Israel could not effect 'deliverance in the earth'. That was accomplished only by the Son of God. John writes in the certainty that it has been accomplished. His description is vivid. He uses the present tense 'cries', and his participles 'travailing' and 'being in pain' (the latter not elsewhere in the New Testament of childbirth; it refers to torture) bring the scene before our eyes. The time of birth is near. Israel is about to give birth to the Messiah. For the early Christians there was an important continuity between the old Israel and the church, the true Israel. Here the woman is undoubtedly Israel who gives birth to the Messiah. But in the latter part of the chapter she is the church who is persecuted for her faith.

3. A second 'sign' (*wonder*) now appears in the sky. The *great red dragon* is undoubtedly a symbol of Satan. It may not be out of place to recall that Pharaoh is called a dragon (Ezk. xxix. 3, xxxii. 2 mg.), for there is a good deal of symbolism associated with Egypt in this book. We have already seen that the language about the plagues is behind many of the troubles introduced by the seven trumpets. The great city, again, is 'Sodom and Egypt' (xi. 8). By contrast the song of deliverance is the song of Moses (who delivered from Egypt) and the Lamb (xv. 3). Egypt stands for all that is evil, and specifically for the oppression and persecution of the people of God. It is thus natural enough that the *dragon* has a place in Egypt.

We should also bear in mind other Old Testament passages which refer to the dragon and bring him into connection with kindred evil beings, such as Leviathan or Rahab (Jb. xxvi. 13; Ps. lxxiv. 13 f., Is. xxvii. 1, li. 9). It is plain that to those versed in Old Testament scriptures the term *dragon* conjured up many associations of an evil being.

It is not clear why the dragon's colour is *red*, but it may be no coincidence that the beast on whom the great whore sits is scarlet (xvii. 3), as is her clothing (xvii. 4). This *red dragon* is a fearsome creature, with *seven heads and ten horns*. The horn is a symbol of strength, so that ten horns points to the mighty power of the dragon. Evil is strong. Cf. the beast with ten horns in Daniel's vision (Dn. vii. 7, 24). The point of the seven heads is not immediately obvious. But in antiquity several terrible beasts were alleged to have a multiplicity of heads (e.g. the Hydra). The thought may be that of the immense vitality of such an animal. It is very hard to kill. In the same way, opposition to the church on the part of the powers of evil is persistent. No sooner is it defeated in one place than it breaks out elsewhere. We should not overlook the fact that the beast, Satan's chief henchman, also has seven heads and ten horns (xiii. 1, xvii. 3), and is scarlet in colour (xvii. 3). We should understand that the evil we see on earth is made in the image of Satan.

The *crowns*, incidentally, which are on the dragon's seven heads, are crowns of royalty (*diadēmata; stephanos*, which is used in verse 1 and for which see note on ii. 10, may denote rejoicing or victory: Moffatt brings out the difference by translating 'tiara' there and 'diadems' here). John pictures Satan as immensely powerful and as exercising sovereignty.

4. The dragon's tail now dragged *the third part of the stars of heaven* and threw them to the earth. As with a number of the trumpets, *the third part* will denote a significant minority (viii. 7, 8, 9, etc.). The throwing of the stars to the earth (cf. Dn. viii. 10) is perhaps meant to show that the activities of the evil one in other spheres yet have their repercussions here on earth. But all this is apparently no more than a preliminary flexing of his muscles. His primary interest is in devouring the child about to be born. Satan was hostile to Jesus from the very beginning (cf. Herod's attempt to slay the Christ child, Mt. ii. 13 ff.). He sought to destroy Him from the moment of

His birth. It might be asked why the dragon did not simply devour the woman, which would effectually have accomplished his purpose. But John is setting forth spiritual truth in pictorial form, not giving us a chapter in the natural history of the dragon.

5. The woman gave birth to a 'male son', the adjective putting some emphasis on the sex, which is, of course, given in the noun. The child was destined for world dominion. The verb *to rule* is literally 'to shepherd'. It speaks of absolute authority (see note on ii. 27), and the *rod of iron* of firmness (not tyranny, as the English idom might perhaps be held to indicate). Who *caught up* the child to heaven John does not say, nor how it was done without the waiting dragon's being able to prevent it. But in this book God is all-sovereign. He does what He wills. So now John's point is that He protects the incarnate Son from destruction by Satan. The 'how' does not matter. Sovereignty is further indicated by the reference to the *throne*.

Some find difficulty in the fact that there is no reference to any event in the life of Christ. John omits everything between the birth and the ascension. This has been drawn into an argument that John is not composing freely in this section, but taking over a pagan myth. But this is to overlook a feature of his method. John is quite capable of concentrating on one thing at a time so that he omits quite important considerations which are not immediately relevant. Thus he can describe heaven in chapter iv with no mention of Christ. But when he comes to chapter v he emphasizes the central place of the Lamb. Here his subject is not strictly Christ, but the church. He is showing how the incarnation gives encouragement to believers. Satan tried hard to destroy Christ. But he did not succeed. Christ came right through to the ascension. Let believers take heart. God always effects His purpose.

6. *The woman fled into the wilderness.* She was thus protected from the dragon just as surely as was her Son but in a different way. Many draw attention to the flight of the Christians to Pella at the time of the siege of Jerusalem. This does illustrate

the point, but the words, of course, have a much wider application. The woman's place was *prepared of God.* Her flight was
foreseen and provision was made for her. She was nourished
by divine provision (cf. the manna for the Israelites in the
wilderness, and the provision made for Elijah, 1 Ki. xvii. 4).
The agent God employed is not important enough to be
mentioned (as often in this book). For the period of 1,260
days see the note on xi. 2. The period is given here in exactly
the same form as in xi. 3, the time of the prophecy of the two
witnesses. It is not unlikely that we should link the two. God
protects His church during the time of her witness.

b. Satan cast out (xii. 7–12)

This little vision reminds the believer that he is caught up in
a wider conflict than the one he sees. The thought is not quite
that of Paul who spoke of wrestling 'against principalities,
against powers' (Eph. vi. 12). John is speaking of spiritual
forces indeed, but he reminds us that the conflict is not simply
one between demons and men. Angelic forces are also engaged.
Our struggles are not to be shrugged off as insignificant. They
are part of the great conflict between good and evil.

7. *Michael* appears as the leader of the heavenly hosts.
Indeed, they are called *his* angels. This accords with his
description as 'archangel' in Jude 9. Michael is apparently a
warlike angel (Dn. x. 13, 21, xii. 1, Jude 9). His enemies, the
dragon's helpers, are also spoken of as *angels* (the term means
'messenger' and there can be evil messengers as well as good).

8. The result of the battle was the defeat of the dragon and
his party. Their defeat was so complete that *their place* was
not found *any more in heaven.*

9. So *the great dragon* was expelled. *Cast out (eblēthē)* is
perhaps better 'thrown down' (as NEB). In this significant
moment he is given a very full description. In addition to
being *the great dragon* he is *that old serpent,* which is probably
meant to awake recollections of Genesis iii. He is called both
the Devil and *Satan.* The latter is the older name. It transliter-

ates a Hebrew word which means 'adversary'. It is used of human adversaries such as those God raised up against Solomon (1 Ki. xi. 14, 23), and the Philistines used the term of David (1 Sa. xxix. 4). When used of angels it at first had no derogatory associations and it is used, for example, of 'the angel of the Lord' who stood in Balaam's way (Nu. xxii. 22). But the term came to be used of the adversary of mankind, that spirit that accuses men before God. He accused Job (Jb. i. 6), and Joshua the high priest (Zc. iii. 1). The title 'Accuser', 'Satan', thus became attached to him in an exclusive sense.

This name for the evil one would have made a specially strong impact in the first century, for there was a well-known and well-hated figure called the *delator*, the paid informer. He made his living by accusing people before the authorities. *Devil (diabolos)* means 'slanderer'. It is not a large step from 'accuser' to 'slanderer' and thus 'the Satan' is not infrequently referred to as 'the devil'. In addition to accusing and slandering the evil one deceives. John brings out the scope of this activity by saying that he *deceiveth the whole world*. Barclay sums up much when he says of this evil being: 'Satan, as it has been put, stands for the sleepless vigilance of evil against good.' John repeats the information that Satan *was cast out*, this time adding his destination, *into the earth* (cf. Lk. x. 18, Jn. xii. 31), and the fact that *his angels were cast out with him*.

10. John hears yet another *loud voice* and once again the speaker is not named. The words themselves give us some clues, however. The plural *our* shows that it comes from a number, not from an individual. The reference to *our brethren* leads some to conclude that they are not angels. This, however, does not follow, for angels can call men brothers (xxii. 9). It seems that here those outside the human race, and thus angels, are meant. But the point is not really important. The words are an exclamation of triumph. Now there has come *salvation, and strength, and the kingdom of our God, and the power of his Christ*. The co-ordination of these, each with its own article in the original, makes a very impressive list. *Power (exousia)*

means 'authority' rather than 'physical power' (as it does in
ix. 3, 10, 19). Notice the reference to *his Christ*. The complete
sovereignty of God is in mind. At the same time Christ is
brought into the closest connection with God.

The reason for the exclamation of triumph is that Satan
has been overthrown. He is here called *the accuser of our
brethren*, and we see what this means in the fact that he *accused
them before our God day and night*. The picture is one of implacable
hostility on the part of Satan as well as of the complete triumph
of God. He urged the sins of the *brethren* in the very highest
court. But now he has been completely defeated and is powerless against them.

11. Indeed, it can be said that *they overcame him*, the emphatic pronoun putting stress on the fact that *they* did this, as
the aorist tense does on the completeness of the victory. But
the martyrs did not win their triumph themselves. They
overcame *by the blood of the Lamb*. What the Lamb has done
avails for the Lamb's followers. With this is linked *the word of
their testimony*, for the redeemed bear their witness to their
Redeemer. To give way in the face of persecution is to fall away
from Christ and to lose everything. But to stand firm means
final victory over Satan. That John has the martyrs in mind
is clear from the words, *they loved not their lives unto the death*. But
the same quality of devotion is required from all the followers
of the Lamb (cf. Lk. xiv. 26, Jn. xii. 25).

12. Because of what Christ has done, and because His
victory extends to the 'brethren', the voice calls on the heavens
and those who dwell there to be merry (*ouranos*, 'heaven' is
found fifty-two times in Revelation, but this is the sole occurrence of the plural; it is not easy to see why). The verb *dwell*
(*skēnoō*) originally meant temporary dwelling (living in a
tent, *skēnē*), but it has plainly lost all such sense here. It means
permanent home. While the rejoicing is called for from the
inhabitants of heaven it is plain that men of earth can rejoice
too. Their citizenship is in heaven. And, though they suffer
grievous troubles on earth, they are assured that these are
temporary and that already the triumph is being savoured in

heaven. By contrast there is *woe* for them on *earth* and *sea*. The devil has come down to them in great anger, knowing that he has only a little time. This time will be that before the second advent. *Time* is *kairos*, which is perhaps used here in the sense 'a suitable time' (cf. i. 3, xi. 18). Not much time remains suitable for the activities of the evil one. The troubles of the persecuted righteous arise not because Satan is too strong, but because he is beaten. He is doing all the harm he can while he can. But he will not be able to do this for much longer.

c. War between Satan and the woman and her Son (xii. 13-17)

The persistent hostility between Satan and the people of God is developed. The Man Child being delivered from his hostility, Satan turns his attention to the woman and to the rest of her children.

13. The 'war in heaven' (verse 7) appears to be an attempt to destroy the Man Child. Baulked in that attempt *the dragon* turns his attention to the mother. The persecution of the church is not primarily a human affair, but due to the instigation of Satan. In fact it is his reaction to defeat in heaven. Since his activities must now be confined to earth he hits out against those associated with his conqueror.

14. To *the woman* were given *two wings*, though it is not said by whom. That they were wings of a *great eagle* probably indicates ease and speed of flight. The woman was able to flee *into the wilderness* (cf. verse 6), which is *her place*. In this book the great city is 'Sodom and Egypt' (xi. 8) and it stands for opposition to God and to God's people. In days of old God's people escaped from Egypt into the wilderness and Egypt symbolism is in mind throughout this chapter. The members of the church live in the world, the great city. But they do not belong to it. Though they dwell physically in cities their true home and their sure refuge is far from the great city, i.e. in the wilderness.

The eagle's wings call to mind the word of God to His

people, 'Ye have seen what I did unto the Egyptians, and how I bare you on eagles' wings, and brought you unto myself' (Ex. xix. 4; cf. Dt. xxii. 11, Is. xl. 31). The woman is to be *nourished*, though it is not said by whom. That God provides for her is important, the agent He employs is not. For *a time, and times, and half a time*, see note on xi. 2. During this period (the forty-two months may contain an allusion to the forty-two stages in the wilderness wanderings, Nu. xxxiii. 5 ff.) the woman is secure in her hiding place and inaccessible to Satan. He is now called *the serpent* but there appears no real difference from 'the dragon' (verse 13).

15. It is not clear whether the events of this verse follow those of the preceding or whether they are given as an example of the protection afforded the woman. But *the serpent* adopted a novel method of trying to drown her. He cast water out of his mouth *as a flood* ('like a river') so that she might become 'river-borne' (*potamophorēton!*). This descriptive word occurs in a papyrus of 110 BC (MM) and so is not a coinage of the Seer. But no other example appears to be cited of its use of a person. Swete sees in the figure 'the thought of the godly wrestling with a flood of evil'. This thought may well be present, as also a reference to Egypt again, for as they escaped from that land the people of God were in danger from water.

16. The woman found an unexpected ally in the earth, which swallowed the river emitted by the dragon. Ancient literature does not afford an exact parallel, though some remind us that rivers were known to plunge beneath the earth (there was one near Colosse). More apposite is the song of Moses, 'Thou stretchedst out thy right hand, the earth swallowed them' (Ex. xv. 12). In time of difficulty the Lord delivers His servants in one way or another. Some commentators see a reference to natural moral order, and think that there is that in the moral order established on earth which helps the Christian church. This is an unlikely interpetation, for in this book the world and the church are set over against one another. Those outside the church do not help it but persecute it. The church's help comes from God.

17. The woman not being vulnerable to his attacks, the dragon proceeded to vent his rage on the remainder of her offspring (cf. Gn. iii. 15). These are further explained as those who *keep the commandments of God* (cf. xiv. 12) and *have the testimony of Jesus Christ* (see note on i. 2). Satan is at war with all Christians. He is not able to accomplish his purpose against God and therefore he does what he can in opposing God's people.

d. The beast from the sea (xiii. 1–10)

It is accepted throughout the New Testament that in the last days there will be a special outbreak of the powers of evil. Sometimes this is associated with an individual who may be called the antichrist (1 Jn. ii. 18) or 'the man of lawlessness' (2 Thes. ii. 3 RSV). It is this figure who is behind the opening vision of this chapter. John does not name him, but calls him 'the beast'. A wealth of picturesque detail brings out the horror associated with him. He is closely linked with Satan, and indeed is something like an incarnation of the evil one. Many modern scholars see in the beast a reference to the Roman Empire. This seems too simple. We may well see in the Empire a preliminary manifestation of the evil that will one day be realized to the full in the antichrist. But there is much more to the beast than ancient Rome.

1. For *I stood* we should read 'he stood' (mg.). The words refer to the dragon mentioned in the previous verse. He is standing on the shore as his henchman, the beast, emerges. John *saw a beast rise up out of the sea*. The ancient world often associated evil with the sea. Who could tell what existed in its mysterious depths? With its constant change and movement it well symbolized 'the seething cauldron of national and social life, out of which the great historical movements of the world arise' (Swete). For *the beast* see note on xi. 7. The description reminds us of Daniel vii. 2–7, but this beast is more horrible than those of Daniel, for he combines in himself the horrors there distributed among the four. He had *seven heads and ten horns*, as did Satan (xii. 3). That the two had the same appearance probably means that the evil we see on earth is but a counterfeit of the evil one.

The chapter says little about the dragon. He remains very much in the background. He does his work not openly, but through men. John is talking about a more than human evil, but it is an evil that reveals itself in the deeds of men. The modern world, like the ancient, furnishes us with illustrations. Hendriksen sees the beast as signifying 'worldly government directed against the church', and he takes the multiplicity of heads to indicate that this has various forms, as Babylon, Assyria, Rome, etc.

The beast has *ten crowns* on his horns. This appears a curious place for them (Satan has them on the heads, xii. 3), but it is a way of stressing his dominion (*diadēmata* are crowns of royalty; see note on xii. 3) while leaving the heads free for *the name of blasphemy*. It is not certain whether we should have 'the name' or 'the names', the MS evidence being divided. If the former, all the heads have the same name; if the latter, they differ. Either way there is contempt for the things of God (cf. verse 6).

2. *The beast* is now likened to a *leopard* (or 'panther' as some understand *pardalis*). The feet are like those of a bear and the mouth like that of a lion. Since the animal had seven heads the singular, *mouth,* is curious. We should be clear that John's interest is in symbolism. He is not going into detail to help his readers visualize the beast. In fact it seems impossible to put together all the features John mentions to make up one animal. But that is not his intention. He is making use of a variety of the features of the animals mentioned in Daniel vii. His composite beast thus becomes indescribably horrible. He combines in one the terrible features hitherto associated with different beasts. The beasts of Daniel vii are to be understood of the various world empires and it may well be that this is in mind with John's beast. In that case he stands for a final empire in which will be concentrated the frightfulness of all its predecessors. But John does not see the beast as having any power of its own. *The dragon gave him his power.* He also gave him his 'throne' (so, rather than *seat*) and *great authority.*

The combination adds up to a formidable foe. John's readers should not think that the powers of good are opposed to an inconsiderable enemy.

3. John saw one of the beast's heads *as it were wounded to death*. He does not say how the beast received its wound (i.e. here; in verse 14 we find it was 'by a sword'). He does not even say whether it received the wound after it came to land. John's interest is not in how the wound came to be inflicted but in the fact that a wound which appeared to be mortal was healed. He does not tell us how it was healed. He concentrates his attention on the fact that it was healed. Two points only receive emphasis: the deadliness of the wound (*wounded to death*, and then *his deadly wound*) and the fact of recovery. The expression rendered *as it were wounded* (*hōs esphagmenēn*) was used of the Lamb in v. 6, and as the recovery of the beast is clear there may possibly be the thought of death followed by resurrection. This is one of several places in which the evil one is pictured as parodying Christianity.

Those who see in the beast the Roman Empire think of the heads as Roman emperors and usually refer the healing of the deadly wound to the Nero *redivivus* myth. Nero was so evil that many could not believe that death was the end of him. The expectation arose that he would reappear in a resurrected form. Others think that Caligula is meant, for he had a dangerous illness and recovered. What is not often noticed by those who see the Empire as the meaning of the beast is that it is not said that the head died and was restored. Rather it was the beast that suffered a deadly wound, located in one of its heads, and was healed. There is no suggestion that the head was restored. We are justified in reflecting that there is an evil which comes ultimately from the dragon and which is found both in the human heart and in the communities of men. And it apparently cannot be slain. Though wounded it rises again and will do so to the end of time, to the astonishment of men (*all the world wondered*).

4. The effect was to convince the world of the futility of resisting the beast. So men worshipped the dragon, the ultimate source of the beast's power, and the beast also. The connection between the two is obviously close. Swete, who sees a reference to the Roman Empire, comments, 'It was not moral greatness but brute force which commanded the homage of the provinces. The invincible power of Rome won Divine honours for the worst and meanest of men.' Without confining ourselves to the Roman Empire, such a comment shows the sort of thing that is in mind. *Who is like unto the beast?* may be meant as a parody of a similar Old Testament expression (Ex. xv. 11, Ps. xxxv. 10). And in view of the activities of the angel Michael it is possible that we should also detect a reference to the meaning of his name, 'Who is like God?'

5. The verb *was given* reminds us that the beast has no power of his own. He receives the power he exercises directly from his master, the dragon. But John's readers will reflect that ultimately it is God who determines the limits within which he operates. This is further emphasized by the statement that he has power *to continue forty and two months* (for this period see note on xi. 2). Even the horrible and irresistible beast can exercise authority only during the time God permits. The saints are encouraged by the thought that the duration of their suffering has already been determined by God. It is not the beast who decides this point. His power is limited though he speaks *great things and blasphemies*.

6. The blasphemies are particularized. To blaspheme the *name* of God means much the same as to blaspheme *against God*, for the name sums up the whole person (see note on ii. 3). His *tabernacle* means 'his dwelling'. If we read the following *and* (which is omitted in many good MSS) the blasphemy is against God, against heaven, and against all who are in heaven. If we omit it (as seems the most likely reading) God's dwelling is equated with God's people. The blasphemy is then directed against God and those in whom God dwells. To regard the state as supreme (and offer divine honours to the emperor as was demanded in the first century) was not a permissible opinion but the supreme blasphemy. John's words must have come home to his first readers with tremendous force.

7. Once again the verb *was given* (which occurs four times in verses 5–7) stresses the beast's subordinate position. It is important to see that even the antichrist can function only by divine permission. This is all the more significant as it comes in a passage telling of divine honours which were accorded the beast. Divine honours for one who can do only what the God the little Christian church worships allows him to do! On this occasion authority is given for him to make war with the saints (cf. Dn. vii. 21). These words are lacking in some MSS, but should be accepted (see note in *GNT*). As a result of this war he obtains *power* (i.e. authority, *exousia*) over 'all kindreds and people' (so the better MSS), *and tongues, and nations* (see note on v. 9). Incidentally this shows that something more than the Neronic persecution is in mind, for that was not world-wide.

8. With a change to the future tense John looks to the time when full divine honours will be paid to the beast (cf. 2 Thes. ii. 4) by all the earth's inhabitants (for them *that dwell upon the earth* see note on vi. 10). This is a phenomenon which recurs. 'Again and again there emerge bestial forces out of the filmy depths of the nations that fascinate and mesmerize humanity until all the world wonders after and worships the beast, except those whose names are written in the book of life of the Lamb slain before the foundation of the world' (Torrance).

This last point is important. It is true that these men have set themselves in opposition to God. It is true that they are willing worshippers of the beast. But the significant thing is that their *names are not written in the book of life*. John wants his little handful of persecuted Christians to see that the thing that matters is the sovereignty of God, not the power of evil. When a man's name is written in the book of life he will not be forgotten. His place is secure.

The book of life is connected with *the Lamb slain from the foundation of the world*. It is in the capacity of the slain Lamb that Christ brings salvation. There are the two thoughts that it is the atoning death of Christ that is significant and that the salvation He brings is no afterthought. *From the foundation of the world* should be taken with *slain* (cf. 1 Pet. i. 19 f.) rather than with *written* (though some prefer to take it this way and understand it of election as Eph. i. 4). Either way God's eternal purpose is in view and is contrasted with the fleeting might of the powers of evil.

9. John counsels attention in a phrase reminiscent of the Synoptic Gospels and of ii. 7 (where see note). It may refer to what follows rather than to what precedes.

10. There are textual difficulties here. AV takes both couplets to refer to persecutors. Some take both to refer to the saints: 'If anyone is for captivity, to captivity he goes, if anyone is to be killed with the sword, he is to be killed with the sword.' Better is RSV, 'If any one is to be taken captive, to captivity he goes; if any one slays with the sword, with the sword must he be slain.' The first part of the couplet teaches an acceptance of the realities of life. If it is in the providence of God that the Christian is for captivity, then to captivity he will surely go (cf. Je. xv. 2). But the second part has to do with requital. The man who kills with the sword will be killed as he has killed (cf. Mt. xxvi. 52). If the Christian takes the sword he will not establish the faith, for the truth of Christ cannot be defended by violence. He will simply perish by the sword. But when persecuted he can know that the final word is not with his persecutors. This is not fatalism, but the conviction that God is sovereign and works out His good and perfect will. In the days of persecution this is a strong consolation. It is *the patience* (better 'steadfastness'; see note on ii. 2) *and the faith of the saints*. The saints trust a God who works in the manner outlined.

e. The beast from the earth (xiii. 11–18)

The beast is not alone. John turns his attention to a second beast, the henchman of the first. In that he secures worship of the image of the first beast (verse 12) the second appears to stand for a priesthood. Those who find in the Roman Empire an illustration of the first beast see the imperial priesthood in the second. Unhappy results always follow when state power and a false priesthood are allied.

11. The second beast came up *out of the earth*. His origin in the familiar earth makes him less mysterious than the first which came from the sea. He is less fearsome than the first, a fact shown also in that he has but *two horns* whereas the first had ten, and seven heads besides (verse 1). *Like a lamb* may indicate a parody of true religion, which is further brought out later when this beast is described as 'the false prophet' (xvi. 13, xix. 20, xx. 10). It is also possible that we should understand the number *two* of the horns as in contrast with the two witnesses of chapter xi. All in all this beast looks like a dreadful parody of the truth. He spoke *as a dragon*, which we must understand to mean 'like the dragon'. This beast's speech is like that of the evil one.

12. He is formidable. He has *all the power* of his predecessor. But he is in no sense a rival, for he makes men worship him. It is not easy to see what *the earth* means in this connection in distinction from *them which dwell therein*. Probably the combination simply stresses totality. The whole world is made to worship the first beast, characterized again as him *whose deadly wound was healed*. Clearly this made a tremendous impression.

13. Magic was a common practice among first-century priesthoods as a means of impressing the gullible. So this beast does (habitually, present tense) *great wonders (sēmeia)*. This noun is sometimes used in Revelation of the visions John sees (xii. 1, 3, xv. 1), but a number of times also for miracles. In this sense it always denotes miracles wrought by evil powers (so here and in verse 14, xvi. 14, xix. 20), a sharp contrast with the Fourth Gospel where it is a characteristic word for the miracles of Jesus. Perhaps this is a further example of the parodying of the good. The term indicates that the miracles are not aimless wonders. They have deep significance and are part of Satan's plan (cf. Mk. xiii. 22, 2 Thes. ii. 9). An example is the making of *fire come down from heaven*. This is not said to have destroyed the beast's enemies or the like. It is apparently simply meant to arouse admiration.

14. By his miracles he deceives men and establishes his

position. *Them that dwell on the earth* in this book seems to mean unregenerate mankind (see note on vi. 10). The beast can deceive only unbelievers. There is an important spiritual truth here. If a man serves God with all his heart he will not be taken in by the empty miracles of the deceiver. But if he turns from God he predisposes himself to believe the lies of the second beast. *Which he had the power to do* is rather 'which were given to him to do', where the 'were given' characteristically emphasizes the derivative nature of this beast's power. His miracles were done *in the sight of the beast* which may be another example of parody, for the two witnesses stood 'before the God of the earth' (xi. 4), the Greek preposition both times being *enōpion*. There is an implication of a readiness to serve and obey. The second beast instructs his followers to *make an image* to the first, who is characterized yet once more by his recovery from his deadly wound.

15. *He had power* is really 'there was given' (*edothē*). John will not allow us to forget for one moment the derivative nature of the beast's power. The second beast was now permitted to give life to the image of the beast so that it spoke. There are many stories of speaking images in the ancient world. Kiddle reminds us that 'the breath of life' (*life* here is *pneuma*, 'spirit' or 'breath') is associated with the Creator-God, and continues, 'When the priests of Antichrist have thus animated their idol, they have acted a blasphemy exceeding that of all previous idolators; this is the magician's most impious usurpation of God's power.' Grammatically it is the image which causes the death of the non-worshippers. But perhaps we should understand a change of subject so that it is the second beast who made the image speak and caused the death of those who refused to worship it.

16. He now caused a mark to be set on all men *in their right hand, or in their foreheads.* The listing of various classes, *small and great* (for which see note on xi. 18), etc., is a way of stressing totality. No-one was exempt. The choice of right hand or forehead is presumably for conspicuousness. It could not be hidden. It may also be meant as a travesty of the Jewish custom of wearing phylacteries (little boxes containing extracts from the Bible) on the left hand (or forearm) and on the head. The precise significance of the mark is uncertain. Barclay sees several possibilities: if from the branding of domestic slaves, 'it means that those who worship the beast are the slaves, the property of the beast'; if from the custom of soldiers branding themselves with the name of a favourite general, 'it means that those who worship the beast are the devoted followers of the beast'; if from the use of sealing contracts, 'it will mean that those who worship the beast accept the law and the authority of the beast'; if from the mark stamped on coinage, 'it will again mean that those who bear it are the property of the beast'; if from the certificate that a man had sacrificed to Caesar, 'the mark of the beast may be the certificate of worship, which a Christian could only obtain at the cost of denying his faith and being false to his Lord. Once he had that certificate he was labelled as a worshipper of Caesar and a denier of Christ.'

17. *That* (*hina*) denotes purpose, namely that no-one could engage in trade without the mark. *Might* (*dunatai*) is stronger than 'hinder' or the like. It points to a total prohibition, which would make it impossible for people without the mark to get even necessities like food. It is thus impossible for those who oppose the beast even to live. *The mark* is explained as *the name of the beast, or the number of his name* (AV's *or* after *the mark* is lacking in the best MSS and should be omitted; what follows explains what the mark is).

18. *Here is wisdom* is a pause for emphasis (cf. xvii. 9). The following important statement provides a means by which the intelligent reader (*him that hath understanding*) can compute the beast's number. The only clues John gives are that it is *the number of a man* (or 'of man') and that it is 666 (or, as some MSS have it, 616). Most students work from the fact that in the ancient world (where men lacked our convenient arabic numerals) it was usual to employ letters to denote numbers.

In Greek the first nine letters of the alphabet were used for the units, the next for the tens, and so on.[1] The problem then is to find a name which gives a total of 666 when the numbers signified by its letters are added together.

The possibilities are almost endless. In modern times the most favoured solution is 'Nero Caesar' (if the final letter be omitted to give the equivalent of the Latin spelling of the name the total is 616, the variant reading). But to get this result we must use the Greek form of the Latin name, transliterated into Hebrew characters, and with a variant spelling at that (the vowel letter *y* has to be omitted from *qysr*). This solution has its attractions, but no-one has shown why a Hebrew name with an unusual spelling should be employed in a Greek writing. It is also to be borne in mind that in the ancient world when Nero was a considerable figure (the Nero *redivivus* myth is thought by many critics to underlie parts of Revelation), this solution was apparently never thought of. Irenaeus mentions (and fails to adopt) the view that *Lateinos*, i.e. the Roman Empire, was meant. He mentions also *euanthas* and *teitan* (=the emperor Titus?) and favours the latter.

Other solutions are put forward, but none has won wide acceptance. It is possible that such solutions are on the wrong lines and that we should understand the expression purely in terms of the symbolism of numbers. If we take the sum of the values represented by the letters of the name *Iēsous*, the Greek name 'Jesus', it comes to 888. Each digit is one more than seven, the perfect number. But 666 yields the opposite phenomenon, for each digit falls short. The number may be meant to indicate not an individual, but a persistent falling short. All the more is this likely to be correct if we translate 'it is the number of man' rather than 'a man'. John will then be saying that unregenerate man is persistently evil. He bears the mark of the beast in all he does. Civilization without Christ is necessarily under the dominion of the evil one.

[1] There are not quite enough letters for the system to work, and a few other signs are pressed into service. There is a list in W. Gunion Rutherford, *First Greek Grammar*, 1935, pp. 143–145. For a similar system in Hebrew see *Gesenius' Hebrew Grammar*, ed. E. Kautzsch, rev. A. E. Cowley, 1946, p. 30.

f. The Lamb on Mount Zion (xiv. 1–5)

From the forces of evil John turns to those of good. He sees in a vision the triumph of the followers of the Lamb.

1. The scene is vivid (*I looked, and, lo*). John sees on Mount Zion *a Lamb*, or rather, 'the Lamb', and with Him 144,000 who had 'his name and his Father's name written on their foreheads' (RSV). The last point will be in contrast with the followers of the beast who bore his name on their foreheads (or right hand, xiii. 16). These are marked with the mark of God. Mount Zion is sometimes associated with the thought of deliverance (Joel ii. 32) and this is in mind here. God's people are triumphant. Some take the words to refer to the earthly Zion, in which case we must interpret them of the millennial reign. But this seems unlikely. In the first place, that would mean that the Lamb would have made the transition from heaven to earth without any comment being made on it. And in the second, John appears to be referring to the final triumph and not to anything intermediate. We should not overlook the fact that the Lamb is standing on the mountain, whereas the beast stood only on sand (xiii. 1).

For the number 144,000 see note on vii. 4. Here, as there, it is unlikely to stand for a spiritual élite of any sort, such as the martyrs. This number of completeness stands for the whole church of Jesus Christ. We should not miss the note of fulfilment. 'A hundred and forty-four thousand were sealed, a hundred and forty-four thousand were saved' (Kiddle). There they were on earth confronted by enemies. Now they are in heaven and not one of them has been lost.

2. As often, John hears an unidentified voice from heaven. He is fond of this device. It indicates in a general manner that the voice is of divine origin, but leaves it open whether it comes from God Himself or from one of His angels or from some other source. This voice seems to have impressed John, for he describes it with a threefold simile. It is *as the voice of many waters* (cf. i. 15), i.e. like the voice of Christ. It is *as the voice of a great thunder* (cf. vi. 1), i.e. very loud indeed. And it is *as harpers harping with their harps* (not as AV, *I heard the voice of harpers*, etc.). The voice was not only loud, but melodious and attractive. The voice is probably that of the 144,000.

Some think of the heavenly host as singing the song and teaching it to the throng. But the next verse connects it with redemption and no good reason is brought forward for holding that those who have never been redeemed are teaching such a song to those who have. It is more likely that we should see the song as the expression of the joy of the redeemed.

3. For *a new song* see note on v. 9. The name of God is not mentioned but the song is sung *before the throne*, the living ones, and the *elders*, so that it is clear that it is sung in His very presence. The use of *throne* may be a way of emphasizing God's sovereignty. It is not explicitly said why only the 144,000 *could learn that song*. But since John immediately refers to them as *redeemed from the earth* it is a fair inference that the song is connected with this fact. Without the experience of redemption no-one could sing the song. Redeemed *from the earth* indicates redemption from worldly things and worldly men. They are God's.

4. The triple *these* draws attention to three distinguishing marks of this group. The first is that they *were not defiled with women; for they are virgins*. This is surprising, in the first instance because the 144,000 stands for the whole church and it is not easy to apply the first part of the saying to women members, nor the second part to men, and in the second instance because the New Testament does not regard sexual relations as defiling. This idea was found in the ancient world, and in time became prominent in the church. But it is not found in the New Testament. There marriage is a state to be commended and sexual relations are a necessary part of the married state (1 Cor. vii. 4 f.). The most the New Testament writers say is that there are some pieces of Christian service that can be better carried out by the unmarried (1 Cor. vii. 32–34). Some suggest that the verb *defiled* means improper sexual relations (so AG). But our passage seems to mean that the 144,000 had no sexual relations at all (*they are virgins*).

The answer to the difficulties seems that here, as so often, John is using symbolism. Somewhat in the Pauline manner he is viewing the church as the bride of Christ. Now Paul can say of believers, 'I have espoused you to one husband, that I may present you as a chaste virgin to Christ' (2 Cor. xi. 2). Later in Revelation John sees 'the bride, the Lamb's wife' (xxi. 9). But the marriage is at this point future. The virgin must be chaste. So she is described as having no sexual relations at all. It may not be irrelevant to recall that in the Old Testament heathen worship is often likened to improper sexual relations. John is saying, then, that the 144,000 were not unfaithful to their Lord. They glorified God in their bodies (1 Cor. vi. 20).

This is reinforced by the use of the term *virgins*. If *not defiled with women* is a strange expression to use of women, this is an unusual one with regard to men. A few passages are cited wherein it is used of men, but none appears to be earlier than this passage. This is the only one of fifteen New Testament occurrences of the term where it refers to males. We should see the term as symbolical. It means that the people in question have kept themselves completely free from intercourse with the pagan world system. They have lived up to what is implied in their betrothal to Christ. We thus have one expression which strictly applies to men only balanced by another which (as far as our knowledge goes) was used of women only right up to this time. In each case John is concerned with spiritual truth.

The second point about the redeemed is that they *follow the Lamb whithersoever he goeth*. They do not and cannot lay down the place where their service will take them. He leads. It is theirs to follow. The third point is that they were *redeemed from among men* as *firstfruits*. *Redeemed* means 'purchased at a price' (see note on v. 9), and *from among men* that they no longer belong to the world. *Firstfruits* were the first part of the harvest and were holy in a special sense. They could not be put to ordinary secular use. They belonged to God (Ex. xxiii. 19, Ne. x. 35, Pr. iii. 9). Even when the word did not refer to the harvest in the strict sense it usually meant a gift made to a deity (see MM). The thought of belonging to God is the primary idea. James sees the church as 'a kind of firstfruits of his creatures' (Jas. i. 18) and it is something like this that John has in mind. The church belongs to God. Her calling is to be consecrated to Him. There is a close connection between *God* and the *Lamb*, as often (see note on v. 13).

5. *No guile* is better 'no lie' (RSV). Complete truthfulness is a further characteristic of believers (cf. Zp. iii. 13). The contemporary world does not seem to have been exactly over-burdened with men who had a strict regard for truth, and Christians must have stood out (cf. Ecclus. xx. 24). They are summed up simply as *without fault* (we should omit *before the throne of God*), *amōmoi*. This adjective is sometimes used of sacrificial victims, so there may be a hint here that Christian service is sacrificial.

g. The harvest of the earth (xiv. 6–20)

Though John gives it no particular emphasis this seventh sign is itself septiform. Seven angels either proclaim judgment or take some part in bringing judgment about. The series culminates in a dreadfully final picture of the earth as drenched in blood. We may regard the messages of the three angels and of the voice from heaven as an interlude between the sixth and seventh signs (cf. the interludes between the sixth and seventh seals and between the sixth and seventh trumpets).

i. Three angels proclaim judgment (xiv. 6–12). As three angels in succession proclaim judgment the saints are assured once more that the triumph of evil will be short-lived. God will certainly bring judgment upon evildoers, but in His own good time.

6. *Another angel* is difficult because there has been no preceding angel since xii. 7. Perhaps it differentiates this angel from those mentioned later, and *another* is common in this chapter (verses 8, 9 in the best MSS, 15, 17, 18). Earlier an eagle flew in *the midst of heaven* (viii. 13, where see note) proclaiming a threefold 'Woe' to earth's inhabitants. Now an angel proclaims there an (not *the*) *everlasting gospel*. This is the only place in this book where *gospel* occurs.

At first sight there is not much of the 'good news' about the message this angel brings. But two things should be said. One is that judgment is a necessary implication of the gospel (cf. Rom. ii. 16). The words in fact constitute a last appeal for repentance from those about to be judged (cf. Mk. i. 15, Acts xiv. 15, etc.). The other is that John was writing to Christians facing persecution. For them it was indeed good news that all men, their persecutors included, would be called upon to give account of themselves, and that the time of the power of evil was determined. Torrance comments, 'It is impossible for the Church at any time to come to easy terms with the contemporary order . . . as long as the Cross is in the field and the everlasting Gospel is preached, God's love will strike in judgment at all the defence-works of evil thrown up in state and society and history by the banding of men together in massive reaction and perverted self-defence against the will and Word of God.'

Everlasting points to a message that is permanently valid, while *them that dwell on the earth* (see note on vi. 10) and *every nation*, etc. (see note on v. 9) show that it is universally applicable.

7. The angel speaks *with a loud voice* for his words go out to all mankind. He calls on men to *fear God*. Evildoers have much to fear (cf. vi. 15 f., xi. 11, 13). But the angel's message is not basically negative and he calls on men to *give glory* to God, and to *worship* Him. God is characterized as Creator, and *heaven, and earth, and the sea, and the fountains of waters* are singled out for mention. Everything that exists comes from the hand of God. Those who oppose Him are in a hopeless position. The worshippers of the beast had been impressed by his power (xiii. 3, 7 f., 13, 15). Now they are compelled to recognize real power. 'Here is the bitter irony of their lot: though they damn themselves eternally by their refusal to face the truth, one day they will be *forced* to face it. Sooner or later the "glory" they refuse to "give" the Creator willingly will be torn from them by the spectacle of His wrath' (Kiddle).

8. A second *angel* announces that *Babylon is fallen* (cf. xviii. 2). The verb comes first in the announcement. It is in the aorist of completed action, and it is repeated. All this combines to give the impression of imminence and certainty. There can be no doubt about the fall of the city. This is the first mention of *Babylon* in this book (again in xvi. 19, xvii. 5, xviii. 2, 10, 21). In every case Babylon is called 'great'. There is no reason for holding that John means the Mesopotamian city of this name (though he may well have in mind Je. li. 7 f.). In the first mention of this city in the Bible (Gn. xi. 9, but cf. Gn. x. 10) we read that after the Flood man tried to scale the heights of heaven by building a mighty tower. The name thus stands for the pride of man and for the heathen city-empire. For John, Babylon is the great city, the symbol of man in community opposed to the things of God. Sometimes in other writings Babylon means Rome (2 *Bar.* xi. 1, *Sib. Or.* v. 143, 159, 434, possibly 1 Pet. v. 13). John does not go as far as this, though doubtless to men of the first century there was no better illustration of what Babylon means than contemporary Rome. John is looking forward to the overthrow of all the evil that Babylon stands for.

The reason for her fall is her bad influence. She made all nations *drink of the wine of the wrath of her fornication* (again in xviii. 3). John is combining two thoughts: first, that Babylon makes the nations drink the wine of her impurity, i.e. she corrupts them with her evil ways, and second, that this impurity brings down upon it the wrath of God (cf. Je. xxv. 15). 'The nations, having drunk the wine of the fornication of Babylon, have really therein drunk the wine of the wrath of God' (Charles).

9, 10. *The third angel* spoke *with a loud voice.* He concerns himself with those who worship the beast and his image and who have his mark (xiii. 16). They will be the objects of the divine wrath. John uses two words for wrath here: *thumos*, which is rendered *wrath*, and *orgē* (see note on vi. 16), which is

translated *indignation*. These two words do not differ greatly
in meaning, but *orgē* more readily denotes the kind of anger
that rises out of a settled disposition and *thumos* anger of a more
passionate kind. It accords with this that in the New Testament
orgē is the usual word for the divine wrath. Indeed, outside
Revelation *thumos* is used of the divine anger only once. But
as it is the more vivid word it is not surprising that it occurs
often in this book (xii. 12, xiv. 8, 10, 19, xv. 1, 7, xvi. 1, 19,
xviii. 3, xix. 15). Stählin can say, 'But one might very well
say that *thumos*, to which there clings the concept of passionate
outburst, was well adapted for describing the visions of the
seer, but not for delineating Paul's concept of the wrath of
God.'[1]

The wine of God's wrath *is poured out without mixture*. The
word rendered *poured* really means 'mix', and it is used of
preparing wine for consumption by mixing it with spices,
water, or whatever was needed. It is paradoxical to say it is
'mixed without mixing', but this is John's way of saying that
it is not broken down in any way. The wrath of God will be
visited on these sinners with no mitigation (cf. Ps. lxxv. 8, and
for this verb and adjective, *Ps. Sol.* viii. 15). The effects are
torment with *fire and brimstone*. This, of course, is to be taken
symbolically, but seriously. The modern vogue of dispensing
with hell has no counterpart in Revelation. John is quite sure
that the consequences of sin follow sinners into the life to come.
Here on earth they may rejoice over their misdeeds. There
they will suffer for them. This will take place in the presence
of *holy angels* and of *the Lamb*. Christians who suffered for their
faith did so in the presence of crowds of onlookers. Ultimately
their tormentors will be punished in the presence of more
august spectators 'in keeping with many other scenes of this
book where the deepest sting that bitter conscience is dealt is
that it must suffer while utter purity is looking on' (Love).

11. The torment mentioned in verse 10 is eternal. The
beast's worshippers *have no rest day or night*. This is in contrast

---

[1] *TDNT*, V, p. 422. See further my *The Apostolic Preaching of the Cross*[3],
pp. 180 ff.

to the four living ones of whom exactly the same expression is used to describe their unceasing worship (iv. 8). John spells out the identity of the sufferers: those *who worship the beast and his image*, and anyone who receives *the mark of his name*.

Some complain about John's handling of this theme, feeling that the topic should not be dwelt upon. But John is not gloating over the sufferings of the wicked as some later Christians have done. He is not describing suffering for suffering's sake in the manner of the horror thriller. He has a sense of serious purpose. Motives of self-interest impelled many to try to escape martyrdom. They thought it would be easier for them if they denied the faith. John wants them to be under no illusions. Such 'self-interest' is fatal. There are ultimate realities with which his readers must reckon. And, despite the hesitation of modern men, he must reckon with them, too. One may shut one's eyes to facts, but this does not do away with them.

12. A consideration of ultimate realities sustains the people of God. They must pass through troubles, but they know that their troubles are temporary whereas those of their tormentors will be eternal. This sense of values keeps them calm. It issues in steadfastness (see note in ii. 2). *The saints* are characterized by their keeping of *the commandments of God, and the faith of Jesus*. Both ethical conduct and reliance on the Saviour are important.

ii. The dead which die in the Lord (xiv. 13). Now comes an interjection detailing the blessedness of those who die in Christ. Man's natural tendency is to think of blessedness in terms of this life. But in a persecution situation John wants it to be clear that there are more important things than life.

13. Once more John hears from heaven a voice he does not identify. It has the highest authority, but whether it comes direct from God or through an intermediary he does not tell us. It pronounces blessed those who *die in the Lord*. This is one of seven such beatitudes in this book (see note on i. 3). This is a noteworthy piece of encouragement in a situation where the steadfastness of the saints was most important. God's people may be grossly maltreated even up to and including the infliction of the death penalty. But they, and not their tormentors, remain blessed. It is not easy to see whether we should take *from henceforth* with what precedes or with what follows. Grammatically it could go with either, but the difficulty of attaching it to *Yea, saith the Spirit* leads most to take it with the preceding. Yet those who die in the Lord are always blessed, and not only *from henceforth*, and so some suggest we should link it with resting from their labours. This would be attractive were it not for the intervening words. If the text be accepted as it stands, AV is probably correct. NEB may, however, be right in reading, ' "Henceforth", says the Spirit, "they may rest from their labours" ' (this omits *Yea*, which makes it almost necessary to take *henceforth* with what follows; see the textual note in *GNT*). That the speaker is *the Spirit* adds solemnity to the words. The Spirit does not often speak in this book but He does in the letters to the churches (ii. 7, 11, etc.) and in the final invitation (xxii. 17).

The word *labours* (*kopōn*) means 'labour to the point of weariness' and sometimes merely pain. It is in this latter sense that we should understand it here. Heaven is not so much a place where no work is done as one where pain has ceased. The believer rests from his *labours*, but his *works* (*erga*) go into the life beyond the grave. This gives dignity to all the work in which Christian men engage. They are occupied in no insignificant task.

iii. The reaper on the cloud (xiv. 14–16). John sees an angel with a sickle sitting on a cloud. The harvest of the earth is ripe and is reaped. This vivid way of speaking about the end of the world would come home with great force in an age when men were more familiar with agricultural processes than they are now. The harvest is the climax. Three angels have already announced judgment. This builds up to the moment when the angel sitting on the cloud plunges his sickle into the earth's harvest. There is drama and finality about the action.

14. For *I looked, and behold,* see note on vi. 2. John sees the scene vividly before him. There is dispute as to the identity of the one *like unto the Son of man* (better, 'a son of man'). The name, the fact that he sits on a cloud (cf. Dn. vii. 13), and his wearing of *a golden crown* all lead some to identify him with Christ. The holding of a sharp sickle would not be out of character. But a command is issued to him in rather peremptory terms (verse 15), and this is very hard to reconcile with this identification. We could, perhaps, regard the command as coming from God and the angel as no more than a messenger. In the Gospels the Son does not know the time of the End (Mk. xiii. 32). Jesus said that this is a matter for the Father Himself (Acts i. 7). Yet when full allowance is made for this it remains curious that the exalted Christ should receive a command in the peremptory words of verse 15. And it is more than curious that the Lamb who is in the midst of the throne, and who throughout this book is depicted as in the closest communion with the Father, should need an angel to tell Him of the Father's will. That the incarnate Jesus should be ignorant of the time of the End is explicable. That 'the Lamb which is in the midst of the throne' should be ignorant of it is not.

It is also unlikely that John would depict the glorious Christ as doing essentially the same thing as an angel does (in verse 19). A small point is that if this were Christ we would have six angels in the series, whereas it is much more in keeping with John's method that he should have seven. We should also bear in mind that, whereas to modern Christian ears 'one like a son of man' sounds like a reference to Christ, it is not a strange designation in apocalyptic. There it is a normal way of referring to an angelic being, men being usually symbolized by animals of some kind. It is best to think of the holder of the sickle as an angel.

15. The familiar description, *another angel,* introduces the fifth in the series. He comes *out of the temple* (or 'sanctuary') which means from the very presence of God. His words are addressed to one person alone, the angel sitting on the cloud, but he cries *with a loud voice*, as befits an angel. *The time is come* (lit. 'the hour came') is not unlike certain passages in the Fourth Gospel, where 'the hour' is an important concept. It denotes the inevitability with which things come to their climax. There, however, the cross is in view. Here it is the end of the world, as *the harvest of the earth* makes clear.

Is ripe (*exēranthē*) points to the drying off of plants when the crop is fully ripe. The time for the intervention of him who bore the sickle is not chosen arbitrarily. He puts in the sickle at exactly the right moment. Persecuted believers may know that if God's intervention is delayed this is only because it is not yet the right moment to reap. Reaping is certain as soon as the harvest of the earth is ripe. Some take this to refer to the gathering in of the righteous with the symbolism of wheat harvest (cf. Mt. xiii. 30, 38, Mk. iv. 29). They see the wicked in the next section where grape harvest, with its treading out of the grapes, is more suitable imagery for the judgment of the wicked. This is possible. But it is usually supported by seeing Christ as the Reaper who gathers in the saints, a suggestion which, as we have already noticed, is not soundly based. Moreover there is nothing in the context to show that the righteous are in view. Wheat is not even mentioned, for example. It is better to see the harvest as general.

16. The angel on the cloud did as he was told. He reaped the earth. This is not explained and we are left to apply the imagery for ourselves.

iv. The vintage (xiv. 17–20). Reaping is now taken a stage further and we move on to grape harvest. This with its treading of grapes is a very suitable figure of judgment.

17. There now appears another sickle-bearing angel, the sixth in the series. Like his predecessor he came out of the sanctuary. And, as with the first-mentioned reaper, it is specified that his sickle was sharp.

18. The seventh angel came *out from the altar* (see note on vi. 9). The altar has earlier been associated with the prayers of the saints and with judgment (viii. 3–5, where see note).

This may well be in mind here also. John sees the judgment as God's final answer to the prayers of His suffering saints. This angel has *power* (*exousian*) *over fire*. This is not explained, but fire and judgment are often closely connected. He commands the angel with the sickle to *gather the clusters of the vine of the earth*, adding the information that *her grapes are fully ripe* (cf. verse 15). It is not clear why a sickle should be used for the harvesting of grapes. But John is not concerned to give exact viticultural information. A sickle is a word with grim overtones, and this is the important point. John may have in mind here the words of Joel iii. 13: 'Put ye in the sickle, for the harvest is ripe: come, get you down; for the press is full, the fats overflow; for their wickedness is great.'

19. The angel obeyed. He reaped the earth's vine and hurled what he gathered *into the great winepress of the wrath of God* (cf. xix. 15). This is a vivid description of judgment on the wicked.

20. John does not say who trod the winepress, nor what was the city outside which it took place. Presumably neither is of great concern. For treading out the winepress, cf. Isaiah lxiii. 3, and for action outside the city we might compare 'without the gate' (Heb. xiii. 12). John's major concern is to show that there will be a cataclysmic destruction of mankind at the end of the age. The vast quantity of blood (cf. 1 *Enoch* c. 3, 'the horse shall walk up to the breast in the blood of sinners') points to the blotting out of all mankind. The earth has come to a final end. John is doing no more than allude to this at this point. He develops the idea later.

A thousand and six hundred furlongs (RSV 'stadia') is a distance of about 184 miles. But John's interest is rather in the number than in the precise distance it represents. Of the explanations suggested perhaps best is that which sees it as the product of sixteen (the square of four, the number of the earth which is the abode of the wicked) and one hundred (the square of ten, the number of completeness). Blood stretching for 1,600 stadia thus stands for the complete judgment of the whole earth and the destruction of all the wicked.

VII. THE SEVEN LAST PLAGUES (xv. 1–xvi. 21)

More than once John has taken us through the whole range of God's judgments, as in the visions of the seven seals and of the seven trumpets (see note at the beginning of chapter v). Each time he was telling us something of what will happen in the end-time and something of what goes on in human history. Now under the imagery of seven angels pouring out the contents of seven golden bowls he does something of the sort again. This time, however, there is a marked stress on finality. These are the last plagues. Judgment is complete. This does not mean that they have no relevance to our situation. While they refer especially to the End, yet 'whenever in history the wicked fail to repent in answer to the initial and partial manifestation of God's anger in judgments, the *final* effusion of wrath follows' (Hendriksen).

a. Preliminaries (xv. 1–8)

It is in keeping with his method that John has some preliminary remarks to make (chapter v is a preliminary to the seals, and viii. 1–5 to the trumpets). Here he stresses the majesty of God who is over the whole historical process.

1. For *sign* see note on xii. 1. This sign is described as *great and marvellous*, which marks it as outstanding. Such a description is not given of any other portent, but these adjectives are used of God's own works (verse 3). The plagues these angels deal with are *the seven last plagues* (for *plagues*, cf. ix. 18 and see note, ix. 20, xi. 6). The word is quite general. From the meaning 'blow' or 'stroke', the word 'plague' comes to be used of misfortunes generally. But there is an air of finality about this description. These plagues are the last earth will know. In them God's wrath (see note on xiv. 10) *is filled up* (*etelesthē*; i.e. reaches its *telos*, its end or aim).

2. John's habitual reserve comes out when he sees not 'a sea of glass', but *as it were a sea of glass* (cf. iv. 6 where see note). This time it is *mingled with fire*, an unusual combination of images. The mention of fire may be due to the fact that the context deals with wrath and judgment. 'The red glow on the Sea spoke of the fire through which the Martyrs passed, and yet more of the wrath about to fall on the world which had condemned them' (Swete). Kiddle sees the Exodus symbolism again: 'A heavenly Red Sea! . . . The "sea" has been forded by the martyrs. It is now about to submerge their foes.'

John sees also those who had obtained the victory which he spells out as *over the beast, and over his image, and over his mark, and over the number of his name* (see note on xiii. 18). Nothing evil can triumph over God's people. It is perhaps worth noticing that in the early church the day of a man's martyrdom was often called the day of his victory. Barclay comments, 'The real victory is not to live in safety, to evade trouble, cautiously and prudently to preserve life; the real victory is to face the worst that evil can do, and if need be to be faithful unto death.' These conquerors stand on or by (*epi* could denote either) the glassy sea. *Harps of God* is an unusual description of harps (but cf. 'the trump of God', 1 Thes. iv. 16). It will indicate that the victors enjoy their triumph song only because of what God has done for them.

3. *They sing* (presumably to their own harp accompaniment) *the song of Moses the servant of God, and the song of the Lamb*. This indicates the harmony between different phases of the revelation. Moses is not in opposition to Christ, nor the law to the gospel. Paul can speak of the law as a schoolmaster to bring us to Christ (Gal. iii. 24), and it is co-operation of this kind that is in mind here. Moses is described as *the servant of God*. While this usage is found in the Old Testament it may not be fanciful to recall that 'the servant of the Lord' is a theme of prophecy, more particularly in Isaiah. Perhaps John means us to think that the prophets as well as the law are caught up in this song. Certainly the Exodus imagery will be in mind, as often in this book. The great deliverance wrought under Moses forms the pattern for the great deliverance wrought by the Lamb. In strictness the repetition of the words *the song of* should mean that there were two songs, one of Moses and another of the Lamb. Indeed, some exegetes have understood the expression in this way. They suggest that the song of Moses is that given in Exodus xv, and the song of the Lamb here. But it is much more likely that there is but one song referred to with the double title.

Almost all the song is composed of Old Testament expressions. This is the one song in Revelation to show the parallelism so characteristic of Hebrew poetry. It begins by characterizing God's works as *great and marvellous* (cf. Pss. xcii. 5, cxxxix. 14). The inhabitants of the earth have marvelled at the beast and his wonders. But what are truly great and marvellous are not such trifles, but the works of God. So God is hailed as *Lord God Almighty*. His power is incomparable. From power the thought moves on to justice. God's *ways* are *just and true* (cf. Ps. cxlv. 17). The last word evokes recollections of 'doing the truth' in John's Gospel (Jn. iii. 21) and First Epistle (1 Jn. i. 6). God is addressed then as 'thou King of the nations' (or 'King of the ages', as RSV, NEB; see Tasker's note in *GNT*. *King of saints* is based on inferior MS attestation.) God's universal sovereignty is in mind (cf. Je. x. 6 f.). John keeps on bringing out this point, which must have been exceedingly important for his troubled readers.

4. In view of God's greatness the rhetorical question is asked, *Who shall not fear thee, O Lord, and glorify thy name?* (cf. Ps. lxxxvi. 9, Mal. i. 11). The *name* stands for the whole person (see note on ii. 3). The song comes to its end with three statements each introduced with *for*. The first declares that God only is *holy* (cf. 1 Sa. ii. 2). The word is *hosios*, used in Revelation only here and in xvi. 5 (see note *in loc.*), both times of God. It conveys the idea of perfect purity. The second statement forecasts that *all nations shall come and worship before* God (cf. Ps. lxxxvi. 9). The final statement is that God's *judgments are made manifest*. The term *judgments* (*dikaiōmata*) is often understood in the sense 'righteous acts' (e.g. RV). But there is reason for holding that the term has to do with legal acts and we should understand it here of 'the judicial sentences of God in relation to the nations either in the way of mercy or condemnation' (Charles).[1] At the last God's judicial sentences will be made plain to all.

Before leaving this song it is worth noticing that, though it is sung by the victors, there is no word in it about themselves or the way they overcame. Those who triumph in Christ fix all their attention on Him. 'Heaven is heaven because in it at last all self, and self-importance, are lost in the presence of the greatness and the glory of God' (Barclay).

5. *The temple of the tabernacle of the testimony* is an expression found here only (but cf. xi. 19, Ex. xl. 34). But the Greek words rendered *the tabernacle of the testimony* form the LXX translation of the Old Testament expression 'the tent of meeting' (AV, 'the tabernacle of the congregation'). It would seem that John wants us to discern a reference to the wilderness once again. He is using a symbol of the very presence of God Himself. At the same time he introduces once more the thought of witness which means so much to him and to the churches to which he writes with their 'martyrs'.

6. When this sanctuary was opened there came out *the seven angels* who had *the seven plagues*. These plagues thus come with the fullest divine sanction, for they are brought by angels who have come from the very presence of God. Some attention is paid to their appearance, which is not usual in this book. They are clothed in *pure and white linen*. The word translated *linen* (*linon*) is not usual for a garment, and some accept the textual variant *lithon* ('stone'). This is possible in the sense in which the king of Tyre can be saluted, 'every precious stone was thy covering' (Ezk. xxviii. 13). But this, too, is unusual, and since *linon* is sometimes used of clothing (AG) it seems best to accept this sense here. The angels have *their breasts girded with golden girdles*. Some hold that this means a priestly rather than a military girding, but the point is not proven (see note on i. 13). But at the least the appearance of these angels symbolizes their spotlessness. It emphasizes the purity from which the wrath is poured out on the world. This is no

---

[1] For a discussion of this word see my *The Apostolic Preaching of the Cross*[3], pp. 287 ff.

bestial thing, evil with passion. It is a pure concern for the right.

7. The bowls which convey the last plagues are given to the angels by one of the four living ones. These have their place close to the throne of God, so this origin for the bowls will indicate that they come with the fullest divine sanction. This is brought out also in the explicit statement that the bowls are full of *the wrath* (see note on xiv. 10) *of God*. God is spoken of in terms of eternity: He *liveth for ever and ever*. This contrasts with the earth's inhabitants, for they are in time. These plagues coming upon them are 'last' plagues (verse 1).

Vials renders the Greek *phialas* (for which see note on v. 8). It was used of the container which held the prayers of the saints (v. 8) and it is not at all impossible that John wants us to bear that passage in mind. More than once he brings out the thought that the prayers of God's people which seem so insignificant are important. They may initiate great divine judgments. They have their part to play in bringing about the final state of affairs.

8. *The temple was filled with smoke from the glory of God* (cf. Ex. xl. 34, 1 Ki. viii. 10, Is. vi. 4, Ezk. x. 4, xliv. 4). At this solemn moment God's glory is especially manifested. With *glory* there is linked *his power*, which is very much in place in a book so full of the might of the Lord. John tells us that nobody could enter *the temple* (i.e. the sanctuary) until the seven plagues *were fulfilled*. He does not say that the smoke, etc. brought this about, though this may be in mind. But the main point is the inevitability of the plagues. When God's good time has come nothing can stop final judgment.

b. The first bowl (xvi. 1, 2)

The seven angels proceed to pour out their bowls on the earth, thus releasing the seven last plagues. They are described in rather more succinct form than were the seals or the trumpets. And, whereas there was an interlude between the sixth and the seventh members of both earlier series, the interlude between the sixth and the seventh bowls is much less prominent.

There are some clear resemblances between the plagues in Egypt and the judgments released by the bowls, as also between the latter and the trumpet judgments. But there are also differences, which Swete sums up in these words: 'The Last Plagues have features peculiar to themselves; the fourth is entirely new, the rest are more or less freshly conceived. On the other hand the differences are deeper and more suggestive. While no personal suffering is inflicted on Man by the first five of the Egyptian plagues or by the first four of the Trumpet-visitations, he is attacked at the very outset of the present cycle. Again, while the first four Trumpet-plagues affect only a third of the earth, the sea, the fresh water supply, and the lights of heaven, no such limitation appears in the account of the Seven Plagues now about to be described. They are not tentative chastisements, but punitive and final.'

It is this air of finality which sets this series of plagues off from all the others. Others might refer to one country (Egypt), or to a third of the earth. These are universal. They point us to God's overthrow of all that is evil. There is another point. Though there is stress on the severity of these plagues we should not overlook the implied call for repentance. John keeps on pointing out that men reacted in the wrong way, refusing to repent of their evil (verses 9, 11, 21).

1. As often, John hears a voice which he does not identify for us. It is *a great voice*, which is suitable for the announcement of the release of the last plagues. When John uses this expression he usually has the adjective follow the noun in the Greek, but here it precedes it. The unusual order puts some stress on *great*. This voice came *out of the temple*, so that its origin is with God. Indeed we might go further and reason that the voice must be the very voice of God, for we have just been told that no-one could go into the sanctuary until these judgments were fulfilled (xv. 8). This seems to exclude angels or the like. If this is the way the passage should be understood, John is telling us that the last plagues are released by none less than God. For *vials*, or rather 'bowls', see note on v. 8, and for *the wrath of God* on xiv. 10.

2. *The first* angel *went,* i.e. 'went away' (*apēlthen*) and *poured out* his bowl. The impression left by the choice of this verb is that the angels did not, so to speak, step forward and pour out their bowls, and then return to their places, but rather that, having discharged their tasks, they disappeared from the scene. The result of the pouring out of the first bowl was that *a noisome and grievous sore* (i.e. a painful ulcer) appeared on the beast's adherents. We are reminded of the plague of boils in Egypt (Ex. ix. 10 f.; cf. Dt. xxviii. 35). The recipients are described as those who had *the mark of the beast* and who *worshipped his image.* These are the things which specially characterize them and mark them off from other men. There are then some evils which afflict those who give themselves over to wickedness but do not affect other men.

c. The second bowl (xvi. 3)

3. The second angel directed his efforts toward the sea, which *became as the blood of a dead man* (cf. Ex. vii. 17–21). It is peculiar that in the Greek *as* precedes *dead man,* not *blood,* i.e. it means 'blood as of a dead man' rather than 'as blood of a dead man'. But this can scarcely affect the general meaning. It is worth recalling that when the second trumpet was blown something like a mountain was hurled into the sea, and a third of the waters became blood and a third of the creatures in and on the sea died (viii. 8 f.). On this occasion there is no mention of one third or any other proportion. We are now face to face with the last plagues. Everything in the sea died, this being expressed in a full and unusual fashion, *every living soul . . . in the sea.*

d. The third bowl (xvi. 4–7)

4. When the third trumpet was blown the rivers and fountains were affected, and this is the case here. But there is an intensification. On that occasion one third of the waters was affected (viii. 10 f.). Now there is no mention of one third. On that occasion there was no mention of blood, the waters simply becoming 'bitter'. Here all turns to blood. It is true that it is not said here that men died, but that presumably is only because other judgments followed so swiftly. Without water to drink there is no future for man.

5. John heard *the angel of the waters*, a designation which appears to be found nowhere else. Among the Jews angels were often thought to be responsible for specific areas of the universe (for classes of angels see the Index to Volume II of Charles's *Apocrypha and Pseudepigrapha of the Old Testament*). Thus there is nothing surprising about the expression. Indeed, there is at least one passage which speaks of angels (plural) as set 'over the powers of the waters' (1 *Enoch* lxvi. 2). But there is certainly nothing like it anywhere else in the Bible.

The angel of the waters saw in these proceedings an excellent example of making the punishment fit the crime. He speaks of God as *righteous* and regards this activity as one of judging. The pouring out of the bowls is not a series of arbitrary actions. It is a solemn act of judgment. God is spoken of in terms of His eternity (for *which art, and wast* see note on i. 4). In the better MSS there is no *and shalt be* which accords with the fact that the consummation has arrived. There is no point in speaking of a future coming. Instead the reading is 'the holy One', which perhaps should be taken in the sense 'O Holy One' (RSV: the article is equivalent to a vocative). For 'holy' see note on xv. 4.

6. The 'punishment fits the crime' theme becomes explicit. The sinners in question *shed the blood of saints and prophets* and because of that *thou hast given them blood to drink*. Since they delighted in shedding blood it is fitting that they should now drink blood. The meaning may be that those who so readily shed the blood of Christ's followers now find themselves caught up in fighting one another and consequently in bringing about the shedding of their own blood. We shall see later in this chapter and again in xvii. 16 that the forces of evil are not thought of as presenting a united front. There are hatreds and divisions and strifes among its members. The crisp *they are worthy* (Moffatt, 'As they deserve') puts an emphasis on their receipt of what they deserve as the final touch. Kiddle reminds us that 'experience has an abundant store of examples to prove to whatever nation cares to pay heed that communities do suffer proportionately to their crimes, and that often enough there is a grim and obvious aptness in the ill effect of an ill cause'. Preston and Hanson bring this up to date by saying, 'The comment is not unlike that which many people are making today about the atom bomb: "thou hast given them blood to drink". God has allowed us to discover one of nature's greatest secrets, and we look like celebrating the event in blood.'

7. For *the altar* see note on vi. 9. This is the only place in Revelation where the altar is said to speak, though we have heard before of a voice from the horns of the altar (ix. 13). It may be relevant that the altar is especially connected with the prayers of the saints (viii. 3) which introduced judgments of God (viii. 5). The angel who commanded that the vine of the earth be reaped came from the altar (xiv. 18), a further link between the altar and judgment. The altar interjects its agreement with the angel. It does this first with *even so* (*nai—'yes'*), followed by an address to God as *Lord God Almighty*, a most appropriate address in view of the divine power put forth in the judgments under consideration. Then secondly the altar speaks of God's judgments as *true and righteous*. The same adjectives, though in the reverse order, were used of God's ways (xv. 3; *dikaiai* is there translated 'just' and here as *righteous*).

e. The fourth bowl (xvi. 8, 9)

8. The fourth angel now poured his bowl on the sun. The familiar *was given* (there is nothing corresponding to *power* in the Greek; it simply reads 'and it was given') reminds us once more that God is over the whole process. There is no independent power in the sun. If the sun is to scorch men it is because God gives it the power to do so. In previous sections of the book there have been signs in the sun. But they have all been concerned with restricting it in whole or in part (vi. 12, viii. 12, ix. 2). This time, by contrast, the sun scorches men with a heat so fierce that it can be said to be *with fire*.

9. The effect of the sun is strongly emphasized with the use of the adjective *great* and the use of the cognate accusative ('scorched a great scorching'). But sinners would not learn the lesson. They simply *blasphemed the name of God*. They did not repent. They gave God no glory (*to give* links these two thoughts; had they repented the ascription of glory would inevitably have followed). John brings out God's sovereignty once more with *God, which hath power over these plagues*. It is very important to him (and to us) that God is over the whole process right to the end.

f. The fifth bowl (xvi. 10, 11)

10. *The fifth angel* made his attack directly on the beast's citadel. He poured out his bowl *upon the seat* (i.e. 'throne', *thronon*) *of the beast*, with curious results. The beast's *kingdom was full of darkness* (cf. ix. 2, Ex. x. 21-23). Further *they* (obviously the beast's adherents, though this is not said in set terms) *gnawed their tongues for pain*. Just as there is no mention of what caused the darkness, so there is no mention of what brought about the pain (though possibly it is the result of the previous plagues; the first gave men ulcers, and the fourth burns from the scorching heat). John is not giving a detailed report, but simply highlighting the important points. In this case they are the darkness and the pain. It is not without its interest that the fifth trumpet plague had something similar. Smoke came out of the abyss and darkened the sun and the air, and this was accompanied by the appearance of locusts who tortured men (ix. 1 f., 5 f.). It is possible that we should take the darkening in this plague to denote a waning of the power of the beast, and this will be further stressed in the remaining plagues.

11. As was the case with the previous bowl, the sinners reacted in the wrong way. They blasphemed God. John brings out something of His majesty by calling Him *the God of heaven*. But these earth-dwellers could not recognize the majesty of heaven when they saw it. They were preoccupied with their *pains* (plural here, though singular in the previous verse). One pain is singled out, namely the ulcers (the same word as in verse 2, though here plural). John notes once more that despite their troubles these men did not repent. Even grievous pain did not awaken them to the realities of the situation.

g. The sixth bowl (xvi. 12-16)

More is said about the result of the pouring of the sixth bowl than in the case of any of the first five. It resulted in men being prepared for the End. It did not usher in the End, but prepared for it.

12. *The sixth angel* poured out his bowl *upon the great river Euphrates.* The sixth trumpet had also been concerned with this river, being the signal for the release of four angels who were to kill one third part of mankind (ix. 13-15). The effect of the outpouring of the sixth bowl was the drying up of the Euphrates to make ready a way for *the kings of the east.* This is not further explained, but in the Old Testament a mighty action of God is frequently associated with the drying up of waters, as the Red Sea (Ex. xiv. 21), the Jordan (Jos. iii. 16 f.), and several times in prophecy (Is. xi. 15, Je. li. 36, Zc. x. 11). 'It is possible that his mind runs also on the story told by Herodotus (i. 191) of the capture of Babylon by Cyrus, who marched into the city across the drained bed of the Euphrates; a new Babylon is to be surprised, and the drying up of the river marks the removal of the last obstacle to its fall' (Swete).

Beyond the Roman Empire, the east of Euphrates, was for John's readers a great unknown land. Who could tell what mighty kings lurked there? It was known that the Parthians were located in this area and during the first century there was a persistent fear of an invasion from this quarter. This was reinforced by the Nero *redivivus* myth, for this suggested that Nero would put himself at the head of the Parthian hordes and so march into the Empire.

John is suggesting that at the End all these fears and more will be realized. We should bear in mind that Nero and his armies in the myth were not going to ally themselves with Rome, but to attack her. So John is thinking of division among the forces of evil (cf. xvii. 16), not of a united front. But we would be wrong in holding that he is doing no more than voice a contemporary expectation. By appealing to contemporary fears he is making the point that at the end of time the divided forces of evil will engage in a terrible conflict. Curiously, having told us that the way will be cleared for mighty potentates to march westward John does not follow up the thought. He does not speak of the kings as using the way prepared for them. In fact he does not mention them again.

13. John now sees *three unclean spirits* coming out of the mouths of *the dragon, the beast,* and *the false prophet.* This last-mentioned is evidently the beast from the earth (xiii. 11; cf. xix. 20 with xiii. 14). The dirty spirits are *like frogs,* which may be meant to remind us of the plague of frogs in Egypt (Ex. viii. 3). Love sees here 'a devastating caricature of the failure of evil. That which men fear most because it appears to be mighty and eternally entrenched becomes at long last only a ridiculous spawning of sickly creatures of the night.' Frogs have evil associations. They are slimy and ugly. They produce an incessant and meaningless croaking, but no solid achievement. Such thoughts are aroused by the symbolism. The main idea, however, is that these spirits are like the 'lying spirit' who was to entice Ahab into battle (1 Ki. xxii. 21 ff.). But instead of enticing one man these have the much greater task of enticing the whole world into battle.

14. These spirits are 'demonic spirits' (so rather than *the spirits of devils*; as the devils are spirits themselves they can scarcely have spirits). They work *miracles* (*sēmeia*, 'signs', for which see note on xiii. 13). They do not simply do extraordinary things. Their miracles have meaning. The three dirty spirits have one real task to perform, namely that of gathering all men together for the final battle. As they *go forth unto the kings of the earth* it seems that their influence is exerted on rulers rather than on the common man. *The earth* and *the whole world* (for which latter cf. iii. 10, xii. 9) make clear the universal scope of their activities.

But the day to which all this leads up is not the day of the dirty spirits, nor the day of the rulers of the world. It is *that great day of God Almighty* (cf. 2 Pet. iii. 12). This is the most resounding description of the last day. *Great* disinguishes it from lesser days. And it is the day *of God*, not of man or even of the antichrist. It is associated with the culmination of the divine purposes. And *Almighty* reminds us that in the face of the might of the whole earth God's power is supreme.

15. The story of the bowls is interrupted by an interjection from the Lord Jesus Christ Himself in language somewhat reminiscent of that in iii. 3. It is to be seen against the gathering of the forces of evil described in the previous verse. With all evil combining against God, this call from the Lord Himself brings us back to the realities of the situation.

He likens His coming to that of *a thief*, i.e. it is unheralded and totally unexpected (cf. 1 Thes. v. 2). Then he pronounces blessed the man who is ready for that coming (for the seven beatitudes in this book see note on i. 3). There is nothing surprising in a reference to him *that watcheth*. But there is an unexpected twist in the reference to him that *keepeth his garments* and also in the fact that the fate from which he is to be kept is that of walking naked and of his shame being seen. *They see* is an impersonal plural and is equivalent to a passive (cf. xii. 6). We should probably not press the details of this description too closely. Elsewhere the garments stand for God's sentence of justification. We would not be God's people without them. Here, then, the thought is that believers caught unprepared will be put to shame at the critical time in the world's history. They will be like those outside the people of God.

16. John reverts to the activities of the dirty spirits. *He* should read 'they', as RSV. The spirits, then, gathered the kings (and, of course, their followers) to a place whose name is given as *Armageddon*. No place of this name is known, and the term is surely symbolic. But its meaning is uncertain. John tells us that it is a Hebrew word, and the two most favoured suggestions are that it means 'mountain of Megiddo' (*har mᵉgiddô*) or 'the city of Megiddo' (*îr mᵉḡiddô*). The former seems closer to the

Hebrew, but unfortunately no mountain appears to be called 'the mountain of Megiddo'. Many stirring feats took place in the vicinity, but they seem to be connected rather with the plain of Esdraelon than with any particular mountain or with Megiddo itself. In fact Megiddo is but rarely mentioned in connection with battles (Jdg. v. 19, 2 Ki. xxiii. 29, 2 Ch. xxxv. 22). There are Old Testament passages which look for the ultimate battle near mountains (Ezk. xxxix. 1 ff., perhaps Dn. xi. 45), but none that we can identify with the present expression.

It is possible that 'mountain' should not be taken literally, but understood of the great mound on which the city stood, in which case the two suggestions come to much the same thing. Since many great battles have been fought nearby, the city may stand in John's mind for decisive conflict. In that case it will stand here as a symbol for the final overthrow of all the forces of evil by an almighty God. It is not unlikely that the deliverance under Deborah is regarded as setting the pattern. Then Sisera had 900 chariots of iron (Jdg. iv. 13), but in Israel there was scarce a shield or spear among 40,000 (Jdg. v. 8). Israel's position was completely hopeless. But when the battle was joined, 'the Lord routed Sisera and all his chariots and all his army' (Jdg. iv. 15 RSV). So will it be at the last day. However strong the forces of evil may appear, and however hopeless the position of those of good, God will win the victory. He will resoundingly overthrow the evil.

h. The seventh bowl (xvi. 17–21)

The climax comes with the seventh bowl. This speaks of utter destruction. It does not say that all men will be killed. They must still face Almighty God for judgment. But this bowl does mean the complete fragmentation of earthly life.

17. *The seventh angel* poured out his bowl *into the air*, which was held to be uniquely the abode of demons (see note on ix. 2). The evil spirits are being attacked in their own element. John heard another *great voice*, unidentified as is common in this book. But he tells us that it came *out of the temple* and *from the* *throne* so that it has the fullest divine sanction. It signals the moment of climax by saying, *It is done* (one word only in the Greek, as also in xxi. 6).

18. The announcement of the climax caused great excitement. Similar phenomena followed the blowing of the seventh trumpet (xi. 19). For *voices, and thunders*, etc., see note on iv. 5. All this heightens the solemnity of the moment. Special stress is placed on *a great earthquake* which surpasses all other earthquakes. This is first put negatively, *such as was not since men were upon the earth*, and then twice positively, *so mighty* (*tēlikoutos*) and *so great*.

19. *The great city* is a motif we have seen before (see note on xi. 8). It stands for civilized man, man in organized community, but man ordering his affairs apart from God. It symbolizes the pride of human achievement, the godlessness of those who put their trust in man. This *great city* is now shattered. It divides *into three parts* which stands for its complete break-up. And in the break-up of the great city *the cities of the nations fell*. The one implies the other. With *great Babylon* we return to the thought of the great city. John tells us that this city *came in remembrance before God*, with the result that He visits His wrath upon her (see note on xiv. 10). Nowhere in this book is there an expression as emphatic as that rendered *the cup of the wine of the fierceness of his wrath*. John leaves us in no doubt that Babylon is to receive the most wholehearted opposition conceivable from an all-powerful and all-holy God.

20. John reverts to the physical effects of the cataclysm. *Every island fled away*. No mountain was to be found. For the linking of mountain and island cf. vi. 14, and for the disappearance of the mountains Zechariah xiv. 10 (which looks for the whole land to be turned into a plain).

21. Now comes a great hailstorm. Each hailstone weighed *about the weight of a talent*. This is variously estimated at from 45 lbs. to 90 lbs., or even more. We cannot be sure of the exact weight, but John's point that the hail was of enormous size is clear. And for the third time in this chapter we read that the effect of the disaster was that *men blasphemed God*. To bring out his point that this *plague* was unusually severe John uses a word translated *exceeding* which he uses nowhere else in the book (*sphodra*). The disaster must be seen for the decisive event it is.

VIII. THE TRIUMPH OF ALMIGHTY GOD
(xvii. 1-xx. 15)

John now gives himself over to a wholehearted description of the mighty triumph won by God over all His enemies. Hitherto his book has put a good deal of emphasis on God's sovereignty. He has tried to hearten his trembling fellow-believers by showing as plainly as he can that God is not mocked. Again and again he has brought out the point that in the end evil will be completely overthrown. But up till this point his concern has been basically with the here and now. He has shown his readers that, while evil may appear to be strong and they themselves may be helpless before it, in reality evil can do no more than operate within the sphere of God's permissiveness. It exercises only the power that God allows it to exercise. John has been concerned with the paradox implied in the two thoughts that God is almighty and that the people of God are oppressed. The solution he has offered in a variety of ways is that the wicked do and can do no more than God allows them to do.

Now John fixes his eyes firmly on the end-time. He concerns himself not with the apparent triumph of the evil, but with their final and complete overthrow. He sees God as casting down every stronghold and hurling His judgments against the wicked. No might of theirs avails. God is completely triumphant.

a. The judgment of the great whore (xvii. 1-18)

The first act in the final drama of judgment has to do with the fate of one described as 'the great whore'. Plainly this woman is to be identified with great Babylon, as the next chapter makes clear. She stands for civilized man apart from God,

man in organized but godless community (see introduction to
chapter xi, and notes on xi. 8, xiv. 8). This first section on the
judgment has three subdivisions: first John sees the woman,
secondly he receives an explanation of her significance, and
finally he is informed of her punishment.

i. The woman seated on the beast (xvii. 1–6). A preliminary description of the woman makes it clear that she is a
being of great earthly splendour, but also that she is exceedingly
evil and implacably opposed to the people of God. She is
plainly to be understood in contrast to the woman of chapter
xii and 'the bride' of chapters xxi, xxii.

1. This phase of the revelation is introduced by *one of the
seven angels* who had the bowls, though which is not said. The
same description is given later of the angel who showed
John 'the bride, the Lamb's wife' (xxi. 9). It is not unlikely
that we are to think of a connection. Out of God's final
judgments there emerges a single purpose which means both
the destruction of evil and the appearance of the new Jerusalem. God's purpose is consistent, but the result varies
according as it concerns the righteous or the wicked.

The angel now calls John to come. He will show him *the
judgment of the great whore*. Actually we do not come to this
judgment until the next chapter. There turn out to be some
necessary preliminaries. But this is the beginning of the whole
section concerned with the judgment. The woman is described
as *the great whore*. Outwardly she was all glittering splendour
(see note on verse 4). But John sees the glamour as meretri-
cious. It conceals a basic hostility to God combined with a
readiness to seduce men from their rightful allegiance.

The figure of sexual looseness is common in the Old Testament, where it is used in more ways than one. The people of
God is there seen as God's bride, so that unfaithfulness is
likened to adultery (Je. iii. 9, Ezk. xvi. 32). But the prophets
sometimes think of this unfaithfulness as habitual and mer-
cenary. Isaiah, for example, can exclaim, 'How is the faithful
city become an harlot!' (Is. i. 21; cf. also Je. ii. 20, iii. 1, Ezk.
xvi. 15 f., Ho. ii. 5, etc.). This is a vivid way of describing

an unfaithfulness which is horrible. It shows us that sin is first of all a sin against love.

A further way in which the figure is used is to describe insolent and idolatrous world powers as harlots, e.g. Tyre (Is. xxiii. 16 f.) and Nineveh (Na. iii. 4). They are not said to be adulterous, for they are not God's people, His bride. It is significant accordingly that in the present passage the term is *whore*, not 'adulteress'. John is not speaking of the people of God, but of a secular power. It is a secular power of low standards, one which has both committed horrible evils and seduced others into sharing her guilt.

The *whore* is described as she that *sitteth upon many waters*. As the woman symbolizes a city this might refer to its location as well watered, or even to wide-ranging seagoing commerce. Babylon in the Old Testament can be addressed as 'thou that dwellest upon many waters' (Je. li. 13), a description which aptly draws attention to the facts that the Euphrates flowed through that city and that it was the centre of a network of canals. But the Old Testament can also use streams or rivers in referring to peoples (e.g. Is. viii. 7 f., xxiii. 10, Je. xlvi. 7, xlvii. 2, Ezk. xxix. 10). Verse 15 makes it clear that the waters here stand for peoples. For his symbolical Babylon John has taken a conventional description of old Babylon and re-interpreted it along the lines of Old Testament symbolism to give a picture of a world empire exercising dominion over many subject nations.

2. *The kings of the earth* no doubt regarded their dealings with this city as laudable trade and cultural ventures. John saw them as *fornication* committed with this prostitute. They have joined in her sins against God. Their commerce with her involved them in the same basic attitude to the things of God as she had. John changes his imagery when he speaks of *the inhabitants of the earth* (see note on vi. 10) as *made drunk* by her (cf. Je. li. 7). While the kings of the earth take the lead the evil infection is not confined to them. It spreads throughout their peoples. The fact that the wine is *the wine of her fornication* (cf. xiv. 8) shows that sexual impurity is still the basic thought.

Earth's dwellers as a whole are happy enough to be seduced by the harlot.

3. Up till now the angel has spoken about the whore. Now John sees her. For this to take place he is carried *in the spirit into the wilderness*. For *in the spirit* as a state of exaltation and special receptivity brought about by the Spirit, see note on i. 10. The spot chosen for John's standpoint is significant. Throughout this book the *wilderness* is the place for God's people over against the great city (cf. xii. 6, 14). It is the negation of all that the city stands for, and in the wilderness one is safe from all that the great city can do. It is only here, only in detachment from the great city, that God's people can see her as she really is. If they identify themselves with her they will be blind to her essential nature.

From his vantage-point John sees a woman seated *upon a scarlet coloured beast*. That she sits on 'many waters' (verse 1) and now on a beast should not worry us. John never strives for consistency in his visions (see note on i. 17). He has two truths to bring out about this woman. One is given by her position over many waters. Now we come to the other, that she is borne by the beast. John's two pictures simply present us with two truths. We should identify the beast with that in xiii. 1. The woman's posture indicates a close connection and identifies her as one of the forces of evil continually supported by the beast. Underlying the differing manifestations of evil is the continuing reality represented by the beast.

Scarlet is the colour of the 'great red dragon' (xii. 3, where see note; a different Greek word is used). The word used here (*kokkinon*) refers to the dye made from the *kokkos*, 'the female of a scale insect (similar to the cochineal) which clings to the leaves of an oak tree; the dried bodies of these insects, known as kermes, were used by the ancients to prepare a purplish-red dye' (AG). It is a colour of splendour. But also in the Bible, of sin (Is. i. 18). *Blasphemy* is characteristic of the beast (xiii. 1, 5, 6), but this is the only place where the animal is said to be *full* of it. This will indicate blasphemy in the fullest measure. For the *seven heads and ten horns* see note on xii. 3.

4. The woman was royally robed. *Purple and scarlet* are colours of splendour and magnificence. These colours were not for the poor, since the dyes producing them were very expensive. *Purple* denoted the dye made from the murex, a shell-fish. For *scarlet* see note on verse 3. Both were costly to extract, so that the colours always indicate splendour and magnificence even more than the particular shades denoted by the words. The woman was also lavishly adorned. *Decked* is really 'gilded' (*kechrusōmenē*), and points to liberal adornment.

The *golden cup* the woman holds leads to the expectation of a specially satisfying drink. Should not only the best come in such a costly container? But in fact the cup is full of *abominations*. This word originally signified anything detestable, but in the Old Testament is especially associated with idolatry. This will be its significance here. The following *and the filthiness of her fornication* should probably be understood as 'even the filthiness . . .'. The attractive cup is revealed as no more than an enticement to men to join the glittering harlot in her evil ways. It is her method of seducing them from God. The picture is a vivid one, combining regal state with utter moral and religious corruption.

5. Names are written on foreheads quite often in this book. Thus God's servants were sealed in this way (vii. 3, ix. 4), and the servants of the Lamb were marked similarly (xiv. 1, xxii. 4). On the other side the same is true of the adherents of the beast (xiii. 16, xiv. 9, xx. 4). So now the character of the harlot is shown by her name, which is displayed on her forehead for all to see. Charles draws attention to passages in Roman authors informing us that Roman harlots wore on their brows labels inscribed with their names. The whore is thus in character.

Mystery (see note on i. 20) will indicate that the significance of the harlot's name is not open and obvious to all. It is a subject for revelation. And indeed the angel proceeds to reveal it (verse 7). Some students take *mystery* to be itself part of the name, but this is very improbable. It is a way of bringing out the significance of what follows. Moffatt renders 'by way of symbol', a translation which brings out the point that the name has meaning, but obscures the other truth that its significance is not discerned other than by revelation. The angel makes it known to John and John to believers. But the worldly would not know it at all.

The first part of the name is *Babylon* (see note on xiv. 8). Previously we have come across this city as a great city seducing all mankind, and the object of the divine hostility (xiv. 8, xvi. 19). Now we see her singled out as *the mother of harlots*. She is not only a harlot herself, but she spawns evils like herself. With this is linked *abominations of the earth*. As in verse 4, all kinds of abominable things are ascribed to the great city, and not one particular vice only. Barclay cites some vivid statements from Roman writers themselves, such as Juvenal, who describes the way the empress Messalina used to serve as a prostitute in a common brothel, and Seneca, who called Rome 'a filthy sewer'. Barclay comments, 'John's picture of Rome is not in the least exaggerated; it is actually restrained in comparison with some of the pictures which the Romans themselves drew of their own civilisation.'

6. John saw this woman *drunken with the blood of the saints, and with the blood of the martyrs of Jesus* (cf. Is. xxxiv. 5, 7 LXX). The metaphor shows that blood had flowed freely. The harlot had slain not one or two of the saints, but a great number. This figure also implies that she enjoyed the process. When she persecuted the church she did not think of herself as performing a distasteful but necessary duty. She rejoiced in it like a drunkard rejoices in his wine. *Drunken* is present tense in the Greek. John is talking about a continuing state, not merely past history. In this passage there can be no difference between *saints* and *martyrs*, but the placing of the two terms side by side adds solemnity to the indictment. The explicit use of the term *martyrs*, which means 'witnesses', may also be meant to bring out the guilt of the harlot. She was not ignorant of the issues. Witness had been borne.

John adds that when he saw her he *wondered with great admiration*. This last term is used in a sense now obsolete. It means 'wonder', and not admiration in our sense of the word. It reinforces the verb and stresses the greatness of John's astonishment. This may be because of the contrast between what he saw and what he expected. He had been invited to look at the judgment of the city (verse 1). Instead he sees a harlot magnificently arrayed. It is all most perplexing. It is also possible that some of his astonishment comes because he now sees for the first time the true nature of the Roman Empire, the contemporary representative of the great city.

ii. The significance of the woman and the beast (xvii. 7–14). Having shown John the harlot and the beast, the angel proceeds to explain their significance.

7. *The angel* inquired why John had wondered. There is an explanation, which he proceeds to give. He first says that he will explain *the mystery* (for this term see note on i. 20) *of the woman, and of the beast that carrieth her.* Notice that there is but one *mystery* for these two. They belong intimately together and to know the one is to know the other. The beast is again characterized by his heads and horns (see notes on xii. 3, xiii. 1).

8. The beast is the more important of the two and is explained first. It is not easy to understand all that we are told. Part of our difficulty lies in the fact that the symbolism seems to have different meanings. This is probably because the beast is fundamentally the principal henchman of Satan (the great red dragon) and Satan's work is done in different ways at different times.

The beast *was, and is not.* There may be an intentional contrast with i. 4. Again, in xiii. 3 we saw that the beast suffered a mortal wound, but recovered. The evil in mankind may seem to disappear, but it only seems. It always returns again. The Nero *redivivus* myth which many see behind this verse is an excellent illustration of what John means (though it does not exhaust his meaning). Nero lived out his evil life. He died. And in Domitian there appeared one who might be called a second Nero, Nero all over again. That the beast *was* means that he had put in an appearance on the earth. That he *is not* signifies that he is no longer in evidence.

But this does not mean that the last has been heard of him. He *shall ascend out of the* abyss (so rather than *bottomless pit*; see note on ix. 1). This identifies him with the forces of evil and indicates that his final sortie will be the climax of the efforts of the evil one. But it will fail. He will *go into perdition.* Not for one moment does John lose sight of the certainty of the overthrow of evil. But this is not the way it seems to them *that dwell on the earth,* an expression which denotes unregenerate mankind (see note on vi. 10), as the following *whose names were not written in the book of life* makes clear. The reminder that this goes back to *the foundation of the world* is a reminder of God's eternal purpose. But the unregenerate do not discern this. They *shall wonder* at the reappearance of the beast after his disappearance. The beast has a fascination for worldly minds.

9. Now comes the clue, the word to the wise. For *here*, see note on xiii. 18. John is not now speaking of some obvious truth which is apparent to all. But the wise can work it out. *The seven heads* are now said to be *seven mountains, on which the woman sitteth.* This identifies her with Rome, for the seven hills of that city are often mentioned in ancient literature. This does not mean that Rome exhausts the meaning of the symbol. As we have seen, the great city is every city and no city. It is civilized man, organized apart from God. It has its embodiment in every age. 'Babylon, then, is the world as the centre of seduction at any moment of history, particularly during this entire present dispensation. The harlot, Babylon, always opposes the bride, new Jerusalem (Rev. 21: 9 ff.)' (Hendriksen). In the first century, Rome was a striking embodiment of what John means by Babylon. In Rome as nowhere else men could see the city of man bent on its own blasphemous way, opposing with all its might the things of God.

10. *And there are seven kings* should probably be taken in the sense 'they are also seven kings' (RSV). The heads symbolize both hills and kings. Attention moves from the city to the city's rulers. *Five* of them *are fallen*, i.e. they have died. They are out of the way. At the moment of writing the sixth is in occupation of the throne (*one is*). The seventh *is not yet come*. His reign is still future.

What are we to make of all this? Many think that we should look to contemporary Rome as the illustration of these realities which is most prominently in John's mind. In this case the *kings* are the Roman emperors. Most agree that we should start with Augustus, not Julius Caesar. The five are then Augustus, Tiberius, Caligula, Claudius and Nero. The identification of the sixth depends on whether we accept Galba, Otho and Vitellius as emperors.[1] If so, he will be Galba. If not, he will be Vespasian, and Titus will be the seventh who is to have a short reign. Most accept the latter view, though without making it clear how John and his readers would agree on eliminating Galba, Otho and Vitellius.

A different point of view is put forward by, for example, Hendriksen. He thinks that the *kings* symbolize not individual rulers but empires. The five which have fallen are the Old Babylonian, the Assyrian, the New Babylonian, the Medo-Persian and the Graeco-Macedonian. The one that is the Roman, and the seventh, yet future, may stand for 'all antichristian governments between the fall of Rome and the final empire of antichrist'. Since the eighth is 'of the seven', the final kingdom of antichrist may well arise in one of the ancient seats of empire. Either interpretation is possible. Both remind us of the continuing power of the beast.

11. The symbolism becomes very complicated. *The beast* himself (characterized again as one *that was, and is not*, for which see note on verse 8) is now identified with *the eighth*, and is also said to be *of the seven*. If we reject Galba, Otho and Vitel-

---

[1] On the death of Nero, Galba assumed power, i.e. in June AD 68. But he was murdered on 15 January 69. Otho, who followed, was never unopposed and he committed suicide on 17 April. Vitellius followed, but Vespasian declared war against him on 1 July and he was killed on or about 20 December. Thus none of the three was ever able really to establish himself. But each bore the title 'emperor'.

lius, the eighth emperor was Domitian, and Swete reminds us that both pagan and Christian writers likened Domitian to Nero. John may mean that Domitian was 'Nero all over again' (cf. the identification of John the Baptist with Elijah, Mt. xi. 14). A difficulty in the way of this interpretation is how to apply *was, and is not* to Domitian. The answer may be that in one sense he was, and in another he was not Nero.

The eighth, be it emperor or empire, is equated with one of the seven. Now the seven have already been identified with the heads of the beast. So John is telling us that the beast, the basic source of evil, finds a kind of incarnation in each of the seven. In a way he is each of them. And he is especially the eighth. But, whether we interpret the passage in terms of kings or of empires, John is not concerned with the beast's career. Indeed, that is part of the difficulty. He does not say enough for us to make a firm identification. His interest is not in what the beast does, nor in his power. It is in his destruction: he *goeth into perdition.* So ultimately perishes all evil.

12. We move now to the beast's *ten horns* which we now find *are ten kings* (cf. Dn. vii. 24). These are sometimes taken as ten emperors of Rome, either including Galba, Otho and Vitellius, or taking the line a little further down in history. This is to ignore the angel's express statement, these *have received no kingdom as yet.* Their dominion is still future, so that they must be held to differ from the seven, of whom five have already fallen (verse 10). Others draw attention to the Nero *redivivus* myth, which held that Nero would return at the head of large armies from the east. These were often identified as Parthians. But whether this was done or not, it was thought that he would not be alone. He would have the support of other rulers.

It is something like this that John has in mind. At the End the beast will give rise not only to the eight already mentioned, but also to ten others. These may be earthly kings like the Parthian satraps who were practically independent rulers. Or they may be demonic figures. They are not the same as 'the kings of the earth', for these are pictured as mourning over the destruction of the great city (xviii. 9), whereas these ten 'shall hate the whore' (verse 16). They are antichrist's helpers, to be raised up in the last days.

The number *ten* may be their exact number, but it may also be symbolical and point to completeness. Two things are said about their kingly authority. The first is that they *receive power as kings one hour*. This may mean that their reigns will be short as men count time. Or it may mean short as God counts time. To men they may appear great, but to God they reign but for one unimportant hour. They are associated with antichrist. Their day will be as brief as his. The other thing is that they *receive power . . . with the beast*. They do not reign alone or in their own might. They are not to be understood apart from the beast.

13. This last point is underlined. The ten are not a group of independent thinkers. They *have one mind* (*gnōmē*). And their one mind leads them to *give their power and strength* (i.e. 'their might and authority', *tēn dunamin kai exousian autōn*) *unto the beast*. They are willing collaborators, not men forced into an unwelcome association.

14. John looks ahead to the end of time and sees them making war *with the Lamb*, but to no avail, for *the Lamb shall overcome them*. He is the supreme Lord and King, which is brought out by saying *he is Lord of lords, and King of kings* (cf. xix. 16, Dt. x. 17). Against such a Being the minions of the beast are in a hopeless situation. With the Lamb are those who are *called, and chosen, and faithful*. These are His retinue, not His resources. They represent no independent source of aid, for He needs none. Indeed, the very qualities named show that they depend on Him.

iii. The punishment of the whore (xvii. 15–18). This concluding section shows the disunity of the forces of evil, and also the certainty that God's words will be fulfilled.

15. The angel explains *the waters* on which the harlot sits (verse 1). They stand for a multitude of peoples over which the harlot is set (for *peoples*, etc., see note on v. 9). She has a great empire.

16. It is easy to think of the forces of evil as one united phalanx. But there is no cohesion in evil. Wicked men are not just one happy band of brothers. Being wicked, they give way to jealousy and hatred. At the climax their mutual hatreds will result in mutual destruction. There will be hatred between *the ten horns* and *the whore*, a hatred which will issue in deeds. They will *make her desolate and naked*, i.e. they will strip her of every resource (cf. the punishment of the harlot Oholibah, Ezk. xxiii. 25–30). They will *eat her flesh*, i.e. they will prey on her and consume her. And they will *burn her with fire*. She will be completely destroyed.

17. The basic reason for all this is in the divine will. *God hath put in their hearts to fulfil his will*. More. He causes them *to agree*. They will not quarrel and break up their coalition which might allow the harlot to escape. Her doom is from God. He sees to it that the kings have the unity they need for their act of destruction. *They give their kingdom unto the beast* till God's *words* are fulfilled (for the plural *words*, cf. xix. 9, xxi. 5, xxii. 6; it may indicate a multiplicity in the purposes of God). There is treachery on the part of the beast who sustains the whore (verse 3). But God's purposes are not overthrown. The beast may defeat his own supporters. He will never defeat God.

18. The woman's identity is now revealed, albeit in a guarded fashion. John learns two things about her: she is a *great city* and she *reigneth over the kings of the earth*. In John's own day this stands for Rome. But in the end-time it is man in organized community (see note on xi. 8).

b. The judgment of Babylon (xviii. 1–xix. 5)

In vivid and unforgettable language John outlines the judgment of the great city. He describes her fall and its effect on those who were in sympathy with her. There are many coincidences of language with the description of the fall of Tyre (Ezk. xxvi–xxviii) and that of Babylon (Is. xiii, xiv, xxi, Je. l, li). But there is more than similarity of language. John has caught the spirit of the prophetic doom songs. As Kiddle puts it, 'We cannot grasp anything like the full power of John's words unless we are familiar with the passages to which he alludes. The song in REVELATION is a resounding echo of the passionate faith and stormy exulting in the doom-songs of the great prophets . . . chap. xviii. is at once a "new song" in the sense that it has passed through the fire of the prophet's imagination, and also a summary of all prophetic oracles on the doom of unrighteous peoples.'

We miss the point of it all if we conclude with many modern critics that John is concerned only to denounce contemporary Rome. Byron could say,

> When falls the Coliseum, Rome shall fall;
> And when Rome falls—the World.

It is something like this that John has in mind. He is catching up all that the prophets have said as they announce the doom of Tyre or Babylon or Nineveh. But he is thinking not of the fall of one city or empire but of the collapse of civilization. Final judgment means the overthrow of all that opposes itself to God.

i. The fall of Babylon (xviii. 1-3). An angel announces the fall of the great city. We already know that it will be the forces of evil that will bring this about (xvii. 16) and the angel does not repeat this. He concentrates on the result.

1. Once again events are set in motion by an angel, this one being marked out as *having great power* (i.e. 'authority', *exousian*). This is one of few places in Revelation where angels are said to have authority, though authority is often said to be 'given' to various forces of evil. The expression indicates that this angel is particularly important, an impression which is confirmed by the fact that he is possessed of a glory that shone like light over all the earth (cf. Ezk. xliii. 2).

2. He cried *with a strong voice*. This is the only place in the book where the adjective *strong* (*ischuros*) is applied to a voice (though cf. its use in 'the voice of *mighty* thunderings', xix. 6). The adjective is applied to angels (v. 2, x. 1, xviii. 21), and they speak in 'great' (*megalē*) voices. The statement that

Babylon is fallen is repeated, (cf. xiv. 8, where see note, Is. xxi. 9). The city's doom is still future but it is so certain that it can be spoken of as already accomplished. For *Babylon* see note on xiv. 8, and for 'the great city' on xi. 8. The angel speaks of the complete desolation of the city under three heads. First, it has become *the habitation of devils.* It is deserted by men and regarded as a dwelling only by devils. Secondly, it is *the hold of every foul spirit,* the word *hold* being the one rendered *cage* later in this verse and 'prison' in xx. 7. Here it means something like 'haunt'. It is the place where evil spirits have their being. Thirdly, it is *a cage of every unclean and hateful bird.* Such birds commonly haunt deserted places, and this will be the significance of the term. We should perhaps notice that the Old Testament mentions Babylon as becoming the habitation of some curious creatures (Is. xiii. 21 f., Je. li. 37; cf. also Is. xxxiv. 10 ff.).

3. The reason for the desolation is the sin of the city in corrupting others. For drinking *the wine of the wrath of her fornication* see the note on xiv. 8. Not content with sinning herself she brought others to share in her sin. The *kings of the earth* may include here the people over whom they ruled. More probably the thought is that the kings themselves had become wealthy through their countries' trade with the harlot. This is clearly the reason for mentioning *the merchants of the earth.* Strong words are used of both. The kings *committed fornication with her.* The merchants became rich *through the abundance of her delicacies.* This last word *(strēnous)* means 'wantonness', 'luxury' (MM).

ii. A call to leave the city (xviii. 4, 5). Persecuted and harried as they were, the people of God must have been sorely tempted to come to terms with the city. She could not only cause their persecution to cease, but make their lives rich and comfortable. But it is important that they see the issues for what they really are and have nothing to do with unclean things. So they are called to come out of her. Such a call is frequent in the Old Testament from Abram on (Gn. xii. 1,

xix. 12 ff., Nu. xvi. 23 ff., Is. xlviii. 20, lii. 11, Je. l. 8, li. 6, 45, Zc. ii. 6 f.). And it is not lacking in the New Testament (2 Cor. vi. 14 f., Eph. v. 11, 1 Tim. v. 22). Compromise with worldliness is fatal. God's people must, while playing their full role in the community, hold themselves aloof from the world in many of its aspects.

4. Again John hears an unidentified voice from heaven. *Another* shows that it is from a different speaker. The words *my people* make it seem that the voice is from God, but the next verse can scarcely be from Him, though the speaker appears to be the same. Charles suggests that it may be Christ who speaks. The voice calls on God's people to leave the city and not be *partakers of her sins* (cf. Eph. v. 11, 1 Tim. v. 22). In this way they will ensure that they *receive not of her plagues* (cf. Je. l. 8 f., li. 6, 45).

Some critics make much of the fact that the city is regarded as already destroyed in verse 2. They think John has made use of sources which contradict each other or is guilty of careless writing. No such hypothesis is needed. They fail to note that past, present and future tenses are all used of the destruction of the city. This is a song, not a piece of prose carefully arranged in chronological order. This verse follows quite naturally on verse 2. The call to God's people is supremely important. John is writing to believers, some at least of whom did not perceive the urgency of the situation. They were ready to compromise with the vices of Babylon. In a sense this appeal is the key to the whole chapter. John is not gloating over the city's downfall. He is appealing to Christians to see the realities of the situation and to act accordingly.

5. In a vivid figure John depicts the sins of the city as heaped in a pile that reaches heaven (cf. Je. li. 9; the word rendered *reached* means literally 'were glued together'). Then the imagery changes and we are reminded that God does not forget the evils that men do (cf. xvi. 19). From the standpoint of the persecuted church it might seem that evil men were getting away with their sins. From the standpoint of heaven it is plain that God is not mocked. He remembers.

iii. Judgment on the city (xviii. 6–8). The voice calls for
the city to be destroyed completely. Though she had no
notion of the fate that awaits her the speaker is sure that
destruction is coming.

6. It is just possible that a new voice is to be understood
here, a voice breaking in from the earth. But there is no indication of this and it is perhaps best to think of the same
speaker. But there is certainly a change in those to whom the
words are addressed. Verses 4 f. are addressed to the people
of God, but this verse to God's ministers of judgment. They
are commanded to do to the city what she has done to others
(cf. Je. l. 29). *Reward* (*apodote*) has about it the air of recompense. It denotes not revenge but just requital. *Double unto her*
double looks for punishment in full measure (cf. Is. xl. 2).
There is tremendous depth of feeling against the guilty city.
There is also the recognition that the simple 'an eye for an eye
and a tooth for a tooth' is not sufficient. In view of Babylon's
fuller culture and enlightenment, a more severe punishment is
required. She has mixed a cup for others (so rather than
filled; the verb is that rendered 'poured out' in xiv. 10, where
see note). So the voice calls 'mix her a drink of double strength!'
(Phillips).

7. The voice continues to call for condign punishment. It
now looks for torment in proportion to the way the city
glorified herself and 'waxed wanton' (*estrēniasen*; the verb is
found only here and in verse 9 in the New Testament). She
has acted irresponsibly. *In her heart* points to a deep-seated
attitude and possibly one of which she is quite unconscious.
She sees herself as *a queen* supreme over all, and does not
envisage a change. It is curious that she says she is *no widow*,
but this is possibly taken from old Babylon's view of herself
(Is. xlvii. 7 f.). *I . . . shall see no sorrow* looks for the same happy
state to continue, the illusion of the materially prosperous in
every age.

8. This is the reason (*therefore*) for her sudden punishment,
which will take place in one day (cf. Is. xlvii. 9). There is no

warning and no delay. Four *plagues* are singled out. *Death*, of course, should end everything. The meaning may be that, though some men in the city die, the city continues for a time. Or we could translate the word as 'pestilence' (rsv). With this are linked *mourning, famine* and *fire*. Together all this means disaster for the city. And this will certainly happen, *for strong is the Lord God who judgeth her*. The word *strong* is specially emphatic. The might of the Lord must not be overlooked. And *judgeth* is important. This is not an arbitrary display of power. God inflicts on the city merited judgment.

iv. A lament over the city's fall (xviii. 9-19). John proceeds to bring out the total destruction of the great city by picturing the lamentation of those who had cause to mourn her passing, the kings, the merchants, those whose trade was on the sea. None is depicted as loving the city for herself, but only for what they could get out of her. She might seduce and enrich men but there was nothing lovely in her. 'With a touch of grim humour he paints them as standing at a safe distance from the conflagration, and contenting themselves with idle lamentations' (Swete).

Rome was the centre of the world's trade and during the first century engaged in unparalleled ostentation and extravagance. Barclay has a series of quotations from contemporary pagan authors which amply document the senseless waste habitually practised in the city (e.g. Vitellius, emperor for less than a year, managed to spend £7,000,000, mainly on food). Contemporary Rome formed a magnificent pattern for John's Babylon. It shows that John was not a mere fanatic denouncing without cause. It also illustrates the way the whole world may depend on trade with one great centre.

9. Earth's rulers will be exceedingly distressed at the city's overthrow, for they have been closely associated with her in the sins that brought about her fate (for *lived deliciously, strēniasantes*, see note on verse 7). They gaze on the city as she burns.

10. But they keep their distance for fear lest they be caught up in *her torment*. The onomatopoeic word, *ouai, ouai*, doubled for emphasis, brings out their grief. The meaning is rather 'Woe to the great city' (cf. Is. v. 8, 11, 20, etc.) than 'Alas! alas! thou great city' (rsv). Babylon is characterized as *mighty* as well as *great*. The might of Babylon was all too obvious to the little church. But John wants believers to see that no might can stand against that of the Lord God. Even as he mentions her might he speaks of her destruction. In verse 8 the suddenness of her destruction was emphasized as her plagues were seen coming 'in one day'. Now this is intensified, as her judgment is seen coming *in one hour*! It is overwhelming. That the kings speak of judgment shows that they recognize the justice of what is happening.

11. *The merchants of the earth* join in. They wail (*klaiousin* means a loud wailing, not silent weeping) and mourn (note that the verbs are present tense, as in rsv). Their reason? *No man buyeth their merchandise any more*. Financial loss, not esteem for the city, prompts their distress.

12. John gives a list of cargoes for which there will no longer be buyers. *Gold* and *silver* are obvious enough. *Precious stones* is singular and may possibly mean costly stone like granite. If precious stone in our sense, then *pearls* are singled out as specially important. Next comes fine clothing of various sorts. For *purple* and *scarlet* see note on xvii. 3 f. *Silk* was imported to Rome from China in great abundance. *Thyine wood* is 'hard, fragrant and prettily marked and therefore is much esteemed by cabinet makers . . . the Romans called the wood citron wood and like it immensely'.[1] The veining and colour seem both to have varied considerably which may explain the *all*. *Ivory* is included, as also costly wooden vessels. *Brass*, as elsewhere in the New Testament, should be understood as bronze (see note on 1 Cor. xiii. 1, *TNTC*).

13. The list continues with spices of various kinds, then items of drink and food. Rome's *wheat* came largely from

[1] W. E. Shewell-Cooper, *Plants and Fruits of the Bible*, 1962, pp. 121f.

Egypt and so is appropriate in a list used by sea traders. Next come animals, and finally men. *Slaves* is literally 'bodies', an eloquent commentary on the way slave-traders approached their subject. *Souls of men* also means slaves (as in the Hebrew of Ezk. xxvii. 13). It reminds us of another aspect of the evil that was Rome, namely its disrespect for persons. And in various ways all the world's great empires have had their traffic in 'the souls of men'.

14. The city is addressed directly, and informed that her luxuries are things of the past. *Fruits* she *lusted after* are gone. The *dainty* things (*ta lipara*) are 'the oily' or 'fat' things, and so luxuries. The *goodly* (*ta lampra*) are 'the splendid things'. The former refers primarily to exotic foodstuffs, the latter to clothing and decorative objects. Men will no longer find them in the great city. The wealth of first-century Rome, which evidently lies behind this passage, was proverbial. Thus we read in the Talmud, 'Ten *ḳabs* of wealth descended to the world: nine were taken by the early Romans and one by the rest of the world' (*Kidd.* 49b).

15. It is those who have a vested interest in the city who bewail her passing (and the passing of their profits!). First are the merchants. Like the kings, they do not approach to help or to offer comfort. But they will stand (future tense) at a distance for *the fear of her torment.* They, too, wail and mourn (the same verbs as in verse 11).

16. Now comes the content of their dirge. Like the kings, they begin with a doubled 'Woe' and a reference to the great city. But whereas the kings went on to speak of her might, the merchants refer to her clothing and her wealth.

17. Once more they resemble the kings when they say *in one hour.* The suddenness and completeness of the destruction strikes them. Though the city has *so great riches* all has *come to nought.* It is the loss of the wealth, not any concern for people, that the merchants express.

Next it is the turn of all seafarers to mourn (cf. Ezk. xxvii. 28 ff.). First to be mentioned is *every shipmaster* (*kubernētēs*), but it is not easy to be certain exactly who is meant by the following expression. *All the company in ships* is literally 'everyone who sails for a place'. This may be meant to cover all who travel by sea, or perhaps merchants who travel with their wares on board ship and transact their business when they reach port. If this latter can be substantiated we have references to captains, merchants, and sailors, with the final expression ('all whose trade is on the sea', rsv) comprehensive enough to cover all three. All these had secured their livelihood from the activities of the great city and accordingly all lament her passing. But, like the groups previously mentioned, they stand *afar off*. No-one stretches out a hand to help. The great city has brought profit to many but affection to none.

18. They *cried* out; the imperfect tense may denote a continuing action. We have had the future of the mourning of the kings (verse 9), and both present (11, Gk.) and future (15) of the merchants. Now the seafarers stood (aorist, 17), and 'were crying out' (imperfect). The first point in their dirge is the incomparableness of the great city. None was like her (the expression is like the Hebrew of Ezk. xxvii. 32, though lxx differs).

19. The sailors carry their mourning further than the other groups. They *cast dust on their heads* (cf. Ezk. xxvii. 30), they were crying out, wailing and mourning. For the third time we have the conjunction of these two latter verbs (cf. verses 11, 15), for the third time the doubled 'Woe' to the great city (10, 16), and for the third time the suddenness of it all is expressed in the phrase *in one hour* (10, 17). And as with the merchants, what excites this distress is the loss of profits.

v. The destruction of the city (xviii. 20–24). From the forces of evil, attention switches to those of good. First there is a call to rejoicing on the part of the righteous, then an emphatic statement of the complete overthrow of the city, and finally a brief statement of the justification for this overthrow.

20. The call to rejoice at the destruction of the city appals some modern students. But we should notice in the first place that this is not a vindictive outcry. It is a longing that justice be done. And in the second, John and his readers were not armchair critics pedantically discussing rights and wrongs in an academic fashion. They were existentially committed. They had staked their lives on the truth of the Christian faith. Paul could point out that if Christians had nothing to look for other than the things of this life they were more to be pitied than all men (1 Cor. xv. 19).

But John wrote out of a passionate conviction that they were not to be pitied. It was the Almighty God with whom they had cast in their lot. This meant great suffering here and now. It meant that they were persecuted and despised. But it meant also that they were sure of ultimate vindication. It is this vindication for which this verse cries. It is a passionate cry uttered out of the deep conviction that right must triumph and which eagerly welcomes that triumph.

Rejoice is in marked contrast with the mourning of the previous verses. The appeal is comprehensive, being addressed to heaven, the saints (so the better mss), apostles and prophets. Curiously angels are not listed, though they figure so prominently in this book. Perhaps they are included in *thou heaven*. *God hath avenged you on her* is better 'God has given judgment for you against her!' (rsv). The verb is *ekrinen* which is concerned with justice, not vengeance. Wrongs had been done to the saints and these are now put right.

21. *A mighty angel* (*heis angelos ischuros*) does not appear to be paralleled in this book. It is certainly unusual, but in a book concerned with power it emphasizes the might of this representative of heaven. The throwing of a great stone into the sea is a symbolic action like many recorded in the prophets. It recalls Jeremiah's action in having a stone attached to a book cast into the Euphrates, thus symbolizing the destruction of Babylon (Je. li. 63). Here it points to the complete and violent destruction of the city. It *shall be found no more at all* is an emphatic expression for the complete and final overthrow of the city (cf. Ezk. xxvi. 21; here an emphatic double negative, *ou mē*, and the addition of *eti* drives the point home).

22. Now comes a list of things which will no longer be heard or done in the city. First come various kinds of music (cf. Ezk. xxvi. 13). The word rendered *musicians* (*mousikōn*) might be neuter with the meaning 'instruments of music'. But as it is preceded and followed by words denoting performers it is likely that this does too, in which case it probably denotes 'minstrels' (rsv). The city had evidently taken kindly to the arts, but their practice will cease. There is an air of finality about *shall be heard no more at all in thee* (there is a double negative *ou mē*, reinforced by *eti*, and this continues throughout the lists). Like the arts, craftsmanship of all kinds had evidently flourished, but will be no more. The cessation of *the sound of a millstone* points to the disappearance of normal daily life with its routine activities such as preparation of food. Bit by bit John is picturing the stilling of all the life of the great city.

23. Lamps (*luchnos* means 'lamp' not *candle*) will no longer shine. Marriage will cease (cf. Je. vii. 34, etc.). *For* is difficult. It should introduce the reason for the foregoing, but it is hard to see the connection. Perhaps the thought is that Babylon's very greatness has brought about her destruction. The city's merchants were the earth's grandees. Or the thought may be that they concentrated on greatness and interpreted it in terms of material prosperity. They forgot God. The point of the second *for* is plainer. Mingled with their profit-making went all manner of evils. All the nations were deceived by the city's *sorceries* (cf. Na. iii. 4).

24. Babylon was spoken of in the third person in verse 21. Then she was directly addressed in verses 22, 23. Now she is described in the third person once more. In this city was found *the blood* of God's people, specified as *prophets* and *saints*. To this is added *all that were slain upon the earth*. This is another indication that we must take 'the great city' symbolically. There is no one city on earth of which this can be said. Babylon is clearly a symbol for all earthly cities (cf. the similar statement about Jerusalem, Mt. xxiii. 35).

vi. A thanksgiving for the judgment of Babylon (xix. 1-5). The passage on the judgment of Babylon concludes with a mighty thanksgiving in heaven at the conclusion of God's judgments.

1. John tells us that he heard 'as a great voice' (not *a great voice*). This is somewhat puzzling because there seems no doubt but that he is telling us of the song of a heavenly host. We must take it as a further example of his reserve in describing heavenly realities. The singers are not named, but they are probably angels, the throng of v. 11. They sing a song of praise. It begins *Alleluia*. This transliterates a Hebrew expression meaning 'Praise Jah', i.e. 'Praise God'. It is the typical Hebrew note of praise. The word is found four times in this passage (verses 1, 3, 4, 6), and not again in the New Testament. The Hebrew equivalent occurs a number of times in the Psalms, but it is always translated. This is thus the only passage in the English Bible where 'Alleluia' occurs. The song ascribes to God *salvation*, and *glory* and *power* (*honour* is not read in the better MSS). The events just described form an illustration of all three.

2. The first *for* gives the justification for the outburst of praise in a general statement, the second justifies the first with a specific example, the overthrow of the great city. As often, her overthrow is described not in terms of sheer power, but as a judgment (*ekrinen, he hath judged*). Moffatt misses the note of justice with his rendering, 'he has doomed the great Harlot'. But there is more than doom. Justice is done. *The great whore* corrupted the earth *with her fornication*, and all heaven rejoices accordingly at her overthrow.

We must bear in mind in all this our constant readiness to be corrupted. 'The world likes a complacent, reasonable religion, and so it is always ready to revere some pale Galilean image of Jesus, some meagre anaemic Messiah, and to give Him a moderate rational homage. . . . The truth is that we have often committed adultery with alien ideologies, confounded the Gospel with the religions of nature, and imbibed the wine of pagan doctrines and false principles and deceitful practices. We have sought to bend the will of God to serve the ends of man, to alter the Gospel and shape the Church to conform to the fashions of the times' (Torrance).

Ultimately this is of no avail. The great whore is judged. 'The moral law can no more be broken than the law of gravitation; it can only be illustrated!' (Kepler). Perhaps we should add a comment of Love: 'We like to think of a Hallelujah chorus in the style of Handel, where the Hallelujah is the triumphant worship of the reigning Lord. And John comes eventually to such a chorus. But he is realistic enough to know that first there must be the equally triumphant rejoicing over the downfall of evil at the hand of God.' The great whore corrupted the earth. But she did more. She shed the blood of God's servants. She had to be called to account.

3. A second time the throng praised God. It is not clear whether on this occasion the song consists of one word, *Alleluia*, with the information added that the smoke of the city ascended perpetually (cf. Is. xxxiv. 10), or whether the latter is part of the song. Either way we must not think of their attitude as negative. Their God is a Creator. The destruction of the great whore is but the prelude to the new era: 'their hallelujah rings out the old, but it also rings in the new' (Kiddle).

4. The inhabitants of heaven who are closest to God join in the praise. The twenty-four elders and the four living ones prostrate themselves and worship. The specific mention of *the throne* points us to God in His majesty. They utter two words, *Amen*, which indicates their assent to what has been said, and *Alleluia*, the great word of praise (cf. Ps. cvi. 48 for the conjunction of these two words).

5. Yet once more John reports a voice whose speaker is not named. It came *out of the throne*, and so must be thought of as emanating from God. But it is not the voice of God nor of Christ, as the words *Praise our God* make clear. The voice calls on all God's people to join in the chorus of praise. The lowliness of men before God is suggested in the double description *servants* (*douloi*, 'slaves') and *ye that fear him*, while the universality of the appeal is sounded in the *all* and in the *both small and great*.

c. The marriage of the Lamb (xix. 6-10)

The triumph of the servants of God is now brought out with the imagery of a heavenly marriage. The church is seen as the bride of Christ.

6. Once more John speaks of an unidentified voice. This time, however, he describes it in some detail, though with his usual reserve in speaking of heavenly realities. His thrice repeated *as* shows that the voice is not exactly 'the voice of a great multitude', etc. but a voice resembling these things. It is likened to the voice of *a great multitude*, to the sound of *many waters* (cf. i. 15 and the note there), and to *mighty thunderings* (cf. xviii. 2 for the use of *ischuros* of a voice). The voice then is extremely powerful, but it is also musical (cf. xiv. 2). As with others in this chapter, the voice begins with *Alleluia*. The note of praise is strong and sustained. The reason given is not the overthrow of Babylon, though that cannot be out of mind. It is rather that *the Lord God omnipotent reigneth*. The positive rather than the negative is struck. *Omnipotent* renders *pantokratōr* (for which see note on i. 8 where it is rendered 'Almighty').

7. The voice calls on those who hear to rejoice and be exultant (for this combination, cf. Mt. v. 12). After what has gone, we naturally think that glory is to be ascribed to God because His power has been so strikingly displayed in the destruction of the city. But not so. The voice concerns itself not with the past, but with the future. It calls to praise because the marriage of the Lamb is about to take place. The bride has *made herself ready*. This imagery is fairly widespread in the Bible. Israel is often thought of as Yahweh's bride (Is. liv. 6, Ezk. xvi. 8 ff., Ho. ii. 14 ff., etc.), and marriage symbolism is not uncommon in the Gospels (Mt. xxii. 2 ff., xxv. 1 ff., Mk. ii. 19, Jn. iii. 29). Paul sometimes employs this figure (2 Cor. xi. 2, Eph. v. 25 ff.). In Revelation marriage imagery is employed in xix. 9, xxi. 2, 9, xxii. 17 (some think the supper in

iii. 20 may possibly be understood in the same way). We should have expected here the word 'bride' (*numphē*, as in xviii. 23, xxi. 2, 9, xxii. 17) instead of *wife* (*gunē*). Nothing seems to turn on the choice of word, however.

8. The song concludes with the affirmation that it was given to the bride to be clothed in *fine linen, clean and white* (contrast the clothing of the harlot, xvii. 4, xviii. 16). John adds the explanation that this linen is *the righteousness of saints*. This is usually understood in the sense 'the righteous deeds of the saints' (RSV). But the word *dikaiōma* never seems elsewhere to have the meaning 'righteous deeds'. It always denotes 'ordinance', or something of the kind. 'Sentence of justification' would be much more in accordance with New Testament usage (see note on xv. 4). The plural will indicate that many individuals are involved. Such a meaning is demanded in this context by the verb *was granted*. This clothing is given to the saints. It is not provided by them. The white robes of the multitude in vii. 9, 14 were not provided by any righteous acts on the part of the wearers, but were the result of washing in 'the blood of the Lamb'. So is it here.

9. Now comes a command to John to write. Earlier he was commanded to write the contents of the whole book (i. 11, 19), and there is a similar order for each of the messages to the seven churches (chapters ii, iii). John was forbidden to write what the seven thunders said (x. 4), but was instructed to write down the little saying about the dead who die in the Lord (xiv. 13). He will be commanded to write down yet another saying (xxi. 5). For *blessed*, etc., see note on i. 3. Those bidden to *the marriage supper of the Lamb* are described in terms of their call (there may be a hint of permanence in the perfect participle *keklēmenoi*). The divine initiative is important.

The speaker adds that these are the *true sayings of God*, thus adding solemn emphasis. Some have wondered that these particular words should be singled out, for they do not appear to be more than usually noteworthy. But they had great point for the church in the conditions in which she found herself. In the troubled days of the persecutions it did need emphasis that it was the persecuted saints who were blessed, not their persecutors.

10. John prostrated himself to worship the speaker. This can only be because he thought him divine (there are one or two places in the Old Testament where men prostrate themselves before angels, as Nu. xxii. 31, 1 Ch. xxi. 16; but these refer to homage, not worship of the creature). There is no place in Christianity for the worship of any but God. John is immediately checked with 'See not' (*hora mē*). The abruptness of this expression lends emphasis to the prohibition. It is clear that some early Christians were tempted to worship angels (Col. ii. 18). The present passage rebukes and discourages the practice.

The angel links himself with John by calling himself *thy fellowservant*. There are not unimportant differences between angels and men, but the really significant thing is that they are both 'servants' (*douloi*) of their common Lord. The angel further belongs to those who *have the testimony of Jesus*, an expression which is explained as *the spirit of prophecy*. There are, however, ambiguities here. The *testimony of Jesus* might mean 'the testimony which Jesus bore' (and is now committed to His servants), or it might mean 'the testimony borne to Jesus'. If we take the former meaning the whole will signify that the message of Jesus is the spirit, the heart of all prophecy. 'Jesus and his revelation of God, which Paul calls "the mind of Christ", is the content of the prophet's message as it is of what John has been told to write in his book' (Preston and Hanson). If we accept the latter meaning, then the significance is that the true spirit of prophecy always manifests itself in bearing witness to Jesus. The Old Testament prophets, New Testament prophets such as John, and the angels, all alike bear their witness to the Son of God.

It is not easy to decide between these, and it is quite possible that the ambiguity is intentional. At any rate, both meanings are true, and we may profitably see both here. The angel makes one other point when he commands John to *worship God*. Worship is to be offered to Him alone.

d. The final victory (xix. 11–xx. 15)

The great victory has been won. The power of evil has been broken. There remains only to complete the final ordering of things, by putting the wicked away permanently and introducing the righteous to heaven. The preceding section has prepared us for a vision of the Bridegroom. But, as often, John surprises us. He gives us instead a vision of a Warrior.

i. One called 'The Word of God' (xix. 11–16). The vision of 'The Word of God' in all His splendour leaves no doubt as to the final dominion of the risen Lord.

11. John saw *heaven opened* (cf. iv. 1). And he saw vividly (*and behold*) *a white horse.* The colour signifies victory (see note on vi. 2). In the following description almost everything said of Christ has a parallel or a near parallel elsewhere. The one really distinctive thing is the white horse. The thought stressed here accordingly is that the Christ now goes to His final triumph. Some identify the rider here with the one in chapter vi. But there seems no reason for this. The only point in common is the colour of the horse, and this is not sufficient to establish the point.

John gives a detailed description. First comes the name, which is fitting, for the name expresses the person. He was called *Faithful and True* (cf. iii. 14). *In righteousness,* in accordance with the character expressed in these terms, He judges and makes war (cf. Is. xi. 4). The present tenses of the verbs point to His habitual action rather than to any one specific occasion. There is no vindictiveness, no lust of conquest. Both verbs are important for John's readers. That He judges mattered immensely in view of the injustice with which John's readers were confronted. And that He makes war must have appealed to men who, persecuted as they were by the mighty, looked for a strong helper.

12. His eyes are likened to *a flame of fire* (as in i. 14). He searches out all things. Nothing can be hidden from Him. There is also a suggestion of majesty, which is further brought out with *on his head were many crowns* (*diadēmata*, crowns of royalty). He exercised widespread dominion. *He had a name written* (where it is not said), known only to Himself. For the significance of the name in antiquity see note on ii. 3. In verses 11, 13, the name expresses what can be known of Christ's being. Here we are reminded that there are hidden depths. Christ's person can never be completely understood by petty human minds. It is possible that there is another thought. Those who practised magic in the first century believed that to know a name gave power over him whose name it was. John may well be saying that no-one has power over Christ. He is supreme. His name is known only to Himself.

13. He *was clothed* (perfect tense) in a robe *dipped* (perfect again; perhaps both indicate permanent result) *in blood*. This will be a reference to Calvary. Christ overcame by shedding His blood. Some have thought that it is the blood of a defeated foe that is meant, and indeed, Charles thinks that 'the idea that the blood on His Vesture is His own . . . cannot be entertained'. It is not impossible that John has both ideas in mind, but it is more than difficult to hold that he writes of blood without a thought of the blood shed on the cross. In this book he repeatedly makes the point that it is in His capacity as 'a Lamb as it had been slain' that Christ conquers. He overcame, not by shedding the blood of others, but by shedding His own.

Now for the third time we have a reference to His name. He is called *The Word of God* (cf. Jn. i. 1). 'The Word' was an expression full of meaning to men of varied backgrounds in the first century. Its use by certain Greek philosophers, notably Heraclitus and the Stoics, had familiarized men with the idea that the Word was the rational principle pervading the universe, a kind of world soul. Among the Hebrews 'the Word of God' was a reverent periphrasis for the divine name. To both Jew and Greek 'the Word of God' pointed to what was supremely important and supremely significant.[1] This is

---

[1] See further the note on Jn. i. 1 and Additional Note A in my forthcoming commentary on John in the *New International Commentary on the New Testament*.

the only place in Scripture where the full expression 'the Word of God' is applied to Christ (though cf. Jn. i. 1, 1 Jn. i. 1).

14. Heaven's armies *followed him,* also on *white horses.* Their clothing resembles that of the bride in verse 8 (except that *leukon,* 'white', replaces *lampron,* 'bright', 'splendid'). John does not say whether these are saints or angels. Probably they are the latter. The saints are regarded rather as the bride of the Lamb. Swete sees a reference to angels and he comments on the fact that they are clothed in white, whereas their Leader's robe is dipped in blood: 'He only has had experience of mortal conflict; for them bloodshed and death are impossible.' Though they are called *armies* there is no mention of weapons and neither here nor elsewhere are they depicted as taking hostile action. The victory against evil is won by their Leader alone.

15. After this brief glance at His armies we come back to the Word. There is a stern side to His nature, and John speaks of *a sharp sword* as going out of His mouth. This points to the power of His Word (cf. Gn. i for the power of the divine Word). For it is with the Word and not with armies that He smites the nations (cf. Is. xi. 4). The armies play no part except as backdrop to the Word. They are a fitting retinue, but He does not depend on them. *He shall rule them with a rod of iron* (cf. ii. 27, xii. 5) shows that He has absolute authority over the nations. He cannot be resisted. There is an emphatic *he* (*autos*) with both *shall rule* and *treadeth.* He and no other does these things. The figure of treading out the winepress of God's wrath (cf. Is. lxiii. 1 ff.) points to the complete overthrow of those who resist God. Significantly He is spoken of as *Almighty* (see note on i. 8).

16. Now comes a fourth reference to Christ's name, this name being written *on his vesture and on his thigh.* Charles thinks this means that 'as they thunder along, their garments stream behind them, and so on the thigh of the Leader is disclosed the name'. Others think that the name is on that part of the coat which falls over the thigh. But the meaning seems rather to be that the name is written in two places. That on the clothing will mean that this is the name for all to see, but it is difficult to see a reason for its being on the thigh. *King of kings, and Lord of lords* (cf. xvii. 14) refers to Christ in His capacity as supreme Ruler. It accords well with the preceding scenes of conquest and of power. John leaves us in no doubt as to who is supreme Lord.

ii. The overthrow of the beast and of the false prophet (xix. 17–21). John devotes a small section to the final overthrow of the beast and his various helpers. They have had their little day and now are put in their rightful places.

17. John sees 'one angel' (for this form of expression, cf. xviii. 21) *standing in the sun.* The position is apparently a vantage-point from which he can more easily control the birds to whom he cries with *a loud voice.* For *the midst of heaven,* cf. viii. 13, xiv. 6. He calls them to 'the great supper of God' (rather than to *the supper of the great God*). This will mean 'the great supper which God will provide'. Or the expression may be a Semitism with the significance 'a supper great to God', i.e. a very great supper. Either way it is in sharp contrast with the marriage supper of verse 9.

18. The supper is explained. It is to be a feast on the corpses of a great host of earthlings (cf. Ezk. xxxix. 4, 17–20). The description emphasizes universality. It starts with kings, and goes on to officers, to heroes, to horses and riders, and to all men, free and slave, small and great. None is excluded. The overthrow of evil is total.

19. The battle is prepared. John sees the forces of evil drawn up in battle array for their last struggle with the good. The beast is at the head. With him are earth's kings and their armies. Their object is to fight against *him that sat on the horse, and against his army.*

20. John says nothing about the battle. He proceeds immediately from the drawing up of the armies to the seizing of the beast. He may mean that there was no battle. Though the forces of evil appear mighty they are completely helpless when confronted by the Christ. So the beast was forcibly captured (*epiasthē*), and with him *the false prophet* (see note on xvi. 13). He is still characterized by the 'signs' (*miracles* is *sēmeia*; see note on xiii. 13) he did and by means of which he deceived those who had the mark of the beast. This was the significant work of the false prophet. But now neither he nor the beast has any power. *These both were cast alive into a lake of fire burning with brimstone.* Actually it is 'the', not 'a', lake of fire, and it is mentioned again in xx. 10, 14, 15, xxi. 8. Being cast into the lake of fire signifies utter destruction. All that the beast stood for is no more.

21. *The remnant*, i.e. the rest of the beast's followers, perished. They were slain by the sword which went out of the mouth of the Rider on the white horse. That is to say, it was His Word which destroyed them (cf. Is. xi. 4). The picture of destruction is completed with the statement that the birds were sated with the flesh of the slain, a common piece of imagery for final disaster.

iii. Satan bound (xx. 1-3). From the beast John turns to the beast's master. He sees Satan seized by an angel and imprisoned in the abyss for 1,000 years. This brings us to one of the most difficult parts of this entire book. There have been endless disputes, some of them very bitter, over the way to understand this chapter. Evangelicals have divided from one another and sometimes have been quite intolerant of views other than those of their own group. It is necessary to approach the chapter with humility and charity.[1]

Pre-millennialists hold that at Christ's return the Christian dead will be raised, and believers still living on earth will be caught up to meet Him in the air (1 Thes. iv. 17). They will reign on earth with Christ for 1,000 years (the millennium). After this Satan will be released for a time. This short period will be followed by the raising of the rest of the dead. In this way there is an explanation of the two resurrections. Finally

[1] For an excellent account of the divergent views, see Walvoord, pp. 282–290. Walvoord himself favours the pre-millennial view.

there comes the judgment of the great white throne. Post-millennialists differ in seeing the return of Christ as taking place after the millennium. Sometimes they see the millennium as standing for the triumph of the gospel in this present age, some-times as a literal 1,000 years at the end of time. A-millennialists hold that there is no literal millennium. The 1,000-year period is symbolical. It stands for the whole time between the life of Jesus on earth and His second coming. They usually see the first resurrection as the new birth of the believer, his rising from the death of sin.

The idea of a millennium was congenial to Jewish thought. Some Jews certainly held that there would be a Messianic kingdom of limited duration and that only after this would the saved enter heaven. In *4 Ezra* vii. 28 this kingdom is said to last for 400 years. Again, some Jews held that the world's history would correspond to the days of creation. History would last for 6,000 years (one 'day' of history being 1,000 years; cf. Ps. xc. 4, 2 Pet. iii. 8). After this there would be a sabbath of 1,000 years before the final state of blessedness (*2 Enoch* xxxii. 2–xxxiii. 2; cf. *Sanh.* 97a). But there is no mention of the Messiah in these speculations. As far as is known, no-one before John speaks of a Messianic reign of 1,000 years.

John is thus not simply repeating accepted Jewish ideas. The revelation he records is new. We must understand it on its own terms, and not press it into the mould of Jewish specu-lation. If he is in fact referring to Jewish ideas of a Messianic kingdom, his point probably is that what some Jews hoped for would be fulfilled in Christ. But it is far from certain that this is what he is doing. In this chapter he does not speak of a reign of all the saints, but rather of a reign of the martyrs. He does not say that it takes place on the earth and in fact it may well be located in heaven (see on xx. 4). And, most importantly, he does not relate this reign to the second advent. In fact he does not mention the second advent in this chapter at all. Too little attention has been given to this point.

It appears that John is simply taking us behind the scenes as he has done so often before. Despite the persecution of believers, Christ is not defeated, nor are those who have died for His sake. Our peep behind the scenes shows us martyrs reigning and Satan bound. The martyrs only appear to have died. They are alive (the first resurrection). Later in the chapter John speaks of the release of Satan as the way in which the nations are gathered for the final battle. But here he is surely concerned with present realities—the apparent defeat of the martyrs and their real triumph.

1. John says nothing to place this chapter in the time sequence. He simply says that he *saw an angel.* Except that he came from heaven, the angel is not distinguished in any way. John does not describe his appearance. He concentrates on what he does. The final unimportance of Satan is perhaps indicated in the fact that it is not the Father who deals with him, nor the Christ, but only an unnamed angel. The angel had *the key* of the abyss (see note on ix. 1) and *a great chain.* Both are clearly symbolical, for there cannot be a key to the abyss, nor can a spirit be shackled with a chain. But they show that the angel had authority over the abyss and that he could restrain Satan.

2. The angel *laid hold on* the evil one, who is given all four of the titles by which he is designated in this book: *the dragon,* the *old serpent,* the *Devil,* and the *Satan* (see notes on xii. 3, 9). The angel proceeded to tie him up for *a thousand years.* It is likely that we should take this symbolically. One thousand is the cube of ten, the number of completeness. We have seen it used over and over again in this book to denote completeness of some sort, and this is surely the way we should take it here. Satan is bound for the perfect period.

3. The angel threw Satan into the abyss, and proceeded to lock and seal it. Satan is completely controlled (cf. Is. xxiv. 22). *That (hina)* introduces the purpose. Satan is locked up not as a punishment, but as means of curtailing his activities. Those who interpret all this of the end-time object that Satan is so obviously active that it is nonsense to talk of him as bound during the present age. They remind us that elsewhere John stresses his present activity (xii. 12).

But we must bear in mind John's singular ability for concentrating on one thing at a time (cf. his description of heaven with no mention of the Lamb in chapter iv). We must remember also his complete indifference to the possibility of reconciling one of his pictures with another (see note on i. 17). It is true that he can picture all the evil on earth as coming ultimately from a very active Satan. But it is also true that he never thinks of Satan as having a free hand. Again and again he uses the expression 'is given' when he speaks of the authority to do any evil act. Here he specifically tells us that Satan was restrained *that he should deceive the nations no more*. From verse 8 we find that this means that Satan cannot gather the nations for the final cataclysm. The End is in God's control, not Satan's. John may also mean that, though Satan is busy, he is restrained from doing his worst. He cannot destroy the church. He cannot even destroy the martyrs, for they reign with Christ. The period of restraint will end, for Satan *must* (*dei*) be loosed, though only for *a little season*. As verse 8 shows, this is God's way of bringing on the End. Because it is God's plan Satan *must* be released.

iv. The first resurrection (xx. 4–6).

Attention is concentrated now on those who have suffered for Christ's sake. They reign with Him through the 1,000 years. This section is thus contemporaneous with the preceding.

4. John saw *thrones* (cf. Dn. vii. 9 mg.). He does not say where they were. Those who see a literal millennium usually place them on earth (cf. verse 1). But John does not say this. He uses 'throne' forty-seven times in all, and except for Satan's throne (ii. 13) and that of the beast (xiii. 2, xvi. 10) all appear to be in heaven. It would accord with this if he here meant a reign in heaven. John does not say how many thrones there were nor who *sat upon them*. But at the end of the verse he speaks of those slain for Jesus' sake as reigning during the 1,000 years, and so presumably it is these who sit on the thrones.

Judgment was given unto them. The passionate concern for

justice throughout this book (and for that matter throughout the New Testament) is not to be missed. The expression may mean that they were given authority to execute judgment, or that justice was done to them, 'judgment was given for them'. John saw the thrones first and then the souls of *them that were beheaded for the witness of Jesus, and for the word of God*. In that he speaks of *souls* only and not of bodies (contrast 1 Cor. xv) it may be that he is thinking of a temporary state. For the 1,000 years the souls of the martyrs reign with Christ in bliss, but the final state awaits the general resurrection.

Beheaded (pepelekismenōn) strictly means 'killed with an axe'. Under the Roman Republic public execution was by beheading with an axe, but in the Empire this had given way to the use of the sword. But here the word clearly means 'executed', irrespective of the method. We cannot confine it to the beheaded. The words *and which (kai hoitines)* may explain the preceding (so Charles), or possibly introduce another class (so Swete). In the former case the passage is concerned only with the martyrs; in the latter another group is introduced, probably those later called confessors (people who in a persecution were not executed but suffered a smaller penalty such as imprisonment). It seems that the former is almost certainly correct, for from xiii. 15 ff., it appears that those who would not receive the mark of the beast were slain. John's concern here is with the martyrs. For *the witness of Jesus* see note on i. 2 (where the same expression is translated 'the testimony of Jesus'). With this is linked *the word of God*. It will point to much the same activity, but there will be in mind also the fact that this could be used as a designation of Christ (xix. 13).

From the positive things they stood for John moves to the negative. They did not worship the beast nor his image and they refused his mark. John goes on to tell us that these souls *lived (ezēsan)*. This is not the usual word for resurrection (though cf. Jn. xi. 25). It appears to mean that the martyrs, though slain in ignominy, lived on in heaven with Christ. But not only did they live. They *reigned with Christ a thousand years*. They have not lost everything. They have gained royalty and triumph.

5. The martyrs are thus differentiated from others. The rest must await the conclusion of the 1,000 years. Grammatically, *this is the first resurrection* could refer to this raising at the end of the 1,000 years. But the sense appears to require that it be taken to denote the raising of the martyrs to life in glory with Christ. It is a strong point of the pre-millennial view that a *first resurrection* implies a second. Other views make the two resurrections of different types, but the pre-millennial view does not. On the other hand it is also the case that John speaks only of one resurrection. He never speaks of 'the second resurrection' to correspond with the first.

6. For *blessed*, etc., see note on i. 3. To have a part in the *first resurrection* is a singularly blessed and holy experience. One negative blessing and two positive ones are singled out. The second death has no power over such people (see note on verse 14). Positively they are to be *priests of God and of Christ* (cf. v. 10, Is. lxi. 6; note also the close connection between God and Christ). And they are to *reign with him a thousand years*. The supreme joy of the blessed ones is that they are associated with Christ in priesthood and in royalty.

v. Satan's final overthrow (xx. 7–10). John reverts briefly to a theme he has mentioned several times, namely the gathering together of all the forces of evil at the end-time to do battle with God. Here he deals with it very shortly. The triumph of God is speedy and certain.

7. At the end of the millennium Satan will be released. We might have expected an angel to set him free, just as an angel had confined him. But John does not say how it will be done. His *when* is *hotan*, 'whenever', so that the time is also uncertain (as far as it goes this supports a symbolical meaning for the 1,000 years).

8. Upon his release Satan will resume his deceitful activities, but on a larger scale. Like the 'unclean spirits like frogs' he will gather the nations for the final battle (xvi. 13–16). The expression *Gog and Magog* seems to signify all people. Gog is mentioned in the Bible only in a genealogy (1 Ch. v. 4), in a prophecy (Ezk. xxxviii, xxxix), and here. Magog is found similarly in genealogies (Gn. x. 2, 1 Ch. i. 5), the Ezekiel passage, and here. Magog appears to be the land from which Gog came (Ezk. xxxviii. 2, though in LXX Magog seems to be a prince). In later Judaism Gog and Magog were thought of as two leaders. In apocalyptic writings, for example, they often symbolize the forces of evil. For John the combination is another way of referring to the hosts of the wicked. He has in mind the last great attack of evil on the things of God. Satan will gather all his henchmen. He will assemble the greatest possible number to oppose God (*the number of whom is as the sand of the sea*). This is the decisive moment, the final battle (cf. xvii. 14, xix. 19).

9. John changes to the past tense, *they went up*, but it is the same sequence. *The breadth of the earth* is a curious expression in this connection. It probably indicates that their armies were of great extent. They encircled *the camp of the saints*, and *the beloved city*. Both expressions appear to mean the people of God. The *camp* sees them as 'soldiers of God', and there might also be an allusion to the encampments of God's people during their wilderness wanderings. *The beloved city* should surely be understood in opposition to 'the great city'. This latter we have seen to denote man in organized community, man organized against God. The former will then signify spiritual man, man willingly under the dominion of God. John is picturing the hosts of evil as taking up a threatening position over against the servants of God. We are prepared for a great battle. But none comes. Exactly as in xix. 19 f., John goes on immediately to the annihilation of the wicked. This time it is done by *fire* which *came down from God out of heaven* (cf. Ezk. xxxviii. 22). Consistently John thinks of the power of God as so overwhelming that there cannot even be the appearance of a battle when He wills to destroy evil.

10. The devil is now characterized as him *that deceived* (cf. verse 8). *Them* will refer to the nations (verse 8). The devil is now finally thrown into *the lake of fire and brimstone* to join the beast and the false prophet (xix. 20). John adds a note about their torment. It will be 'by day and by night' (*hēmeras kai nuktos*) and it will be *for ever and ever*. There is no intermission and no end.

vi. The last judgment (xx. 11-15). John speaks now of an awe-inspiring judgment. All the dead were judged. This brings us to the final overthrow of wicked men and even of death and Hades.

11. John depicts a scene of infinite majesty. He saw a *great white throne*. He also saw the One who sat on it. Neither here nor subsequently does he tell us whether this was God or Christ. But he usually means God by 'he that sitteth upon the throne' (e.g. v. 1, 7, 13), so it is probably the Father who is meant here (cf. also verse 12). Sometimes we are told that Christ is to be the Judge of all (Mt. xxv. 31 ff., Jn. v. 22), while Paul can refer both to the judgment seat of Christ (2 Cor. v. 10) and to that of God (Rom. xiv. 10, see mg.). We should understand that the Father is the Judge, but that He judges through the Son (He 'hath committed all judgment unto the Son', Jn. v. 22).

Of this scene Kiddle says, 'Every irrelevance is cast aside, until the theme is stated in stark simplicity; nothing is allowed to distract our eyes from the spectacle of the Judge, and the judged. It is John's rare power of laying bare an essential truth, without swerving aside into unnecessary qualification and expansion, that is responsible for the omission of Christ's figure in the last Assize.' John invests the scene with the greatest solemnity. There was something so terrible in the demeanour of Him on the throne that earth and heaven themselves fled away from Him. *There was found no place for them*, i.e. they were completely destroyed.

12. The dead stood before the throne, *small and great*. None was excepted. *Books were opened* (cf. Dn. vii. 10). John does not say what books these were, but the context indicates that they were books in which were recorded the deeds of all men. *Another book* sets this one off from all the rest. As it is called the book *of life*, it is that in which are inscribed the names of those who have eternal life. John proceeds to inform us that the dead were judged according to what was written, *according to their works*. It is common New Testament teaching that judgment is on the basis of works.[1]

13. The separate mention of the sea and death and Hades as giving up the dead in them is a way of indicating that all the dead are included. None is overlooked. It is carping criticism to complain that the sea was destroyed in verse 11 and is in existence here. We have seen many times that John does not try to keep his various visions consistent (see on i. 17). Earlier his thought was that in the end the universe will pass away. Here it is that all the dead, wherever they have died, are included in the judgment. He expresses both ideas vividly as befits a seer relating visions.

Some have said that only the wicked are in mind here, affirming that in Revelation Hades is never neutral but that it always refers to the abode of the departed wicked. This view is sharply criticized by Kiddle: 'If "Hades" is so evil that the righteous may not dwell there, "Death" also is so evil that the righteous may not die; the two are wedded in one phrase. We must set ourselves against such absurdities: "Death" is the common fate of men, Christian and pagan together: and "Hades" is their common destination, until the Judgment day brings release.' Some, again, think that the mention of the dead in the sea separate from those in Hades means that those who perished at sea did not go to Hades. But John is not concerned with the minutiae of the disposal of the dead. He is affirming strongly that all the dead, wherever they are, are included in the judgment. And he repeats that all were judged *according to their works*.

14. Just as the beast and the false prophet and the devil had all been thrown into the lake of fire (xix. 20, xx. 10), so now death and Hades were thrown into the same lake. This is not

[1] For the relation of this doctrine to salvation by grace, see my *The Biblical Doctrine of Judgment*, 1960, pp. 66 f.

an easy idea, but John appears to mean that death and Hades are ultimately as powerless as the other forces of evil. Finally there is no power but that of God. All else is completely impotent. The end of the verse explains that being cast into this lake *is the second death.*

15. The chapter ends with the affirmation that anyone whose name did not appear in the book of life was thrown into this lake. John sees a sharp division of men into the saved and the lost. In the end men will either share in the bliss of heaven or find their place in the lake of fire.

IX. A NEW HEAVEN AND A NEW EARTH
(xxi. 1–xxii. 5)

As he comes to the end of his visions John has a magnificent sight of the final state of things. He speaks of a new heaven and a new earth. There is a good deal of vivid description, sometimes of a very material kind. But when John speaks of streets paved with gold, of a city whose gates are made of single pearls, and the like, we must not understand him to mean that the heavenly city will be as material as present earthly cities. It is his way of bringing out the important point that the ultimate state of affairs will be very precious. He is concerned with spiritual states, not with physical realities.

Caird sees this section as in some ways the most important in the whole book: 'Here is the real source of John's prophetic certainty, for only in comparison with the "new Jerusalem" can the queenly splendours of Babylon be recognized as the seductive gauds of an old and raddled whore.' Preston and Hanson speak of the belief that the ideal set forth is possible and proceed, 'Indeed it is this conviction that has inspired all Christian efforts for the betterment of mankind. If it were not so, these chapters are more akin to the guide book than the profound interpretation of the will of God in human history which we have found throughout the previous chapters of Revelation.' I do not think that John means that human effort can realize this ideal on earth. But the heavenly city is certainly the ideal set before believers and it is their inspiration to work for God and for good here on earth.

a. 'God ... with them' (xxi. 1-4)

1. From the fate of the evil John turns to that of the good. He tells us that he saw *a new heaven and a new earth* (cf. Is. lxv. 17, lxvi. 22, 2 Pet. iii. 13). For *new* see note on v. 9. He is describing a complete transformation of all things, but he uses the language of heaven and earth for he has no other language. And he expressly differentiates the new from the present heaven and earth. He is not looking for a new edition of the same thing. We can understand *the first earth* passing away, but it is curious that *the first heaven* is also marked for dissolution. The point may be that in heaven, as so far described, there are symbols of God's separateness, like the 'glassy sea' (iv. 6). But the final state of affairs will be characterized by God's nearness.

From this John goes on to say that there will be *no more sea*. The sea is never still, a symbol of changefulness. And it is the source of evil, for the beast comes up from it (xiii. 1). 'The wicked are like the troubled sea, when it cannot rest, whose waters cast up mire and dirt' (Is. lvii. 20). We must moreover bear in mind that in antiquity men did not have the means of coping successfully with the sea's dangers and they regarded it as an unnatural element, a place of storms and danger. 'For this element of unrest, this fruitful cause of destruction and death, this divider of nations and Churches, there could be no place in a world of social intercourse, deathless life, and unbroken peace' (Swete). In the end this seething cauldron, fraught with unlimited possibilities of evil, will disappear. No man lives on the sea. It is something to be crossed to arrive at one's destination, but there is nothing permanent about it. The sea is one of seven evils John speaks of as being *no more*, the others being death, mourning, weeping, pain (verse 4), curse (xxii. 3) and night (xxii. 5).

2. John saw *the holy city, new Jerusalem*. The adjectives *new* and *holy* point to characteristics distinguishing it from the present world, whereas *Jerusalem* rather points to continuity.

Great events took place in or near Jerusalem and, specifically man's redemption was wrought there.

That the new city came *from God out of heaven* is natural enough for the new order, but that it came to earth is somewhat puzzling, as is the fact that John envisages a new earth at all. Certainly he is not thinking of the new earth as the place of men's felicity, in distinction from the new heaven as God's dwelling place, for God's dwelling 'is with men' (verse 3). In fact after the new Jerusalem descends there appears to be no difference between heaven and earth. Perhaps John has in mind that there is already a sense in which God's people experience the heavenly city. It is this which is their bliss in the presence of a multitude of earthly distractions and difficulties. And this of which they now experience a foretaste (and which is expressed in the idea of *Jerusalem*) will be perfectly realized hereafter. Heaven will, so to speak, come down to earth. John saw the city *prepared as a bride adorned for her husband* (cf. Is. lxi. 10). A young lady is apt to be thoroughly prepared and looking her best on the day of her wedding. So with those who constitute 'the bride' of Christ.

3. Once again John hears a voice but does not identify it for us. This is the last of twenty occasions on which he speaks of a voice as *a great voice* (once also a 'strong' voice). The loudness of the voice and its origin (*out of heaven*) are fitting for a voice with the tremendous announcement, *the tabernacle of God is with men*. The word *tabernacle* cannot here signify a temporary dwelling ('tent'). It refers to God's very presence (cf. Lv. xxvi. 11, Ezk. xxxvii. 27). It is probably used because it recalls the Hebrew word we transliterate as Shekinah, 'dwelling'. This term denotes the glory of God's presence among men. John is conveying two thoughts, those of God's presence and God's glory (which he reinforces with *he will dwell with them*). They will be His peoples (the better MSS have the plural) which perhaps points to the different races of men. As, however, there is no distinction in Christ (Gal. iii. 28), perhaps this expresses only multiplicity. There will be very many who comprise God's own. John adds that *God himself shall be with* *them*, the third time this thought has been expressed in this verse. He is *their God* (cf. Ezk. xxxvi. 28, Heb. xi. 16). There is an intimate bond.

4. None less than God will be the Consoler of His people. He will *wipe away* every tear. His concern is infinite. John gives a little catalogue of evils which will cease to be. *Death* is first with a certain emphasis. Death has no final triumph and it is well that God's people see that it will ultimately cease to be. This is the reversal of the curse of Genesis iii (cf. also 1 Cor. xv. 54). So also sorrow and wailing and pain will cease. John sees a reason for this, namely that 'the first things passed away'. *Former things* (AV) is not quite right. It is the 'first' things, the things pertaining to the first heaven and earth which have been completely done away. Life as we know it is completely replaced by the new order. John had wept at the thought that there was no-one worthy to open the seals (v. 4). Is there no answer to the problem of earth's evil? His visions have answered that question. The Lamb has conquered. Now he finds that tears, too, have gone for ever.

b. Separation between good and evil (xxi. 5–8)

5. This is noteworthy as one of the very few occasions in Revelation on which God Himself is said to speak (i. 8, perhaps xvi. 1, 17). It is usually an angel or an unidentified voice (as in verse 3). John tells us that now God speaks, but he does not say to whom He speaks. It may be to the heavenly hosts, though it is not easy to see why they would need this saying. But certainly the words are meant for reassurance to the little church of John's day. Its persecuted and threatened members needed these words of hope. *I make all things new* (cf. Is. lxv. 17) of course refers primarily to the final renewing at the End. But the present tense is used and it is worth reflecting that God continually makes things new here and now (cf. 2 Cor. iii. 18, iv. 16–18, v. 16 f., Col. iii. 1–4, etc.). *And he said* is probably an interjection from another speaker (the Greek is *kai legei* which comes between two *kai eipen*). It may be that John was so astounded that he forgot to write and an angel reminded him, telling him that these words (presumably the words about to be spoken) are *true and faithful*, i.e. they are eminently trustworthy. They must be recorded.

6. It appears that we have the words of God again. *It is done* should be read as a plural, 'they are done'. This probably refers to all the events that had to take place. To troubled Christians the future seemed problematical. The firm word of God reassures them. He is in command and in the end all things work out just as He wills. *I am Alpha and Omega* (the first and last letters of the Greek alphabet) followed by *the beginning and the end* (cf. i. 8, xxii. 13) reveals God as the Originator and Completer of all things. *I* is emphatic as the speaker moves on to the satisfying of man's deep spiritual need. The gift is made *to him that is athirst*, and we may fairly conclude that unless a man feels his need he will not seek satisfaction. When he does his need is met from *the fountain of the water of life* (cf. Is. lv. 1, Jn. iv. 10, 14). The adverb *freely* emphasizes that God's gift is not grudging. The thirsty may rely on a full and free supply of their need.

7. *He that overcometh* takes us back to the messages to the seven churches (chapters ii, iii). The victor is now assured that in the final triumph he will inherit all things. He will have no lack. Moreover God will be his God and he will be God's son (cf. 2 Sa. vii. 14). He will have a special relationship to the supreme Ruler of all.

8. The reverse side to this is the evil fate that awaits sinners. John inserts a brief but serious warning. It is not without its importance that the 'cowardly' (not *fearful*, as AV) head the list. In the circumstances in which John's readers found themselves, courage was a prime virtue. All the more is this the case in that John is speaking now of final realities. To be cowardly before the enemies of God at the last is finally to lose the things of God. John is speaking not of natural timidity and fear, but of that cowardice which in the last resort chooses self and safety before Christ. God did not give His people such a spirit of cowardice (2 Tim. i. 7).

It is not unlikely that we should take *unbelieving* in the sense 'not to be trusted', i.e. those who in the testing time have given way. It could, of course, mean those who lack all faith, but it seems that these are in mind throughout the list and are not to be located specially in any one term. The *abominable* are not defined with precision. The term is a general one, covering defilements of various kinds. There is probably the idea that to accept ideas and practices from heathen religions is to be defiled (cf. xvii. 4, 5).

Murderers will have special reference to the persecutors, though, of course, all homicide is in mind. *Whoremongers* strictly denotes male prostitutes, but in the New Testament it refers to sexual sin in general. In this place there is possibly a reference to idol-worship as well. This will also be the case with *sorcerers*, which may contain a side glance at such practices as making the image of the beast to speak (xiii. 15). We should not dismiss the practice of magic as something of no concern to us as long as many who call themselves Christians persist in the use of good-luck charms and the like. The attitude is that of the sorcerers of old. *Idolaters* must be castigated in the ancient world, and we do well in modern times to be on our guard against putting anything in the place of the one true God. Last are *all liars*, for truth is a quality earnestly to be sought. The place for all such sinners is *in the lake which burneth with fire and brimstone*. John has described it as 'the second death' (xx. 14), which he repeats.

c. The holy city (xxi. 9–21)

The most considerable section of this chapter is given over to a description of the holy city. In a series of vivid metaphors John sets out important truths about the life to come.

9. One of the angels who had the bowls full of the seven last plagues comes on the scene again, but we are not told which it was. His words, *Come hither* (*Deuro*), constitute a command rather than an invitation. John is summoned. The angel says, *I will shew thee the bride, the Lamb's wife*. The latter expression puts some emphasis on the final state. The marriage is now not something to look forward to but something which has arrived. *The Lamb* is very prominent in the new Jerusalem, and is mentioned in these last two chapters seven times.

We should not overlook the fact that the angel who shows John the bride is introduced in exactly the same terms as the one who showed him the judgment of the whore (xvii. 1). This can scarcely be accidental. John may even mean that it was the same angel. He may want us to see, as Barclay suggests, that God's servants do not select their tasks. God may send them for judgment or for blessing or for both in turn. But they must go where they are sent. They must speak whatever God tells them to speak. Or John may have in mind that there is but one divine purpose. It issues in the appearance of the bride of the Lamb, but it necessarily involves the judgment of the whore. It is impossible to dwell both in Babylon and in the new Jerusalem. The way into the latter is by way of renunciation of the former. Judgment on sin is the necessary prelude to the establishment of the city of God. Christina Rossetti sees it in this way: 'Hourly, momentarily, there come to me mercies or chastisements. The chastisements themselves are veiled mercies, as it were veiled angels. The mercies I name chastisements are no less merciful than those which at once I recognize as mercies.' Mercy and judgment are inextricably interwoven.

10. John was taken 'in the Spirit' (see note on i. 10), which will signify that he was not transported bodily but saw a vision. It disclosed to him Jerusalem coming down from heaven. The description is very like that in verse 2 (where see note) though 'new' is omitted. Some find a difficulty in this second mention of the descent of the holy city. But we need not think of two originally different narratives put together by a bungling editor, so obtuse that he forgot what he had included eight verses before. Nor need we think that the city was taken up to heaven in the meantime and is now brought down again. Rather as Caird puts it, 'To the crack of doom Jerusalem can never appear other than "coming down out of heaven", for it owes its existence to the condescension of God and not to the building of men.' We should perhaps notice that whereas John was in a 'wilderness' when he saw great Babylon (xvii. 3) it was from *a great and high mountain* that he saw the new Jerusalem. The heavenly city is to be discerned only from an exalted standpoint, perhaps the high point of faith.

11. The city had *the glory of God*. The statement is not elaborated, but it is surely the most striking thing about the city. John proceeds to tell us that its *light* was like precious stone, further defined as *jasper stone, clear as crystal*. The latter expression is found here only in the New Testament. It might mean 'shining like crystal' or 'transparent like crystal'. Jasper as we know it is an opaque stone, which raises the question whether John means the same stone as we do. If it is crystal clear it is not our jasper, and some have thought that diamond is meant. There is often uncertainty on the identification of precious stones in antiquity (see note on iv.3). But whatever our view on the identity of this stone, it is quite clear that John thinks of the luminary of the new Jerusalem as like very costly stone. And as this very costly stone was used in an earlier passage to convey the glory of God, its use here will connect the light of the heavenly city with God its Maker (cf. verse 23). The city's light comes not from sun or star, but from God Himself.

12. The city was surrounded by *a wall great and high*. This probably indicates that it is secure and inviolable. It cannot be meant as a defence, for all enemies have been destroyed. The walls are pierced by *twelve gates*, over each of which is set an angel. This will be a mark of dignity, for an angelic gate-keeper is most unusual. There may also be the thought that the angel controls who goes in and out. Entrance into God's city is not open to anyone who chooses to enter, but only to those to whom God gives the right. The gates bear names, the names of the twelve tribes of Israel (cf. Ezk. xlviii. 31 ff.). This heavenly city is the true fulfilment of Israel's high calling. The ancient people of God is not forgotten in the final disposition of things.

13. The location of the twelve gates is specified. It is natural that three face each point of the compass, but the order in which they are mentioned, east, north, south and west, is a curious one. It is found in Ezekiel xlii. 16–19. Some think it was derived from that passage and even that the names on the gates are those in the prophet (Ezk. xlviii. 31 ff.). Smith does this, and goes on to comment on the marvel that Dan, omitted from the list in chapter vii, is now on what he calls 'the "glory side" of the city'. But this is supposition. John does not mention Dan, and the twelve tribes in mind may well be those named in chapter vii.

14. Under the wall were *twelve foundations*, bearing the names of Christ's apostles. The combination of the twelve tribes in verse 12 and the twelve apostles is a way of saying that Israel of old and the Christian church are united in God's final scheme of things. This truth has been brought out in various places in Revelation and it is emphasized once more in the concluding scenes. *The Lamb* (rather than the personal name) points to the character in which man's salvation is accomplished.

15. The angel had *a golden reed* (better 'rod' in this instance; Moffatt renders 'golden wand'). The purpose (*hina*) was to measure the city, its gates, and its wall. Measuring evidently signifies security and protection (in xi. 2 the outer court which was given over to the Gentiles was not measured).

16. The city was square. When the angel measured it up, the length, breadth and height were all 12,000 stadia. The city is thus more than square: it is a perfect cube. This shape is that of the Holy of Holies (1 Ki. vi. 20) and indicates perfection. It is probable that John wants us to see the heavenly city as itself the Holy of Holies. It is the place where God dwells. There will be the added thought that God's people dwell there too in perfect fellowship with God. The number 12,000 is the number of Israel, twelve, multiplied by the cube of ten, the perfect number. It thus stands for the perfect total of God's people. Twelve thousand stadia is approximately 1,500 miles, the distance between London and Athens, between New York and Houston, between Delhi and Rangoon, between Adelaide and Darwin. A city of this size is too large for the imagination to take in. John is certainly conveying the idea of splendour. And, more importantly, that of room for all.

17. The angel continued with his measurements and found that the wall was 144 cubits, about 72 yards. If we are trying to form a mental picture of all this we are in some trouble. The measurement will surely refer either to the wall's height or its thickness. If the former it is curiously low for a city 12,000 stadia high, and we have already been informed that the wall is 'great and high' (verse 12). If the latter, it needs no builder to discern that a wall 1,500 miles high needs a broader base than 72 yards. Clearly the number is symbolical. Swete takes the 144 cubits to be the wall height and sees it as underlining the point that 'the walls of the City are not for defence—for there is no enemy at large any more (Isa. liv. 14) —but serve for delimitation'. This is probably the way to take it, with perhaps the added thought that 144 is the square of twelve, the number of Israel. John adds that the measure is that *of a man, that is, of the angel.* This appears to mean that the angel used ordinary human measures, not some extraordinary measure of his own.

18. The term rendered *the building* (*hē endōmēsis*) is unusual, but apparently means that of which the wall is built. Thus the wall did not simply have jasper built into it but it was built of jasper. As this stone has already been used as something of a symbol of God (iv. 3) we may say that the wall proceeds from God and in its way reveals God. There is also the thought that it is God who is the city's defence. He is a wall round His people. John adds the information that *the city was pure gold, like unto clear glass.* This is puzzling as gold is opaque. John may be referring to its shining appearance. The gold shone like glass. More probably he is taking *clear glass* as immensely costly. Among the ancients glass was usually very dark; crystal-clear glass was extraordinarily valuable, something fit for a king's court (see note on iv. 6). John is speaking of the heavenly city as built of the most costly materials.

19, 20. *The foundations of the wall* are decorated (the perfect indicates something permanent) with all manner of precious stones (cf. Is. liv. 11 f.).[1] The stones appear to be the same as those in the high priest's breastplate (Ex. xxviii. 17–20). It is true that the names are not always the same, but this may well be, as some scholars suppose, because John is making his own translation from the Hebrew, and there may have been different ideas as to the Greek equivalents of the names in the original.

A further point of some interest emerges from the fact that the stones on the high priest's breastplate were connected, at least by some thinkers, with the signs of the zodiac, as both Josephus (*Ant.* iii. 186) and Philo (*Vit. Mos.* ii. 124–6) inform us. Charles gives a list of the correlations accepted between the signs and the jewels as follows:

1.	The Ram	—the amethyst
2.	The Bull	—the hyacinth
3.	The Twins	—the chrysoprase
4.	The Crab	—the topaz
5.	The Lion	—the beryl
6.	The Virgin	—the chrysolite
7.	The Balance	—the sardius
8.	The Scorpion	—the sardonyx
9.	The Archer	—the smaragdus ('emerald')
10.	The Goat	—the chalcedon
11.	The Water-carrier	—the sapphire
12.	The Fishes	—the jasper

Now the original order, that given above, is the order in which the sun passes through the constellations. But John has reversed this order. The heavenly city of which he is writing is not the creation of men's minds. He is not giving a Christianized version of the 'city of the gods' of pagan speculation. He is repudiating all heathen concepts. He is expressing the thought that in the end God reverses human judgments.

[1] For these precious stones see the articles by J. L. Myres, *EB*, 4799–4812, I. H. Marshall, *NBD*, pp. 631–634, Eleanor F. Jourdain, *ET*, XXII, 1910–11, pp. 448–450.

John's first stone is *jasper*, for which see note on iv. 3. The second is *sapphire*, which may mean the blue, transparent stone which we denote by the term. Most authorities, however, maintain that the ancients referred to the lapis lazuli by this name. The third stone is *chalcedony*. With us this is a variety of quartz, but it is quite uncertain what the ancients understood by it. It may have been our chalcedony, but we can say no more. For *emerald*, see note on iv. 3. It was apparently a green stone. Next comes *sardonyx*, which is usually thought to denote a banded stone, perhaps a variety of agate. The sixth is *sardius*, usually taken to be carnelian (cf. iv. 3). The seventh is *chrysolite* (lit. 'gold-stone'), of which AG says, 'the ancients . . . applied the term to the yellow topaz'. The eighth stone was the *beryl*, 'precious stone of sea-green colour' (AG). Next comes *topaz*, which may have been yellow rock crystal, as Myres thinks (*EB*, 4803 f.). The tenth stone is *chrysoprasus*, 'an apple-green, fine-grained hornstone (variety of quartz), colored by nickel oxide and highly translucent' (AG). The eleventh is *jacinth* or hyacinth (Gk. *huakinthos*). Some understand this to be a blue stone like the sapphire (AG, *NBD*), others hold that it is red (*EB*). Cf. ix. 17, where see note. Finally we have *amethyst*, a purple, transparent quartz crystal.

21. The gates of the city are quite magnificent, each one being a single pearl. There is a rabbinic statement, 'The Holy One, blessed be He, will in time to come bring precious stones and pearls which are thirty (cubits) by thirty and will cut out from them (openings) ten (cubits) by twenty, and will set them up in the gates of Jerusalem' (*Baba Bathra* 75a). John is writing against a background which thought of the heavenly city as containing huge pearls. New Jerusalem is not lacking in this respect. From the gates John moves to *the street*, which was *pure gold, as it were transparent glass* (cf. verse 18 and the note there). It is possible that we should take *as it were transparent glass* not with *gold* but with *pure* (it follows it immediately in the Greek). In transparent glass any flaw would show up. If it were pure it would be really pure. So with the gold of this city.

253

c. 'No night there' (xxi. 22-xxii. 5)

John now emphasizes the glories of heaven by depicting it as a place of light. There is no night there. God provides its light. This enables him to bring out the thoughts that dark deeds are excluded and that there is no lack of life.

22. John *saw no temple* ('sanctuary', *naon*), for God is its sanctuary. The heaping up of the titles, *Lord, God,* and *Almighty* is impressive. Each has been used before, but the cumulative effect adds splendour. In the last state of things it is God's presence alone which counts, and that is not confined to any one part of the city. It is characteristic that John adds *and the Lamb*. The Lamb is at the centre of things throughout this book.

23. Just as there is no need of a sanctuary where God is, so there is no place for light alongside Him. God's glory is the illumination for the blessed (cf. Is. lx. 20). *Sun* and *moon* are superfluous. The city does not need them. *The glory of God* lit it up and *the Lamb* is its light. This latter probably does not mean anything greatly different from the preceding statement, but it is in harmony with the general picture that the Lamb is put on a level with God as the source of light for the heavenly city.

24. *The nations of them which are saved* should read simply 'the nations' or 'the Gentiles'. Taken with *the kings of the earth* the expression stresses the universality and pre-eminence of the city. All look to it and *bring their glory and honour into it* (cf. Is. lx). John does not envisage the salvation of a tiny handful and the destruction of the vast majority of mankind. He sees God as bringing 'the Gentiles' into His holy city. God's purposes for men will not be frustrated.

25. Unlike earthly cities this one does not shut its gates when darkness comes. Indeed it cannot, for within it is perpetual light. John brings this out by saying in the first instance that the gates are not shut *by day*, and then that there will be *no night there*. Thus there is no possibility of the city's being shut.

26, 27. It is hard to see what *the glory and honour of the nations* could bring to the heavenly city. John probably means, not that *the nations* add to its splendour, but that they render their homage. Some things cannot enter the city. *Any thing that defileth* is comprehensive, and John singles out two specifics: 'whoever' (rather than *whatsoever*; the participle is masculine) *worketh abomination, or maketh a lie*. See note on verse 8. *Abomination* probably has special reference to idolatry, and lying is reprobated elsewhere in this book. It is important that men speak truth and act truly. Every 'lie is excluded from the heavenly city. Smith rightly points out that 'one may be guilty of working or acting a lie without saying a single word'. By contrast, those who do enter are those whose names are written in *the Lamb's book of life*. Again there is the thought that salvation depends on what Christ has done.

xxii. 1. *He* is not defined, and is probably the angel who measured the city. He now shows John *a pure river of water of life* (cf. vii. 17, xxi. 6, xxii. 17, and for a river, which apparently indicates no meagre supply, cf. Ps. xlvi. 4). Zechariah saw 'living waters' going out from Jerusalem (Zc. xiv. 8), and Ezekiel a river which flowed out from the Temple and went down to the Dead Sea, growing deeper as it went and bringing life everywhere (Ezk. xlvii). All that was foreshadowed in such visions John sees fulfilled.

Clear as crystal conveys the idea of sparkling brilliance. Life takes its origin from God for the river flowed from *the throne of God*. For the third time in this section John adds *and of the Lamb* to his reference to God. He will not let us miss the supreme significance of the Lamb in the final state of things. But a reference to the Lamb as on the throne is unusual and Swete finds this 'a startling expression'. Usually the Lamb is 'in the midst of the throne' (v. 6, vii. 17), but He sits with the Father on the throne also in iii. 21.

2. The river appears to flow through the broad street, whereas that in Ezekiel's vision flowed from the Temple outwards. This river does not go out of the city, for all the

255

redeemed are there. But it flows through the city supplying their need. On both sides of the river there grows *the tree of life.* Preston and Hanson see an allusion to the tree of life from which men were excluded in the garden of Eden (Gn. iii. 22 ff.). 'Now at last, almost at the end of the great drama of the Bible, man may return and legitimately enjoy the blessing which he was banished for illegitimately desiring.' Both *the river* and *the tree* are said to be *of life*, but nothing is said of the relationship between them. Probably we should not inquire too closely. John is insistent that life comes from God. The river and the tree are useful symbols, but no more.

The tree of life bears fruit every month and it is specifically said to bear *twelve manner of fruits* (i.e. twelve fruits in succession, not twelve kinds of fruit). As there is neither sun nor moon there is of course no 'month'. But John's expression is perfectly intelligible. He is using the imagery to bring out his point that there is an abundant supply. He goes on to tell us that *the leaves of the tree* bring *healing* to the nations (cf. Ezk. xlvii. 12). This provokes the question, 'Healing from what?' We would naturally think of healing from sin were it not that every such thing is excluded (xxi. 27). Walvoord takes the word to mean here 'health-giving', and comments, 'The leaves of the tree promote the enjoyment of life in the new Jerusalem, and are not for correcting ills which do not exist.' For *the nations* see note on xxi. 24.

3. There is no *curse* (*katathema*, here only in the Greek Bible, means 'accursed thing', not 'act of cursing'). This is the fulfilment of a prophecy (Zc. xiv. 11; 'utter destruction' there means 'ban', as mg., or 'curse'; LXX has *anathema*). Instead, *the throne of God and of the Lamb* are there (cf. verse 1), for where these rule there is no accursed thing. On the contrary, God's servants render service. The verb *latreuousin* has overtones of worship, and indeed NEB translates 'his servants shall worship him'. Glasson comments, 'This could be linked with the *name on their foreheads* (verse 4); the high priest in Exod. 28: 36–8 had the words "Holy to the Lord" on his forehead. Now the whole community offers priestly worship.' Heaven is not a place of indolent leisure, but a place where service is done, centring on God.

4. To see the face of God was denied to Moses (Ex. xxxiii. 20, 23), but it is the privilege of all God's servants in the holy city. The consummation of their bliss is in the vision of God. There is nothing between them and Him. More, His name is on their foreheads, as in xiv. 1. They are wholeheartedly attached to God. They bear His name.

5. Once more we are assured that there is *no night there* (xxi. 23, 25; cf. Zc. xiv. 6 f.) and that God gives them light. The section culminates with the assurance that *they shall reign for ever and ever*. It is not said that they will reign over anyone, and, indeed, it is difficult to see who their subjects could be. The term indicates a blessed and exalted state. They share in royalty.

X. EPILOGUE (xxii. 6-21)

John rounds off his book with a series of somewhat miscellaneous observations. The connections here are so loose indeed that some commentators feel that John did not revise this last section and put it into final shape. Be that as it may, this epilogue stresses the importance of the book now concluding and assures its readers that Jesus will be coming again soon.

6. Once again we have the combination *faithful and true* (iii. 14, xix. 11). It is not clear whether this is meant to apply to the preceding words or those which follow, or, as Swete thinks, to the whole book. As we are now rounding off the whole there is as much to be said for this last as for any. The whole book, then, is to be relied on. John goes on to speak of God as 'the Lord, the God of the spirits of the prophets' (see mg.), an unusual expression (cf. xix. 10, and for 'the spirits of the prophets', 1 Cor. xiv. 32). It links God in no uncertain manner with the prophets. John may mean that it is the God who inspired the Old Testament prophets who has given him his visions.

257

More probably it is the New Testament prophets who are in mind. They were being oppressed and this is a reminder to them that God is not ashamed to be called their God. In their trouble He sent His angel to show His servants things to come (cf. i. 1). What was happening was not outside His control. Rather these things *must* (*dei*) *shortly be done*. This does not necessarily mean that everything in the vision would happen very soon. The language would be satisfied if there were no delay in beginning the sequence. Torrance comments on the language of imminence, 'The New Testament does not think of the difference between the presence of Christ here and now and His Second Advent so much in terms of a passage of time as the difference between the veiled and the unveiled. That is why the whole of the New Testament by an inner necessity of personal faith thinks of that day as imminent.'

7. The imminence of the coming is repeated. It is followed by a blessing on him who observes *the sayings of the prophecy of this book*. For *blessed*, etc., see note on i. 3. John is clear that his book is a prophecy. We should beware of classing it otherwise.

8. There is an emphasis about *I John*. The previous verses have assured us of the divine attestation. This one assures us that the human instrument vouches for what he has written. He saw certain things and heard certain things. He is not writing at second hand. John goes on to say that he prostrated himself before the angel who had shown him these things. This renewed attempt at angel-worship is curious in view of the fact that a similar impulse had been so recently rejected (xix. 10). It is likely that among the recipients of Revelation there were some who were tempted to this kind of worship. John may wish to make it clear that he sees its attractiveness but it is forbidden. So he repeats the prohibition.

9. The impulse to worship is checked sharply. The angel gives as the reason that he is John's *fellowservant* (*sundoulos*= 'fellow-slave'!). He is also of *the prophets* and of those who *keep the sayings of this book*. It is an intriguing thought that angels tell forth the Word of God like the prophets do, and that they too keep such words as are recorded here. We should not miss the importance of these words for an understanding of the proper dignity of the prophets. They rank with angels as servants of God. But even the greatest of God's servants are not to be worshipped. That is reserved for Him alone. Further, it is salutary to reflect that even one who has seen all the visions of this book may go astray. We are warned to be alert lest we fall into temptation.

10. The angel adds another injunction. *Seal not* (see note on x. 4) means 'do not put a seal on', 'do not keep hidden'. The words of this book are intended for publication. They are not hidden wisdom (contrast Is. viii. 16, Dn. viii. 26, xii. 4, 9). Once again John calls his book prophecy, and once again stresses imminence (cf. i. 7, and note on verse 6).

11. The angel continues by calling on men to pursue their characteristic course. He singles out on the one hand the *unjust* and the *filthy* (cf. Dn. xii. 10, and for *filthy*, Jas. ii. 2), and on the other the *righteous* and the *holy*. He probably means that the Lord's coming will be so swift that there will be no time for change. As they are at the moment, so will the Lord find them. The words are clearly meant as an encouragement to believers. Though the evil continue to pursue their way, let them carry on. The Lord's return is sure and soon. The last word is not with the wicked. The saying may also be meant as a challenge to repentance now. John is saying that there will be no opportunity for a last-minute repentance. The Lord will come too quickly for that. But now there is time. Let men repent while they can.

12. The promise of a speedy return of Christ is repeated from verse 7 (cf. verse 20, iii. 11). To it is added the thought of the exact requital He will give to every man. The returning Christ will bring 'wages' (*misthos*, *reward* means 'what is due'). The verb *to give* (*apodounai*) also signifies requital. *Every man* is involved. There will be no escaping in that day. As we have seen elsewhere, judgment according to works is insisted upon throughout the New Testament.

13. In i. 8 (where see note) and again in xxi. 6 the Lord God has said that He is *Alpha and Omega, the beginning and the end*. Now the identical expression is applied by the risen Christ to Himself, with the addition *the first and the last*. All three expressions mean much the same and they set Christ apart from all created being. None other than God could share in these titles of God.

14. There is a change of speaker, apparently back to John, though this is not said in so many words. A blessing (see note on i. 3) is pronounced on them 'that wash their robes' (mg.; cf. iii. 4, vii. 14, 1 Cor. vi. 11). The present tense is used, pointing to a continuous washing. There is a sense in which the saved are washed once and for all (e.g. vii. 14 where the tense is the aorist). But we so easily defile ourselves day by day as we live in the pressures of this world, that it is necessary for Christ's own to be cleansed continually (1 Jn. i. 7). We are reminded of the soiled robes of those in the church of Sardis. John brings out the effect of the washing in terms of two pieces of imagery he has already used: those who wash in this way *have right to the tree of life* (cf. verse 2), and they *may enter in through the gates into the city* (cf. xxi. 27).

15. There is a contrast with those outside. *Dogs* are evil men (cf. Ps. xxii. 16, 20, Phil. iii. 2), but exactly what evil men is not clear. Swete suggests the 'abominable' (xxi. 8). For *sorcerers, whoremongers, murderers* and *idolaters*, see notes on xxi. 8. The separate mention of loving and making lies makes up a total of seven types of sinner, quite in John's manner. It is interesting to have this conjunction of attitude and act (cf. Je. viii. 10). Precisely where these sinners were is not said; indeed, after the destruction of the evil it is hard to imagine. But John's point is that such things are not to be found in the holy city. Let his readers take warning accordingly.

16. The emphatic pronoun *egō* puts emphasis on the fact that *Jesus* is the speaker. He tells us that the angel has spoken on His authority (cf. i. 1). That He can send an *angel* shows that this authority is great. The angel was sent *to testify*, an important concept in this book. *Unto you* is plural, which is a little unexpected, for the angel spoke to John. But the message was not a private one. It was for Christians at large, and so the plural is meaningful.

For *the root . . . of David* see note on v. 5. Here *root* is joined with *offspring* to emphasize the Davidic descent. Right to the end the point is made that Christ is of David's line. The *bright and morning star* heralds a new day, a new day so sorely needed by John's hard-pressed readers; cf. Beckwith, 'It seems to denote the one who is to bring in the perfect day of God.' Some see a reference to the coming of 'a Star out of Jacob' (Nu. xxiv. 17), an idea which is taken up in later Jewish writings (e.g. *Test. Levi* xviii. 3, *Test. Judah* xxiv. 1).

17. *The Spirit* presumably means the Holy Spirit, here speaking through the prophets. *The bride* is the church. Farrer is impressed by the linking of the two: 'The Spirit and the bride are one voice—what inspiration prompts, the body utters.' These then say *Come*. But to whom are they issuing the invitation? And who is meant by *him that heareth* who is urged to say *Come*? Taking the latter point first, the expression ought to apply to unbelievers, because believers are all included in *the bride*. But if this were the case, the response should surely be 'I come', not an invitation to Christ or to other unbelievers to come. It may be best accordingly to take the expression as referring to the individual church member. It would harmonize with the emphasis on the second advent in these closing words (cf. verse 20) for the invitation to be addressed to Christ to return. But that necessitates a sudden change, for there can be no doubt but that the end of the verse has to do with unbelievers.

It seems best accordingly to understand the invitation as issued by the church and every member of the church to the outsider. This is made specific with *let him that is athirst come* (cf. Jn. vi. 35, vii. 37) and the further invitation to anyone who wills to *take the water of life freely*. Man's deepest needs will be met, though those needs must be felt. *Freely (dōrean)* means 'as a gift', 'without charge'.

18, 19. Now comes a solemn warning that *the words of the prophecy of this book* are not to be tampered with. Notice that it is called *the prophecy*. It is more than the product of human genius. It comes from God. Some hold these two verses to be an instruction to future scribes who will copy out the book. They are not to tamper with these God-given words. This kind of instruction seems to have been not uncommon, a well-known example being in the *Letter of Aristeas*, with reference to the translation of the LXX: 'And when the whole company expressed their approval, they bade them pronounce a curse in accordance with their custom upon any one who should make any alteration either by adding anything or changing in any way whatever any of the words which had been written or making any omission. This was a very wise precaution to ensure that the book might be preserved for all the future time unchanged' (311).

Yet we should notice that John does not address the words to copyists, but to *every man that heareth the words*. It seems likely that we should take the exhortation as addressed to the same hearer as in the previous verse. In other words, they are a strong exhortation to heed what is written. It is not to be modified or evaded (cf. Dt. iv. 2, xii. 32, Pr. xxx. 6, Je. xxvi. 2). If anyone adds to the book's teaching, John says, God will add to him *the plagues that are written in this book* (there is an air of finality about the perfect, *gegrammenas*, 'which stand written'). If anyone takes away part of the book's teaching God will take away *his part* out of the blessings the book has so glowingly depicted. The same verb is used of the man's taking away from the words of the prophecy as of God's taking away *his part*. There is a fitness about it all. The punishment fits the crime.

20. Again we have the thought of testimony, an important concept in this book and in the Johannine writings generally. The Witness here is plainly the Lord Jesus. He affirms that He is coming speedily, and His words are greeted with the fervent prayer that He will do just this. *Amen* is the transliteration of a Hebrew or Aramaic participle with a meaning like 'confirming'. It indicates assent to what the previous speaker has said. This is reinforced with the prayer, *come, Lord Jesus* (*even so* is omitted in the better MSS). Charles points out that the Greek here is the equivalent of the Aramaic transliterated as *Maranatha* in 1 Corinthians xvi. 22. There is an air of certainty and of eager longing about the references to Christ's coming. The designation *Lord Jesus* is found in the whole book only here and in the next verse.

Preston and Hanson see significance in the fact that the last note struck in this book, a note which resounds in many places in the New Testament, is the longing for the Lord's return. John's confidence is finally not in human efforts for the betterment of mankind, but in 'an active, living God, whose love and whose wrath are alike revealed in the events of human history, a God who has played the decisive part in that history when he sent Jesus Christ among us'. They add, 'Only if we hold this faith can we retain any real hope in this present world. . . . It is the only faith that can dare to hold its own in the atomic era.'

21. *The grace of our Lord Jesus Christ be with you all* is unusual as an end to an apocalypse, but the normal close to a first-century Christian letter. There is some doubt about the concluding word or words, for the MS evidence is sharply divided. Some read 'with the saints', some 'with all', some 'with all the saints', some 'with you all' (there are other variants also). On the whole 'with all' seems the most probable reading. It puts the emphasis on universality. John looks for grace for all God's people. He closes his book by reminding us that all Christians, not just some, depend on God's free grace.